Penguin Books
The Great Siege: Malta 1565

Ernle Bradford was born in 1922 and
educated at Uppingham School. He
joined the Navy in 1940, served most of
the war in destroyers in the Mediterranean,
and was mentioned in dispatches. In
1946 he became the founder editor of the
Antique Dealer and Collectors' Guide. He
spent most of the years between 1950 and
1960 sailing his own small boats in the
Mediterranean, and also crossed the
Atlantic three times under sail. In 1960–61
he was researching and completing *The
Great Siege* in Malta, an island which he
had first known in 1942 during the
second great siege in its history.

His books include *Four Centuries of
European Jewellery* (1953), *The Journeying
Moon* (1958), an autobiography, *Southward
the Caravels* (1961), a biography of Henry
the Navigator, and *Ulysses Found* (1963).

Ernle Bradford died in 1986.

Ernle Bradford

The Great Siege

Malta 1565

With four text illustrations

Penguin Books

PENGUIN BOOKS

Published by the Penguin Group
Penguin Books Ltd, 27 Wrights Lane, London w8 5TZ, England
Viking Penguin, a division of Penguin Books USA Inc.
375 Hudson Street, New York, New York 10014, USA
Penguin Books Australia Ltd, Ringwood, Victoria, Australia
Penguin Books Canada Ltd, 2801 John Street, Markham, Ontario, Canada L3R 1B4
Penguin Books (NZ) Ltd, 182–190 Wairau Road, Auckland 10, New Zealand

Penguin Books Ltd, Registered Offices: Harmondsworth, Middlesex, England

First published by Hodder and Stoughton 1961
Published in Penguin Books 1964
20 19 18 17 16 15 14

Copyright © Ernle Bradford, 1961

Printed in England by Clays Ltd, St Ives plc
Set in Monotype Baskerville

Contents

Contents

Foreword

I first came to Malta in 1942, at a time when the island was enduring the second great siege in its history. I was then a naval officer, the navigator of a destroyer, and too busy to care about the island's past, or that other great siege which had preceded the one in which I was involved, by nearly four centuries. In 1943 I revisited Malta during the invasion of Sicily. It was then that I saw the island fulfilling the role which Soleyman the Magnificent had envisaged for it in 1565. From Malta, the Allied Forces stormed and captured Sicily and Italy.

I returned to Malta in 1951, this time at the helm of my own small sailing yacht. I now had the leisure to learn something about Malta's history, and about her first great siege. I was fortunate that Captain John Tothill, D.S.C., Royal Navy, was at that time Captain of Fort St Angelo. It was he who kindly allowed me to berth my boat in the small harbour that lies behind the fortress. For five months I lived in that narrow stretch of water which was once the moat separating St Angelo from the village of Birgu. It was here that the galleys of the Order were moored during the great siege.

During that time I grew to know every detail of the fortress, its bastions, its chapel, and its Council Chamber; as well as those long tunnels and caves beneath it, where the galley-slaves were formerly incarcerated. I did my daily shopping in the narrow streets and alleys of what is now called Vittoriosa, 'The Victorious City', but which is still 'Birgu' to the Maltese – as it has been for centuries. I visited all the places which had figured in the great siege of 1565. It seemed to me at times

7

more real, and vivid even, than that second siege of only a few years ago.

Since then I have revisited Malta many times – in spring, summer, autumn, and winter. I have lived in several parts of the island, and have sailed all round the small archipelago. I have grown to know and respect its people. Without their kindness and assistance I would have found it difficult, if not impossible, to undertake this book.

The Great Siege of Malta was one of the decisive actions in the history of the Mediterranean – indeed, of the Western World. 'Nothing is better known than the siege of Malta,' remarked Voltaire. The fact remains that very little has been written on the subject in English – and this, notwithstanding that the island was confirmed a British possession as long ago as 1814. This lack of interest on the part of English-speaking historians may perhaps be traced to the fact that the English Langue of the Order of the Knights of St John had been dissolved several years before the siege took place. Certainly the bibliography is extensive in French, Italian, and Spanish. I have indicated at the end of this book the principal sources upon which I have drawn. I would in no way pretend that this is anything approaching a complete bibliography. The late Major H. E. Balbi, M.B.E., was collecting material for such a bibliography at the time of his death. It remains for some other student or research historian to complete his work.

In the recent past, Malta and its remarkable history have tended to be somewhat neglected – perhaps because the island's name has been automatically associated with a naval and military garrison. It is noteworthy that it is only within the last ten years that the first comprehensive work on its architecture has been published: architecture which in many respects is more deserving of attention than that of many better known, and publicized, islands of the Mediterranean.

It is to be hoped that Malta has now withstood its last siege. With the current change in its status – from a fortified castle, as it were, to a country residence – it is likely that many historians, students, and art lovers will visit this remarkable small island. For Malta, as the traveller Patrick Brydone wrote to William Beckford in 1773, is 'the epitome of all Europe'.

Maltese is a difficult language to read. For this reason I have not been logical in my orthography. I have, for instance, referred throughout to the main southern harbour of the island as Marsasirocco (the Italian place name) rather than Marsaxlokk. Similarly I have used the name Marsamuscetto for the large harbour to the north side of Valetta, rather than Marsamxett.

Malta, in fact, had no written language or dictionary even, until the nineteenth century, when the Roman alphabet was adopted. The language which is Semitic by origin, stemming possibly from the Phoenician, does not easily lend itself to this system. I have referred throughout to the ancient capital of Malta by its Maltese name 'Mdina', rather than Città Notabile (as it was known to the Knights). The name Mdina undoubtedly derives from the Arabic – Medine or El-Medina (The City). The second main peninsula of Grand Harbour I have called Senglea, rather than L'Isla – the name the Maltese have always given it. The village of Senglea was founded by Grand Master Claude de la Sengle (1553-7). On the other hand, where no English or Italian equivalent exists, I have kept the modern Maltese spelling of place names, such as Ghain Tuffieha (the 'Gh' is silent). Translated literally it means: 'The Fountain of the Apples'.

For assistance and encouragement at various times, and over a number of years, I would like to express my thanks to many people: Sir Hannibal Scicluna, M.B.E., who first allowed me to consult his unique library in 1951; to the Malta Government Tourist Bureau, and the Director of Public Works; and to The Hon. Dr L. Galea, C.B.E., Q.C., for his assistance in the early stages of my research. I would like to record my particular thanks to Dr Vincent DePasquale, Librarian of the Royal Malta Library, for all his kindness and help over many months, also to Mr Joseph Galea and Mr E. R. Leopardi. I owe an incalculable debt to Dr Joseph Spiteri, LL.D., who, in many conversations, has enlightened me on aspects of Maltese custom, legend, folklore, and language. I also owe a debt of thanks to the Librarians of the Garrison Library, Malta, and the British Council Library.

I dedicate this book to the memory of my father, Major Jocelyn Ernle Sidney Patton Bradford, M.B.E., M.C.

E.B.

St Paul's Bay, Malta
16 April 1961

De dehors on lui cria; des remparts on répondit. 'Malte d'or, Malte d'argent, Malte de métal précieux, Malte, nous ne te prendrons pas, même si tu n'étais que courge, même si tu n'étais protégée que de peau d'oignon.'

'– Je suis celle qui a décimé les galères du Turc, tous les braves de Constantinople et de Galata.'

From a sixteenth-century Cypriot ballad, translated by Hubert Pernot

Chapter 1

The Sultan of the Ottomans

Soleyman's titles resounded through the high Council chamber like a roll of drums:

Sultan of the Ottomans, Allah's deputy on Earth, Lord of the Lords of this World, Possessor of Men's Necks, King of Believers and Unbelievers, King of Kings, Emperor of the East and West, Emperor of the Chakans of Great Authority, Prince and Lord of the most happy Constellation, Majestic Caesar, Seal of Victory, Refuge of all the People in the whole World, the Shadow of the Almighty dispensing Quiet in the Earth.

His ministers, admirals, and generals prostrated themselves and withdrew. It was the year 1564, and Soleyman the First, Sultan of Turkey, was seventy years old. He had just taken the decision to attack the island of Malta in the spring of the following year.

His had been a life of unparalleled distinction from the moment when he had succeeded his father, Selim, at the age of twenty-six. Known in his own country as the Lawgiver, and throughout Europe as Soleyman the Magnificent, he had truly earned these appellations. He had reformed and improved the government and administration of Turkey, and had made her the greatest military state in the world. He was unequalled as a statesman, and was a poet in his own right.

If the Turkish people for these reasons called him 'The Lawgiver', the people of Europe for their part had good reasons for conceding to him the respectful title of 'The Magnificent'. His conquests alone justified it, and Europeans have always lavished more respect upon conquerors than upon lawgivers. In the course of his Sultanate, Soleyman had added to his dominions, Aden, Algiers, Baghdad, Belgrade,

Budapest, Nakshivan, Rhodes, Rivan, Tabriz, and Temesvar. Under him the Ottoman Empire had attained the peak of its glory. His galleys swept the seas from the Atlantic to the Indian Ocean, and his kingdom stretched from Austria to the Persian Gulf, and the shores of the Arabian Sea. Only at the walls of Vienna in 1529 had his armies faltered.

At the age of seventy, with so many resounding triumphs behind him, it might have been expected that the Sultan would wish to take his ease and watch the decline of day over the Golden Horn. But to Soleyman in his old age there remained only the desire for power, the ambition to extend his conquests. Even if he had not been ambitious himself, those who surrounded him would never have allowed him to rest.

'So long as Malta remains in the hands of the Knights,' wrote one of his advisers, 'so long will every relief from Constantinople to Tripoli run the danger of being taken or destroyed . . .' 'This cursed rock,' wrote another, 'is like a barrier interposed between us and your possessions. If you will not decide to take it quickly, it will in a short time interrupt all communications between Africa and Asia and the islands of the Archipelago.'

It was forty-two years since Soleyman, in the prime of his life and at the head of a vast fleet and army, had driven the Knights of St John from their island fortress of Rhodes. He had felt for them, then, an unwilling but respectful admiration. Had he not said in the presence of his advisers, 'It is not without some pain that I oblige this Christian at his age to leave his home'? It was the sight of the seventy-year-old Grand Master, Villiers de l'Isle Adam, preparing to embark with his Knights from the captured island that had prompted this reflection. Now, at the same age himself, the Sultan was less moved by chivalry, and more by a desire for vengeance.

The sandstone rock of Malta had proved an even greater irritant than Rhodes. Rhodes had been so close to the shores of Turkey that, in the last years of their residence there, the Knights' sallies had been almost neutralized. The movement of the Order's galleys had been quickly made known to the captains of the Sultan's warships and merchantmen. Yet, even so, they had still managed to harry the trade of the Levant, and interrupt the shipping between Alexandria and Constantinople. Malta, however, was worse, because it was so far distant from Constantinople that it was less easy to spy upon the Order's movements. Furthermore, the island's position in the very heart of the Mediterranean gave it the command of the east–west trade routes. Everything passing through the channel between Sicily, Malta, and North Africa was at the mercy of the Maltese galleys. They let few opportunities slip through their fingers.

To a ruler who had added thousands of square miles to his empire, the possession of an almost barren island might seem unimportant. To a ruler whose daily bread was adulation, who had grown weary of the title, 'Conqueror of the East and West', the island and its Knights were an irritation hardly to be borne.

It seemed as if the Knights, like gadflies, were determined to provoke the anger of the lion. Soleyman might mistrust the advice of his ministers. He could hardly, however, ignore the words of the greatest Mohammedan seaman of his time, the corsair Dragut.

Dragut, although a pirate, was allied to the Porte and in recent years had been careful to pay his duties and respects to the Sultan. He was, like Soleyman himself, a fighter and an opportunist. Soleyman heeded him more perhaps than his own Admiral Piali. When Dragut said: 'Until you have smoked out this nest of vipers you can do no good anywhere,' the Sultan was prepared to listen.

Recent events had confirmed Dragut's opinion. When the Spanish Emperor, Philip II, had mounted an armada against the port of Peñon de la Gomera, the Knights of Malta had assisted him with their galleys, and had added the weight of their experience, seamanship, and military ability, to the Spanish forces. Peñon de la Gomera, which lay on the North African coast due south of Malaga, had long been a favourite port and anchorage for the corsairs of the Barbary coast. Its capture by the Christians was as much a blow to Moslem pride as its economic loss was important. The Knights had successfully attacked one of the Sultan's ports on the Greek coastline. Ranging south of Malta, they had also captured a number of Turkish merchantmen. Soleyman was reminded that, 'The island of Malta is swollen with slaves, true believers, and that among the distinguished men and women held there to ransom are the venerable Sanjak of Alexandria, and the old nurse of your daughter Mihrmah.'

Soleyman's daughter, Mihrmah, was one of the chief advocates of an attack on Malta. The child of his favourite wife, the Russian-born Roxellane, Mihrmah never ceased to remind Soleyman of the account that still had to be settled with the Knights.

The capture of a great merchant ship belonging to Kustir-Aga, chief eunuch of the seraglio of the Sultan, was the ultimate provocation. It was an act which led Mihrmah and all the other members of the harem to raise their voices in protest. This merchantman, whose freight was estimated by the contemporary Spanish writer Balbi as being worth 80,000 ducats, was seized between the islands of Zante and Cephallonia by three Maltese galleys led by the greatest sailor that the Order of St John possessed, the Chevalier Romegas. The ship was bringing valuable luxuries and merchandise from Venice to Constantinople and, in the manner of the time, the principal ladies of the Imperial harem had taken shares in the venture. Captured and towed back intact to Malta, together with all its cargo, its loss mocked the Sultan's favourites. Kustir-Aga, the chief eunuch, a personage of great power in the 'boudoir politics' of imperial Turkey, was not likely to lose any opportunity of reminding his lord and master of the constant depredations of the Knights.

The odalisques of the harem prostrated themselves before the Sultan, crying for vengeance. The Imam of the great Mosque, prompted no doubt by members of the court, was not slow to remind Soleyman, that True Believers were languishing in the dungeons of the Knights. They were being flogged like dogs at the oars of the very galleys which were raiding the empire's shipping.

'It is only thy invincible sword,' the Imam proclaimed, 'that can shatter the chains of these unfortunates, whose cries are rising to heaven and afflicting the very ears of the Prophet of God. The son is demanding his father, the wife, her husband and her children. All, therefore, wait upon thee, upon thy justice, and thy power, for vengeance upon their, and your, implacable enemies!'

It was unlikely that the Sultan, whose prudence and ability had been proved in as many council chambers as battlefields, was swayed entirely – if at all – by this clamour for vengeance. Malta was small, but, as he knew well, it was the keystone of the Mediterranean. Within its magnificent harbours he would be able to shelter his fleets, which would then be free for the conquest of Sicily and Southern Italy. The island was small, but it could be the fulcrum to the lever with which he might make the Mediterranean a Turkish lake. From it he could strike at what a later war-leader called 'the soft underbelly of Europe'. The capture of Kustir-Aga's merchantman, the effrontery of the attacks on his merchant shipping and coastal ports were additional factors, but irrelevant to his grand design.

Soleyman was well aware that the Knights of St John were not like other Christians. They were men who had dedicated their lives to an eternal war against his religion, and against everything that Turkey, as the leader of the Moslem world, represented. He had fought them at Rhodes and he knew that death in battle was something they sought as ardently as did his own Janissaries. He knew their reputation as sailors and corsairs. He had questioned his own sea-captains who had been in action against the Knights.

'Their vessels,' he had been told, 'are not like others. They have always aboard them great numbers of arquebusiers and of knights who are dedicated to fight to the death. There has never been an occasion when they have attacked one of our ships that they have not either sunk it, or captured it.' His sea-captains were in error there, for the records of the Knights show a number of occasions when their attempts on Turkish vessels were unsuccessful. In the main, though, it was true that in skill, seamanship, and fighting ability, there was no single vessel in the Mediterranean that could compare with a galley commanded by one of the Knights from Malta. Soleyman knew enough of their prowess to respect them as adversaries. Even as an old man, he would never have decided to attack their island-base purely on a matter of pique or prestige.

In October 1564 at a formal council, or Divan, presided over by the Sultan, the question of Malta and of a possible siege of the island formed the issue of debate. Not all of those present were in favour. Some envisaged an extension of the empire beyond Hungary and pressed for a large-scale military campaign in Europe. Others were for driving straight at the heart of their chief Christian adversary, and making an attack on the coast of Spain. Others, again, urged the capture of Sicily. Soleyman was reminded of the poverty and insignificance of Malta. 'Many more difficult victories,' they said, 'have fallen to your scimitar than the capture of a handful of men in a little island that is not well fortified.'

It was the Sultan himself who pointed out that Malta was the stepping stone to Sicily, and beyond that, to Italy and southern Europe. He envisaged the day when 'The Grand Seignior, or his deputies, master of the whole Mediterranean, may dictate laws, as universal lord, from that not unpleasant rock, and look down upon his shipping at anchor in its excellent harbour.' Piali, admiral of the fleet, and Mustapha, Pasha of the army, were not slow to grasp the sound strategy behind Soleyman's desire to attack the island. When the Divan concluded, the decision had been taken to invest Malta in the spring of the following year.

The edict went forth. The might of the Ottoman Empire – 'that military state *par excellence* . . . built upon an ever-extending conquest –' was to be deployed against the minute island of Malta, and against the Knights of the Order of St John. The Sultan himself had spoken: 'Those sons of dogs whom I have already conquered and who were spared only by my clemency at Rhodes forty-three years ago – I say now that, for their continual raids and insults, they shall be finally crushed and destroyed!'

Chapter 2

Malta of the Knights

The Maltese archipelago consists of two main islands, Malta
and Gozo. Malta, the larger of the two, is only eighteen miles
long by nine wide, while Gozo is no more than eight miles by
four. The islands lie on an axis running north-west to south-
east, and are divided from one another by a narrow channel
in which lies the islet of Comino. Cominotto, a small rock
adjacent to Comino, and Filfla, another rocky outcrop, a few
miles south-west of Malta, complete the group. Fifty miles
south of Sicily, commanding the main channel through
which all shipping between east and west must pass, they are
almost equidistant from Gibraltar, on the one hand, and
Cyprus on the other.

The islands had been presented to the Order of St John by
the Emperor Charles V of Spain in 1530, 'in order that they
may perform in peace the duties of their Religion for the bene-
fit of the Christian community and employ their forces and
arms against the perfidious enemies of Holy Faith'. On the
face of it the gift was highly acceptable, for the Knights had
been homeless since their expulsion from Rhodes eight years
before. The annual presentation of a falcon to the Viceroy of
Sicily, and a guarantee that they would never make war upon
his Kingdom was all that was required of the Knights in
return.

Charles V was not magnanimous by nature, and the aged
Grand Master Villiers de l'Isle Adam may well have mur-
mured '*Timeo Danaos et dona ferentes*' when he saw that, along
with the gift of the Maltese islands, went that of the seaport of
Tripoli in North Africa. Tripoli, a Christian outpost in the
middle of the hostile Moslem states on the notorious Barbary

Coast, was a gift that Charles V could well afford to make. De l'Isle Adam was right to hesitate when he saw it in the Emperor's rescript. He had yet further grounds for hesitation when the report of the commission, whom he had sent to investigate the Maltese islands, came before him.

'The island of Malta,' they said, 'is merely a rock of soft sandstone, called Tufa, about six or seven leagues long and three or four broad; the surface of the rock is barely covered with more than three or four feet of earth, which is likewise stony, and very unfit to grow corn and other grain.' On the other hand, they agreed that 'it produces an abundance of figs, melons, and different fruits; the principal trade of the island consisting of honey, cotton, and cummin, which the inhabitants exchange for grain. But, except for a few springs in the middle of the island there is no running water, nor even wells: the want of which the inhabitants supply by cisterns . . .'

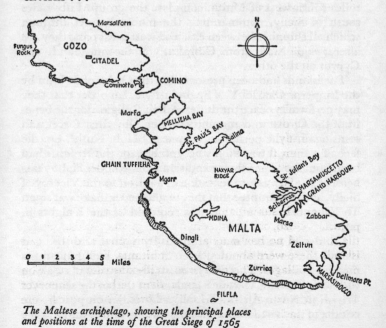

The Maltese archipelago, showing the principal places and positions at the time of the Great Siege of 1565

After fertile and fruitful Rhodes, one of the loveliest islands in the Mediterranean, Malta had been something of a shock to the eight Commissioners. Wood, they reported, was so scarce in Malta and Gozo that it was sold by the pound. Cowdung or wild thistles were used as fuel for cooking. The capital, called Mdina in the Maltese language, or Città Notabile in Spanish, was situated upon rising ground in the centre of the island. Most of its houses were uninhabited. There were no ports, bays, or coves on the western side of the island, and the shore was studded with rocks and shoals. On the eastern side, though, there were a number of useful coves and inlets, as well as two spacious and very fine harbours. These were capable of housing the largest of fleets. Unfortunately, they were at the moment very ill-protected. A small castle called after Saint Angelo guarded part of the largest harbour, but it was furnished with only three small cannons, and a few mortars.

The Knights must certainly have known of Malta's two great harbours in advance of the report, for they had been constantly used by European fleets for many centuries. It was they, in fact, which turned the scale and decided the Grand Master in favour of accepting Charles V's gift. The Knights of St John at that time lived by what can only be called 'organized piracy', and a good harbour was their prime necessity. There was nothing to equal the harbours of Malta until one came to Syracuse in Sicily, or Taranto in southern Italy.

Apart from their favourable comments on the two main harbours, the Commissioners had found everything else disagreeable. There were about 12,000 inhabitants in Malta, most of them poor peasants speaking a kind of Arabic dialect. The climate in summer was torrid and, indeed, almost insupportable. Gozo, on the other hand, was greener and more fertile, but had no harbours at all. In this smaller of the two islands there were about 5,000 inhabitants, living mostly in primitive villages. There was also an ill-constructed castle on the highest point, to which the natives withdrew whenever the Moslem corsairs raided their shores. These raids were common, said the Commissioners, and the inhabitants of the

Maltese islands were long resigned to the almost annual arrival of Moslem pirates, who carried off to slavery any Maltese who fell into their hands.

If the Order had not been desperate for a new home, there is little doubt that De l'Isle Adam would have tactfully declined the Emperor's gift. For more than seven years, however, he had made the round of the European courts asking for assistance. Minorca, Ibiza, Ischia – innumerable islands and ports had been considered by the European sovereigns as potentially suitable for the Knights. For one reason or another, all the more fertile and prosperous islands had been deemed by their owners as unsuitable for the Order.

The fact was, that respected though it might be for its fighting prowess, the Order was not popular. Its Knights, drawn from every nation in Europe, owed direct allegiance to the Pope and were thus insusceptible to national allegiances. They were, indeed, constrained by their rules never to fight against other Christians, but only against the Moslem enemy.

In the sixteenth century, when nationalism was becoming the dominant force in European affairs, such an international Christian Order was somewhat suspect – particularly when it was known how rich it was, and how influential its members. But, quite apart from the difficulty of finding another home, De l'Isle knew how hard it had been to keep the Order together after its expulsion from Rhodes. If many more years were passed in exile the Order was likely to disintegrate. Whatever his Commissioners might say, he realized that it was Malta and Gozo – together with the unwelcome gift of Tripoli – or nothing.

In the autumn of 1530, the Knights of St John of Jerusalem sailed in their galleys from Sicily, across the Malta channel, and took possession of their new home. After Rhodes, 'The Garden of the Mediterranean', they found Malta as unwelcome as were they themselves to the old rulers of the island. It is doubtful whether the Maltese peasants, for their part, cared who was technically their master. Their lives of back-breaking toil, interrupted by the savage attacks of the Moslem corsairs, could scarcely have been harder. The island nobility,

on the other hand, the Inguanez, the Manducas, the Sciberras and others, who were descended from, or related to, the
principal families of Sicily and Aragon, viewed the newcomers with anything but good grace.

Gibbon's remark that 'The Knights neglected to live but
were prepared to die, in the service of Christ' was not entirely
untrue. By the mid sixteenth century this militant Christian
Order was beginning to be something of an anachronism. If it
is true that, during the great siege of Malta, the Knights
attained their finest hour, the fact remains that this fruit was
(as is the case in nature) the last achievement before winter
stripped the leaves from the tree. A Maltese historian, pre-
judiced no doubt by a natural bias, has given this account of
the Knights of St John at the time when they occupied the
islands:

> By the time the Knights came to Malta, the religious element in
> their foundation had fallen into decay. Their monastic vows were
> usually regarded as mere form, and they were remarkable for
> their haughty bearing and worldly aspirations. The Maltese, on
> the other hand, grown accustomed to be treated as freemen,
> greatly resented the loss of the political liberties which had been
> conceded to them . . . It is not, therefore, surprising that there was
> little love lost between the Maltese and their new rulers.

The local nobility had no option but to accept the fact that
the Emperor – contrary to an agreement made in 1428 – had
disposed of the sovereignty of their islands to these proud and
haughty newcomers. They withdrew into their palaces in the
old city of Mdina and maintained as little contact as possible
with the Knights. To their surprise and, no doubt, also to their
relief, they found that the Knights had no intention of settling
in their capital. The Knights, whose service was on the sea,
and who had accepted Malta only because of its fine natural
harbours, preferred to settle in the small fishing village of
Birgu – just inside the entrance of what is now Grand Harbour. Here they began to enlarge and restore the fortifications, and to build in the narrow streets the Auberges of their
order. During two centuries in Rhodes they had evolved a
plan and pattern for their island-living. Now, with the
instinct of men whose minds have been formed in a

conservative tradition, they began to repeat in Malta the pattern of their old home in Rhodes.

These armoured, dedicated men, who move across the history of Malta and Rhodes like visitors from another planet, represented the last active element of the three great military orders which had sprung out of the Crusades. The most powerful of the three, The Templars, had been suppressed in the early fourteenth century. The second, the Teutonic order, had never really recovered from the defeat inflicted upon it at Tannenberg in 1410. It was only the Order of St John of Jerusalem that preserved, into the renascent Europe of the sixteenth century, something of the fire and ardour which had existed in the great era of the Crusades. The Order stemmed from a Benedictine hospital for pilgrims dedicated to St John the Baptist, which had been established in Jerusalem in the eleventh century. In 1113, in gratitude for the services which this hospital had rendered to the crusaders, Pope Paschal II had taken the Order and its possessions under his protection. Unlike the Templars, who were a purely military order dedicated to fighting the Moslem infidel, the Knights of St John were primarily a nursing brotherhood.

The building, furnishing, and improvement of hospitals, research in medicine, and the training of doctors and surgeons, remained the prime motive of the Order. As well as the mother foundation in Jerusalem, daughter houses were maintained in a number of European cities lying on the pilgrims' way to Palestine. Part of the Order's function was also the defence of pilgrims. It was this which led to the emergence of its military side, when the renewed activities of the Saracens and, later, of the Turks made the pilgrim's passage to Jerusalem and the holy places difficult and perilous. Yet even in the sixteenth century, when the aggressive policies of the Turkish sultans had forced the military side of the Order to become predominant, it still continued its original duty. One of the first activities of the Knights, upon their arrival in Malta, was to establish a hospital.

In 1291, after the fall of the last Christian strongholds in Palestine, the Knights of St John had emigrated first to

Cyprus and then in 1310, to Rhodes. For over two centuries, until the great siege in 1522 when Soleyman had driven them from the island, the Knights had evolved the special characteristic of their order. From being hospitallers first and soldiers second, they had become sailors first and hospitallers second. In Rhodes, leaning like a spear against the side of Turkey, they had become the finest seamen the Mediterranean had ever known. Unable to pursue their war against the enemy by land, they had turned themselves into Christian corsairs.

It was in Rhodes, too, that the Knights had perfected the form of their Order, a form which they brought unchanged to Malta. They were an amalgam of all the European nations – a foreign legion of militant Christians, 'the most remarkable body of religious warriors that the world has ever seen . . .' The eight-pointed Cross they bore (which, because of its long association with the island has now become known as the Maltese Cross) was symbolic of the Eight Beatitudes. Its four arms were held to represent the four virtues – Prudence, Temperance, Fortitude, and Justice.

The men who formed this unique body were divided into five distinct groups, yet all – whether fighting man or serving priest – were united by the same vows of Chastity and Obedience. First, came the Military Knights, or Knights of Justice. It was they who, in a sense, dominated the Order, and gave it that quality of patrician arrogance which the Maltese nobility found so distasteful. The Military Knights were the sons of the great houses of Europe. Before being admitted to the Order, it was necessary for them to prove noble birth, on both sides of their family, for at least four generations. That there was no disputing the necessity for these proofs of nobility, can be seen from the archives of the Order in Valetta. No matter how important or wealthy a family might be, no taint of illegitimacy (at any rate in these early days), or suspicion of common blood, could pass the scrutiny of the Grand Master and his Council. It was they who investigated the claims of all potential members of the Order. Novices for their first year after acceptance, the young Knights then joined the Convent, as it was called, for military service. By

The Great Siege

the time that the Order came to Malta this was usually held to mean service as an officer in the galleys. A complete year of this duty was termed 'a Caravan'. After three years of Caravan duty, the Knight had to reside for at least two years in the Convent. After that he became eligible for higher posts – the Bailywicks, Commanderies, and Priories. Not all the Knights, after completing their duties with the Order, remained within the Convent. Many returned to their estates

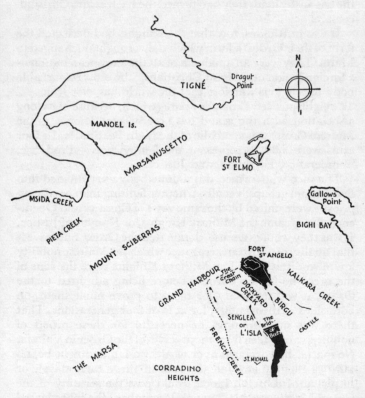

Grand Harbour, Marsamuscetto, and the defences of Malta in 1565

and duties in Europe. It was they whom – on any occasion of dire peril to the Order – the Grand Master was entitled to summon to his headquarters. A failure to report on such an occasion might mean dismissal from the Order, with all its consequences of social and religious disgrace.

The second division of the Order consisted of the Conventual Chaplains, or Chaplains of Obedience, for whom there were no restrictions on birth. Though not exempt from duties in the Caravans, they were, in fact, usually employed in the Hospital and Conventual Church. All of course were ecclesiastics, and were eligible for elevation to Priors or even to Bishop of the Order.

In the third category were the serving brothers who again were not required to be of noble birth, but only, as it was termed, 'respectable'. Their service was only of a military nature. The fourth and fifth divisions, Magistral Knights, and Knights of Grace, were honorary Knights who had been nominated by the Grand Master.

At the head of the Order came the Sacro Consiglio, the Supreme Council, presided over by the Grand Master – himself a Knight, who after years of service, had progressed through the major positions of the Order, and had then been freely elected by his brethren. The Supreme Council consisted of the Bishop, the Prior of the Church, the Piliers or Deans of each national Langue, the Priors, the Conventual Bailiffs, and the Knights Grand Cross.

It was a Council that combined the wisdom and experience of the most distinguished members of both aspects of the Order – the temporal and the ecclesiastical. The Vice-Chancellor, assisted by two priests, acted as Secretary. The Bishop himself was chosen from three candidates whose names were submitted by the Grand Master to the Emperor's Viceroy in Sicily. He, in his turn, submitted one of them for recommendation to the Pope. It can be seen that, although the Knights of St John were by their very nature independent and aristocratic, there were a number of checks placed upon their constitution, intended to ensure that only the best and most efficient rose to the responsible positions. In later centuries, as the Order declined in morale and power, many abuses crept in. But in the sixteenth century, under a strong and selfless Grand Master like La Valette, the constitution operated efficiently.

Apart from the divisions of duties within the Order, the Knights were also divided into eight Langues, or Tongues, consisting of the eight European nationalities from whom its members were primarily recruited. These Langues were Auvergne, Provence, France, Aragon, Castile, England, Germany, and Italy. The French influence in fact, predominated, with its three Langues – Auvergne, France, and Provence. In view of this numerical superiority it was not surprising that many of the most notable Knights over the centuries were of French blood. The three greatest Grand Masters the order ever possessed were all French: Guillaume de Villaret (1310) who led the Knights to Rhodes and established a home which lasted for over two centuries; Phillipe Villiers de l'Isle Adam who brought the Order to Malta in 1530; and Jean Parisot de la Valette.

'Entirely French and a Gascon', as the Abbé de Brantôme described him, La Valette was the greatest Grand Master the Order ever knew. Under him it reached its highest peak of glory. It was against this greatest of Grand Masters and his Knights, that Sultan Soleyman the Magnificent proposed to send the might of his army, and the largest fleet that the Ottoman empire could muster.

Chapter 3

Grand Master La Valette

Jean Parisot de la Valette was that rarest of human beings, a completely single-minded man. Born in 1494, he had joined the Order of St John of Jerusalem when he was twenty. He came from a noble and ancient Provençal family, descended from the first hereditary Counts of Toulouse, and could count among his ancestors Knights who had fought in the Crusades with St Louis. It was a family which had already given several knights to the Order, but La Valette was more dedicated to his vows than most of his ancestors. He never revisited his family estates, or returned to his native country. From the day that he joined the Order, he never left the Convent except on its duties.

As the Abbé de Brantôme described him, 'He was a very handsome man, tall, calm, and unemotional, speaking several languages fluently – Italian, Spanish, Greek, Arabic, and Turkish.' The last two languages he had learned when, suffering a fate not uncommon in those days, he had been captured and made a Turkish galley-slave. It was in action against the corsair Abd-ur-Rahman Kust-Aly in 1541 that Valette was badly wounded and lost his ship, the galley *San Giovanni*. For a year he lived and survived in the terrible world of the galley slave. Only an exchange of prisoners between the Order and the corsairs of the Barbary coast secured his release.

In that century, a man adventuring by sea in the Mediterranean was likely to find the wheel of fortune turn full circle in a matter of a few hours. Dragut, greatest of all the corsairs after Barbarossa, saw La Valette when he was a galley slave and secured for him slightly more favourable conditions.

The Great Siege

Eight years later, when Dragut himself was captured by the Genoese admiral Giannettino Doria, Valette happened to be present. He sympathized with the corsair's anger and remarked: 'Monsieur Dragut – it is the custom of war.' To which Dragut wryly replied, 'And change of Fortune.' Valette's own captor, Kust-Aly, was in turn taken by La Valette, then chief admiral of the Order's fleet, in 1554, and sent to the oars along with twenty-two other prisoners.

Men like these were early inured to the vicissitudes of fate and, if they survived the rigours of their life to be ransomed and returned to their companions, they were of a physical hardiness and endurance difficult for twentieth-century city-dwellers to comprehend. Life in the sixteenth century, no matter what class a man came from, was a question of the survival of the fittest. The weakling died in childhood, and it was only the toughest and most resilient who could hope to see old age. In 1564, the year that Soleyman the Magnificent decided upon the siege of Malta, La Valette was seventy, the same age as the great Sultan. To have attained such an age after a life of constant warfare a man had to be fantastically hard. To have attained such an age with physical strength and mental ability unimpaired, a man had to be almost super-human. If at the same time he were motivated by a fanatical religious faith, there was little that could stand against him. In the great siege of Malta there were men of this calibre on both sides, men hardened by years of warfare and equally convinced of the rightness of their cause.

During his long service with the Order, La Valette had held nearly all the important positions that existed. He had been, successively, Governor of Tripoli – a post so onerous that it had been declined by all the other eligible Knights – Bailiff of Lango, Grand Commander and Grand Prior of St Gilles, Lieutenant to the Grand Master, and General of the Fleet. The last post was equivalent to that of Commander-in-Chief afloat, and Valette, as Baudouin tells us in his History of the Order, 'was unanimously elected although he was still not a Grand Cross but only the Pilier of his Langue'. This in itself was evidence of the respect accorded him.

Even more, this was the first time that the office of General of the galleys had ever gone to anyone not of Italian blood, the position normally being considered an Italian monopoly.

A born soldier, of whom it was said: 'He was capable of converting a Protestant or governing a kingdom,' La Valette soon proved as general of the galleys that his brethren's trust in his skill and prowess was well justified. It was during these years that the galleys of the Order, ranging far and wide from Malta, created that disorganization in the shipping lanes of the Ottoman empire which to some extent provoked the Sultan's decision to attack the island. These raids on enemy shipping were carried out in much the same manner as 'destroyer sweeps'. The fast, heavily-armed galleys, with their trained gunners and sharp-shooters, haunted the Moslem shipping lanes, descending like eagles on their prey. Whether it was a lone merchantman or an escorted convoy, they swept in to the rhythmic beat of the great oars, holding their fire until almost alongside the enemy. Then, after the first discharge of artillery and the first coordinated volley from the arquebusiers, the Knights and men-at-arms boarded the enemy and engaged them with cold steel. From one raid alone, La Valette brought back in tow behind his galley 'three merchant ships whose cargo was worth a prince's ransom, 250 prisoners (destined if unransomed for slave labour in the galleys or on the fortifications of Malta), not to mention numerous pieces of artillery'.

If the great siege of Malta was primarily a land operation, the fact remains that it was a sea-borne invasion. It was a battle for the sea-control of the Mediterranean, and it was the maritime activities of the Knights which had provoked the attack. One cannot write of La Valette, or the Order, or the siege, without considering, however briefly, the ships in which both Knights and Moslem corsairs lived and fought.

Typical Mediterranean galleys of the period, whether Turkish, Maltese, or Algerian corsair, followed much the same lines. They were direct descendants of the classical Greek and Roman galleys and had changed little over the centuries. Long and narrow, they had little freeboard and a shallow draught. (Something like their lines, in miniature, can still be seen in the small fishing boats working out of Malta and southern Sicily to this day.) Their overall length might be as much as 180 feet but, because of the graceful rake of stem and stern, they were often no more than 125 feet between perpendiculars. On a length of 180 feet a galley would have only about 19 foot beam and a depth of hold of only $7\frac{1}{2}$ feet. A sleek greyhound designed for the long calms of Mediterranean summer, they were unsuited to the winter weather. All over the Mediterranean (just as in classical times) September marked the end of the sailing year. Not until spring was securely established did the galleys take to the sea again. During the winter months the Order's galleys in Malta were normally secured in what is now Dockyard Creek, with their bows towards the peninsula of Senglea, and their sterns to Birgu where the Knights had their Convent.

Mobility was the outstanding characteristic of the galley and it was this which had kept so essentially unseaworthy a vessel in use throughout the centuries. Too light and shallow to be a merchantman, the galley was as inbred and specialized a tool of war as a motor-torpedo-boat. At her fastest, it has been calculated that a galley could make about four and a half knots. This could only have been in short bursts, since even the hardened muscles of the galley slaves could not have maintained a fast stroke for any length of time. An average speed was about two knots, adequate for the tideless Mediterranean, but clearly of little use in the fast-running tidal streams around the British Isles or Northern Europe. (It was for this reason that the main development in sailing vessels came from Holland, Scandinavia, and Britain.)

In a Maltese galley, the captain was a Knight of the Order, assisted by a professional sailing-master, with a second officer, or first lieutenant, who was also a Knight. On twenty-six rowing benches were disposed 280 galley slaves. A similar number of professional fighting men were also carried. The main armament was a bow cannon firing a 48-pound ball. There were also four other small guns (about 8-pounders) and fourteen light anti-personnel weapons which fired showers of stones and scrap-metal.

Barras de la Penne, a French naval officer, wrote a vivid description of the life of a galley-slave.

Many of the galley-slaves have not room to sleep at full length, for they put seven men on one bench; that is to say, on a space about ten feet long by four broad; at the bows one sees some thirty sailors who have for their lodging the floor space of the *rambades* (the platform at the prow) which consists of a rectangular space ten feet long by eight wide. The captain and the officers who live on the poop are scarcely better lodged ... the creaking of the blocks and cordage, the loud cries of the sailors, the horrible maledictions of the galley slaves, the groaning of the timbers are mingled with the clank of chains. ... Calm itself has its inconveniences, as the evil smells which arise from the galley are then so strong that one cannot get away from them in spite of the tobacco with which one is obliged to plug one's nostrils from morning till night.

It is not surprising that pestilence and plague often followed the galleys.

If there happened to be a fair wind from anywhere abaft the beam, the galley could set two lateen sails on her short masts. But mostly she was driven and held on her course by the human machinery of her slaves. The life that La Valette knew during his period of captivity aboard the ship belonging to Kust-Aly has been described by Jean Marteille de Bergerac, another Frenchman who was condemned to the galleys some half a century later.

[The galley slaves] are chained six to a bench; these are four foot wide covered with sacking stuffed with wool, over which are laid sheepskins that reach down to the deck. The officer in charge of the galley slaves stays aft with the captain from whom he receives his orders. There are also two under-officers, one amidships and one at the prow. Both of these are armed with whips with which they flog the naked bodies of the slaves. When the captain gives the order to row, the officer gives the signal with a silver whistle which hangs on a cord round his neck; the signal is repeated by the under-officers, and very soon all fifty oars strike the water as one. Picture to yourself six men chained to a bench naked as they were born, one foot on the stretcher, the other lifted and placed against the bench in front of him, supporting in their hands a vastly heavy oar and stretching their bodies backwards while their arms are extended to push the loom of the oar clear of the backs of those in front of them . . . Sometimes the galley slaves row ten, twelve, even twenty hours at a stretch, without the slightest rest or break. On these occasions the officer will go round and put pieces of bread soaked in wine into the mouths of the wretched rowers, to prevent them from fainting. Then the captain will call upon the officers to redouble their blows, and if one of the slaves falls exhausted over his oar (which is quite a common occurrence) he is flogged until he appears to be dead and is thrown overboard without ceremony . . . .

This was the existence that La Valette had once endured and which had gone to shape his character. This was also the death-in-life which every defender of Malta knew that he might expect if he were captured by the Turks.

That the men who survived the galley slave's existence were not necessarily crippled by it, but even hardened to endure to a great age, is proved by La Valette himself. De Bergerac, whose description of the galley slave's life has been quoted, attained the ripe old age of ninety-five. A man who had survived his sentence at the oar-bench was, like the salt-pickled oak of an old ship's keel, practically indestructible.

Like Ulysses, La Valette had 'Endured many things'. His initial baptism of fire was at the age of twenty-eight when he had fought throughout the great siege of Rhodes – that siege which prompted the Emperor Charles V to remark: 'Nothing in the world was ever so well lost as was Rhodes.' La Valette, in company with the other survivors, had embarked from their much-loved island on a winter day when the snow swept down the valleys and the mountain peaks were lost in leaden clouds. He had accompanied his Grand Master, Villiers de l'Isle Adam, through the long years of exile when the Knights, temporarily housed in Rome, had watched their Grand Master make the rounds of the European courts. Valette knew how De l'Isle Adam had begged in vain for the Christian princes and monarchs to help him recapture Rhodes. He knew how De l'Isle Adam had then brought all his brilliant powers of persuasion to bear, to secure another port or island from which the Order could operate. He had lived through that time of bitterness when the English Langue ('So rich, noble, and important a Langue' as Giacomo Bosio described it) had been disbanded on the orders of Henry VIII.

It was only four years after the Knights had taken up residence in Malta that Henry VIII, in conflict with the Pope, had decreed the spoliation of the English branch of the Order. At a blow, the eight venerable Langues, which had for so many centuries worked and fought together, were reduced to seven. Although many of the English Knights remained loyal to their faith (some even being beheaded in England for refusing to deny the Pope's supremacy), 'The Ancient and Noble Tongue of England' was only a shadow. At the time of the Great Siege, England was only represented by one Knight. He was Sir Oliver Starkey, Valette's Latin Secretary, and his close friend and adviser during the dark months of 1565.

It was in 1557 that, on the death of Grand Master La Sengle, 'the universal voice was in favour of La Valette, under whose government the Order recovered its ancient authority.' Almost the first action of the new Grand Master was to take stock of his small kingdom, and to set about improving its fortifications. He was well aware that the day was not far distant when the Turks would attempt to repeat their success at Rhodes.

Chapter 4

Defences of the Island

In the twenty-seven years between the Knights' arrival in
Malta and La Valette's becoming Grand Master, the island
had changed greatly. It had not, however, changed enough
to satisfy a soldier and disciplinarian of Valette's calibre.

Convinced that one day the island would almost certainly have to withstand a siege, he began to improve the
existing defences as well as construct completely new ones.

From the moment that the Order had arrived in Malta,
De l'Isle Adam had begun to enlarge the defences of St
Angelo, the fort commanding the southern side of Grand
Harbour and protecting the fishing village of Birgu. He had
also seen that the walls of the old capital city of Mdina were
strengthened. He had done little else for, as last Grand
Master of Rhodes, he could never efface the memory of that
green island, indulgent to nectarine, fig, and vine. It was his
constant hope that one day, with the help of Christian
Europe, he might be able to recapture the Order's former
home. As the years passed, these dreams faded. Yet even La
Valette was not always satisfied with Malta as a base for the
Order. He had at one time proposed that Tripoli should
become the headquarters, but the loss of the city in 1551
extinguished this hope.

In 1552 when Juan d'Omedes was Grand Master, Leo
Strozzi, a famous commander of the time, made a survey of
Malta's defences and commented on the weakness of various
positions. Thereupon the Grand Master and the Council
appointed a Commission to report in detail and to prepare
plans for the improvement of the defences. The first and
most obvious weakness was the fact that the main entrance

to Grand Harbour was undefended on its northern side. At this point, where the rocky headland of Mount Sciberras (the site of modern Valetta) terminates, it was decided to build a fort. At the same time, another fort was to be built at the end of the peninsula now known as Senglea or L'Isla. This fort, designed by the Spanish engineer Pedro Pardo, was star-shaped and commanded the southern section of Grand Harbour as well as combining with Fort St Angelo to give crossfire over the entrance to Dockyard Creek, (where the galleys of the Order were moored). Called Fort St Michael, it was quickly completed.

The fort on the end of Mount Sciberras was a much more difficult undertaking. A watch-tower and a chapel existed there already, and it is likely that for many centuries there had been a tower and a beacon at this point. The Maltese name Sciber-Ras means literally 'the light on the point', and it is quite probable that there had been some form of beacon there since Phoenician times when the Punic traders had used Grand Harbour. It was they who had given the island the name *Maleth*, 'A Haven', which was later corrupted by the Greeks into *Melita* ('Honey') from which the modern name of Malta derives.

On the site of this old watch-tower at the point of Sciberras, another star-shaped fort was built in 1552 under Pardo's supervision. This new fort, called St Elmo, not only commanded the entrance to Grand Harbour but also the entrance to Marsamuscetto, the other important harbour on the northern side of Mount Sciberras. Small, and in shape a four-pointed star, the fortress of St Elmo had high walls of sand- and limestone. It was built upon solid rock so that no attacker could hope to undermine it. Unfortunately, having been erected in a hurry, the stone used was not of the best quality. There was also no time to build causeways and dikes within the walls to protect the defenders, once an enemy had begun to bombard the interior. Deep ditches, however, were dug around it and, on the landward side, facing Mount Sciberras a counterscarp or ravelin was built. The purpose of this type of defence was to provide a strong check-point against an advancing enemy, where he could be held up as long as possible, until retreat to the fort proper became necessary. On the seaward side to the north there was a further defensive erection, a cavalier. This was a strong point, raised higher than the battlements, and able to dominate the surrounding area with cannon and musket fire.

The weakness of Fort St Elmo lay in the fact that, being at the very tip of the peninsula, it stood on comparatively low ground. From the slopes of Mount Sciberras, an enemy could dominate the fort with his artillery. The total defensive line of the new Fort of St Elmo was about 800 metres.

In the very year in which it was decided to build St Elmo, the Knights had a clear indication that they might expect a large-scale attack in the near future. Dragut landed at Marsamuscetto, and marched round towards Birgu and St Angelo. There was fighting on Mount Sciberras and in the Marsa, the low-lying land at the end of Grand Harbour. Dragut, finding the opposition too strong, re-embarked and sailed north to Gozo. He devastated the small island, and carried off into slavery a large number of the inhabitants.

This raid which revealed the weakness of the Marsamuscetto harbour, hastened the work on Fort St Elmo. It was not, however, until La Valette was Grand Master that one of the fort's main weaknesses was eliminated. On the Marsamuscetto side, where it was quite easy to approach the cavalier and fort, an additional ravelin was hastily built of earth and fascines. Some idea of the difficulties under which the Knights laboured, can be judged from the fact that all the wood and earth used in building this ravelin had to be imported by sea from Cape Passaro in Sicily. Both the cavalier and the ravelin were connected with the main fort, the former by a drawbridge and the latter by a narrow fixed bridge. The ravelin was only just completed by the time that the Turkish Armada reached the island.

The money required for these new fortifications, as well as for improving the existing ones, had to come from the funds of the Order, and at the time La Valette became Grand Master its finances were low. So was the morale of the Knights. The years of exile, and the disillusionment they had felt when they compared Malta to Rhodes, had both contributed to this state of affairs. Worse still, had been the demoralization following upon the fall of Tripoli in 1551, during the Grand Mastership of Juan d'Omedes. The Grand Master had made Marshal De Vallier, the Governor of Tripoli, the scapegoat for the loss of the city, and De Vallier was imprisoned upon his return to Malta.

It is significant that one of La Valette's first actions upon becoming Grand Master in 1557 was to have Marshal De Vallier released. Two years later, La Valette made him the Grand-Bailiff of Largo, one of the Order's most responsible positions. Valette knew that it was not Marshal De Vallier's fault that Tripoli had fallen. He had been Governor of Tripoli himself and had pressed in vain for improvements in the defences. The loss of Tripoli was largely due to Grand Master Juan d'Omedes, who had failed to heed the warnings of his governors, and had failed to supply the necessary men and material to make Tripoli secure.

Realizing that a considerable sum of money must be spent on the defences of Malta, Valette immediately set about restoring the Order's finances. The historian Boisgelin recorded that...

... under [Valette's] government the Order recovered its ancient authority, which was greatly diminished in some of the provinces of Germany, and in the Venetian States. He likewise succeeded in his endeavours to recover from thence the revenues which were due to the treasury, but which for a great length of time had not been paid in.

Between 1551, the nadir of the Order – with Tripoli fallen, Rhodes irrecoverable, and morale low – and 1565, La Valette achieved a complete transformation. As a disciplinarian, he would tolerate none of the abuses which had been allowed to creep in by lax Grand Masters – private duelling, living outside the confines of the respective Auberges, or drinking and dicing. 'The seal of a hero was on his brow', it was said, and there was nothing he demanded of his Knights that he himself could not, and did not perform. Meticulous in his religious observances, he was also the finest general and admiral that the Order had known in many years.

Apart from the work on the new fortifications, those of Birgu (where the Order had its home) were strengthened. The small fishing village on the low neck of land had altered beyond all knowledge in thirty years. Its narrow streets had been adapted to take the separate Auberges of the Langues. The church of the Order, with the relics brought from Rhodes, formed the hub around which their life revolved. There also were the arsenals, the magazines, and the Hospital. Chapels of Devotion had sprung up among the flat-roofed Arabic-type houses of the Maltese fisherfolk, and in Fort St Angelo a large grain store had been constructed. In the solid rock on which the fortress rested, tunnels had been quarried, where the galley slaves had their quarters.

St Angelo itself was cut off from Birgu by a narrow ditch, and had two tiers of artillery-platforms which commanded the entrance to Grand Harbour. Birgu was surrounded by a line of continuous defences with an overall length of three kilometres. Where the defences faced the south, or landward side, a high rampart wall contained two bastions, as well as two demi-bastions at either end. Beyond this formidable defence work, a large ditch had been carved out of the solid rock.

By the late autumn of 1564, Valette knew for certain that an attack on his island fortress was impending. He had agents in Constantinople, Venetian merchants for the most part, from whom he learned of the feverish activity in the shipyards and arsenals of the Grande Porte. Immediately after the Sultan's Council in October, preparations had begun for the spring campaign – for the vast Armada destined for Malta. Activity on such a scale could not be concealed from visiting foreign merchants, and soon the news began to filter back hidden in the cargo lists and documents of merchantmen. (Invisible ink made of lemon juice, was used to hide, 'between the lines', the information so essential to the Grand Master.)

La Valette could now be sure that a sea-borne invasion of this magnitude could only be destined for Malta. Despite

the season of the year, ships were at once sent north to
Sicily to acquaint the Viceroy of that island, Don Garcia de
Toledo. The message was soon being passed through
Europe, reaching Knights of the Order who were absent on
their estates, or attendant on the Courts of their respective
Sovereigns. By sailing boat and by sweat-stained horseman,
the news was carried to the absentee brethren of the Order
of St John: 'Report to the Convent before the spring. The
Sultan intends to besiege Malta.'

One thing La Valette did not know, was that the Sultan
also had his spies. 'Two renegade engineers, one a Sclav-
onian, the other a Greek' had visited Malta in the guise of
fishermen. They had 'noted every gun, and measured every
battery there; and got back safe to the Golden Horn, where
they assured the Sultan that Malta could be taken in a
few days . . . .'

Chapter 5

Preparations

In the early months of 1565 the island was bustling with activity. Turkish slaves were hauling newly cut blocks of stone into position along new, or recently enlarged, ramparts. The ditches on the landward side of Birgu and Senglea were deepened, and the walls that protected the two peninsulas were being strengthened. The fort of St Michael, at the end of Senglea, was provided with larger cannon. These had sufficient range to command the heights of Corradino on the one hand, and the open ground at the foot of Mount Sciberras on the other.

On the top of Gozo's castle (restored after Dragut's raid of 1551) a warning beacon was erected, and at Mdina, St Angelo, and St Elmo, other signal fires were built and manned. Old watch-towers along the coast, which had been in existence for hundreds of years, were hastily restored, and furnished with brushwood and faggots. Inside Senglea and Birgu, the houses, storerooms, and chapels of the Knights and the Maltese, were reinforced and new buildings completed. With memories of Rhodes in mind, La Valette wanted to avoid a collapse of morale through the civilian quarter being reduced to rubble.

It was now that 'that abundance of easily quarryable stone', upon which the first Commission sent to Malta had commented so favourably, proved its worth. If at first they had commented that 'a residence in Malta appeared extremely disagreeable, indeed, almost insupportable, particularly in the summer', the Grand Master and his Council could now see that the whole island was a natural fortress. Its barrenness, its bleakness, and its scanty soil, meant that any invader would have to bring almost all his provisions with him. Unlike Rhodes, the Turkish army would find it impossible to live off the country.

During January and February – the bad months when the North-East Gregale hurls the great rollers against the rocky coast-line – they began to prepare the galleys. As soon as a break in the weather afforded an opportunity, ships must get north to Sicily. Grain and reinforcements must be brought in, as well as any Knights who had made their way overland through Europe.

One thing Valette knew, was that he and the Order could expect little, if any, help from the Christian princes. Francis I of France was even allied to the Sultan (a formal treaty between the two powers having been signed as long ago as 1536). This did not mean that France would assist the Sultan against Malta, but it did mean that she would do nothing to help the Knights – even though many of them were of the noblest blood of her nation. The Emperor of Germany, for his part, was far too concerned about his own land frontiers (which Soleyman was consistently ravaging) to look as far south as Malta. England, under her Protestant Queen, Elizabeth I, was unlikely to send help. In any case, England's main concern at this time was with the imperial policy of Spain. Malta was, in a sense, a Spanish dependency.

It was only from Spain, then, and from her ruler Philip II that La Valette could expect any assistance. Malta had been a Spanish gift to the Knights and, if the island fell, it was the lands and dominions of the Spanish crown that were immediately threatened – first Sicily, and then the Kingdom of Naples. The Pope, of course, could not willingly allow the Order, which came under his personal jurisdiction, to collapse. Pius IV sent them financial assistance – no more than 10,000 crowns. This sum, while it was useful for buying provisions, powder, and armaments, did not solve La Valette's problem. What the Grand Master needed above all was men.

Contemporary records, including that of the Spaniard Francisco Balbi who fought in the siege, give a fairly accurate account of the numbers available for the defence of the island.

By the early spring of 1565 La Valette had under his command 541 Knights and servants-at-arms. This was the hard core of the Order, and did not include the chaplains of the Auberges or the other clergy who, in theory, at any rate, were never permitted to bear arms. The main body consisted of three to four thousand Maltese irregulars, a hardy race, experienced from youth in skirmishes against Moorish corsairs, but little trained for the long drawn-out exigencies of siege warfare. The Order's galley slaves numbered 500 but they, being nearly all captured Moslems, could only be used – under the lash of their overseers – to restore defences, build walls, and act as a labour force. There were a further 1,000 slaves available for the same purpose. All these slaves had, of course, to be continually guarded since, given the opportunity, they would naturally have risen against their Christian masters.

As the winter weather softened into spring, and the flowers and clover began to bloom in the small rocky fields, the galleys went north to Sicily. They brought back with them, as well as stores, powder, artillery, and provisions, a number of Knights and followers who had collected in Messina over the winter. By April, La Valette reckoned that he had 600 members of the Order (later to increase to some 700) and a total force of 8,000 to 9,000 men. With this, he must withstand the full weight of the Turkish navy and army.

On 9 April the Viceroy of Sicily, Don Garcia de Toledo, sailed down to Malta with a fleet of twenty-seven galleys. Seeing the ships approaching, the Grand Master may well have hoped that he was about to receive substantial reinforcements. Unfortunately, almost all that the Viceroy was able to bring was the promise of troops, sometime in the future. He confirmed that he had asked the Emperor Philip II for 25,000 infantry, but both he and La Valette must have known that Spain, with all her commitments, would never be able to produce so many men. A thousand Spanish foot soldiers, at any rate, were promised in the near future. As earnest of his good faith, the Viceroy left under the Grand Master's care his own son, Frederic, 'a promising youth who took the habit'.

If Don Garcia de Toledo had little to give in the form of troops, he had at least some sound advice. La Valette may not have needed it, but he listened with his customary patience. After all, the Viceroy was a distinguished soldier and had led the successful attack on the Moslem port of Peñon de Velez.

'Restrict your Council of War to a bare minimum, and let them all be well-tried veterans,' the Viceroy said.

Both he and the Grand Master knew that one of the bugbears of warfare was a large council, with divided interests and aims.

He also advised him to husband his limited strength and not allow skirmishes and sorties. Every man would be needed for resisting the enemy's main assault on the prepared defences. 'Above all,' he went on, 'take care of your own person. The death of the sovereign has too often been the cause of defeat.'

It was only this last piece of advice that Valette was to neglect. With his fanatical faith and his imperious nature, it was unthinkable to him that he should not willingly hazard himself.

When the Viceroy's fleet returned to Sicily it took aboard as many old and infirm Maltese as possible. The evacuation from the island of all its useless mouths was still proceeding when news that the Turkish fleet had left Constantinople put a halt to all further sea movements. Meanwhile, the training and exercising of the defenders went ahead.

'Each individual was required to fire three musket shots at a target, with a premium for the best.' It was little enough practice, perhaps, for some of the Maltese militia whose experience of firearms was slight. But, from now on, powder had to be sparingly used. In St Elmo, and in the granaries of St Angelo and St Michael, the grain brought down from Sicily was being poured into the great underground chambers, each sealed with its heavy sandstone plug. From the natural springs of the Marsa and just outside the old city of Mdina, thousands of clay water-bottles were filled and ferried to the respective fortresses. Only Birgu had its own water supply, 'a spring which was found almost by a miracle'.

In the arsenals and powder-mills they were preparing the charges, the incendiary bombs and the anti-personnel fire-works with which the besieged would defend their walls. The armourers' shops rang with the clash of hammers repairing and refurbishing the suits of mail, the casques, and the riveted leather doublets of the garrison. Arrangements were being made for the disposition of the galleys as soon as the attack started. The great Turkish merchant ship of Kustir-Aga was securely berthed in the creek between Birgu and Senglea.

Night and day the activity in the threatened island never ceased. Night and day the anvils rang, the masons cut stone, the blacksmiths hammered and the gunners tested their weapons. The commanders of the forts inspected their defences, and concentrated on making good the weaknesses that were inevitable after so short a time to prepare. Rhodes, they reminded themselves, had belonged to the Order for over two hundred years. At the time of its siege, it had been considered the perfection of fortress architecture in the world.

Valette knew that he could expect no real assistance from Garcia de Toledo, or the Spanish Emperor, until June. He also knew that he might expect the attack sometime in May, for such was the information he received from his agents in Constantinople. In any case, it was a matter of common sense for the Sultan's ships to sail as soon as spring began. This would give them the whole summer in which to subdue the island, and consolidate their gains.

Unlike modern wars, which have tended to start as soon as the harvest is in, invasions and land campaigns in the past usually began with the spring. This was particularly true of any sea-borne attacks, where the known inadequacy of the ships to cope with winter weather was of major importance.

Bearing in mind Garcia de Toledo's promise, the Grand Master might have expected to undergo a siege of no more than a month's duration. But not for nothing had he been present at Rhodes as a young man, and not for nothing had he been engaged in siege and sea-battle for nearly fifty years.

He knew that the promises of princes, and even more of their subordinates, must be viewed in the light of circumstances. Rhodes had withstood its last siege for nearly six months – but Rhodes was so close to the Turkish mainland, and so fertile, that the invaders had been easily able to support themselves. Malta, he calculated, would have to be taken before the autumn. After September, with such long lines of communication, the invaders would find it difficult to provision themselves and winter in the island.

If Malta fell, 'The Religion', the Order of St John, was doomed. There was nowhere else for it to go. 'It was his fate then to defend the bare rock to the end.' There could never be, as at Rhodes, another courteous capitulation and an arranged withdrawal elsewhere.

Throughout the winter of 1564-5 the Turkish army and fleet was also making its preparations. The Sultan, suffering from the torments of the gout which afflicted his old age, went down to the arsenals and the shipyards of the Golden Horn to inspect the armada. The death of his favourite wife, Roxellane, the rebellion in 1561 of his son Bajazet, and the eternal pressure of seraglio intrigue, had left little time for Allah's Regent on Earth to enjoy his empire. He had, in any case, been of a serious nature all his life. By his last years nothing could change his impassive approach to matters of state. When – a few years previously – Piali, the admiral whom he had now placed in command of the fleet, had returned in triumph from the capture of Djerba on the North African coast, even this great success over the hated Christians had hardly succeeded in moving the Sultan to any signs of satisfaction. As Von Hammer, the historian of the Ottoman Empire, wrote:

He assisted at this spectacle without altering his normal serious and solemn character. Neither the arrogance that victory produces, nor the intoxication of triumph could change his countenance – so much had the pains of his private life shut his heart against the joys of fortune. At the same time, they had armoured him with courage against all blows that might befall.

Mustapha Pasha, in command of the army, came from

one of the oldest and most distinguished families in Turkey, an ancient dynasty which claimed descent from Ben Welid, the standard-bearer of the Prophet Mahomet himself. He had fought against the Knights at Rhodes, was a veteran of the Hungarian and Persian wars, and a fanatic in religion. Devoted to the Sultan, he was renowned for his violence and brutality. Any Christian who fell into his hands could expect no mercy. Ambitious, as was natural for one of his profession, he hoped to seal a triumphant career by driving the Knights of St John once-and-for-all out of the Mediterranean.

As co-commander with Mustapha, the Sultan appointed his admiral Piali. Unlike Mustapha, who was born a Turk, Piali was of Christian parents. He had been found as a child in 1530, abandoned on a ploughshare outside the city of Belgrade, which Soleyman was then besieging. Brought up in the Sultan's seraglio, Piali had early discovered a vocation for the sea, and had earned a formidable reputation for his successes over the Christians. He was married to the daughter of Selim, Soleyman's son, and the future Sultan. At the time of the siege he was at the height of his powers, about thirty-five years old, favoured by Soleyman and his father-in-law, and celebrated as the victor of Djerba. Among his numerous maritime successes had been the great raid of 1558, when he and the corsair Dragut had laid waste great stretches of the Italian coastline and carried off thousands into slavery.

Assisting these two outstanding commanders were El Louck Aly, Governor of Alexandria, and El Louck Aly Fartax. The former was a redoubtable sea-captain of Turkish stock, the latter a former Dominican brother, a renegade who for many years had been the most active Turkish pirate in the Aegean. Salih, the Rais of Salik, and Hassem, Governor of Algiers, were also commanded to assist with all the ships and troops at their disposal.

Aware perhaps, that with so distinguished a gathering of sea and army captains, and with a command divided between Mustapha and Piali, there might well be dissension, the Sultan gave special orders that the two supreme commanders must work together in everything. Piali, he ordered to 'reverence Mustapha as a father', and Mustapha, to 'look upon Piali as a beloved son'. He gave further instructions that both of them should wait, before beginning the main assault, until the arrival of Dragut. The latter was – in effect – given a watching brief over his two senior officers, Mustapha and Piali. Such an arrangement cannot have been popular. Still less so was the division of the command between Mustapha and Piali. As the Grand Vizier, the jovial and ironical Ali, remarked on seeing the two commanders make their own way down to the assembled fleet:

'Here are two men of good humour, and always ready to savour coffee or opium, about to undertake a pleasure trip together in the islands.'

It was on 29 March 1565 that the Turkish fleet made its way out of the Bosphorus and came down off the golden city to embark the army and the stores. Soleyman was there in person to view the power and pride of his Empire afloat on the waters of the Golden Horn. One hundred and eighty-one ships, not counting a number of small sailing vessels, formed the armada. One hundred and thirty of them were the long, oared galleys, and thirty were galliots or galleases – the latter being one of the largest vessels of the period, carrying something like 1,000 men. Eleven large merchant ships accompanied the fleet, one of which alone carried 600 fighting men, 6,000 barrels of powder, and 1,300 rounds of cannon ball.

To the boom of time-keeping gongs, the shrill whistles of the overseers, and the creak and groan of the great oars, the fleet made its stately way to the dockyards and embarkation points of Constantinople. The sun shone on the minaretted city as the Sultan watched them. He reflected, perhaps, that at the oars of these galleys bound for Malta were Knights and men-at-arms captured from that detestable Order in other battles.

Chapter 6

Invasion Imminent

It was April and the sea was calm when the fleet sailed from Constantinople and made its way by easy stages down the Aegean. Admiral Piali had no wish to cross the long open stretch of the central Mediterranean until May gave them the security of its settled weather.

It was not long before La Valette, waiting anxiously in his threatened island, had news of them. By merchants from Constantinople, by fishermen and trading ships who had seen them pass, he gained some idea of the force which was being sent against him. He heard how they had left the Grande Porte with the large sailing ships in tow behind the galleys. He heard how at one point, during a calm, some of the ships had been carried on to a sandbank and how one of them had been lost with 1,000 men drowned, and another with several cannon and 8,000 barrels of gunpowder. These losses, which had in no way interfered with the fleet's inexorable progress, gave him some indication of the size of force that was on its way to Malta. Perhaps, even in his most pessimistic moments, the Grand Master could not have guessed just how many were the ships and how large the army that the Sultan had raised against him.

Historians differ about the size of the Turkish force, but even the most conservative put it at no less than 30,000 men and most contemporary chroniclers estimate it as 40,000. These were all trained fighting troops. The numbers given do not include the sailors, slaves, or other supernumeraries required to provision and supply so large an army. Six thousand three hundred Janissaries formed the spearhead of the fighting troops, all trained arquebusiers and the picked élite of the Ottoman army. The Janissaries at this period numbered about 40,000 men – the finest troops in Turkey – so it is reasonable to assume that the 6,300 sent to Malta were the élite of an élite.

About 9,000 Spahis from Anatolia, Karamania, and Roumania formed the main body of the force. There were also 4,000 Iayalars, another special corps, composed of religious fanatics, trained to hurl themselves into the breach regardless of death. Four thousand volunteers and about 5,000 levies completed the bulk of the army. A considerable number of renegade Greeks, Levantines, and Jews, followed the fleet in their own or chartered vessels. These, and other camp-followers, hung on the heels of the armada like jackals behind a lion.

Apart from the troops, the ships carried 80,000 rounds of shot, 15,000 quintals (150 cwt) of powder for cannon and siege weapons, as well as 25,000 quintals for the arquebuses and small arms. They came well-prepared for a siege which the Sultan's spies had informed him 'should only take a few days'. In other respects the commissariat of the Grande Porte had not forgotten the nature of the terrain that they were about to invest. Sacks of wool, cotton, cables, tents, and horses for the Spahis, and sails – as well as provisions – had been embarked in the merchantmen. They knew that at Malta 'they would find neither houses for shelter, nor earth, nor wood'.

In the van of the fleet went the two galleys of the Commanders. The one which bore Mustapha was a personal gift from Soleyman. Designed for the Sultan's own use, it was built of fig-wood, called the *Sultana*, and had twenty-five banks of oars. Two hundred Turks, freemen, not galley slaves, were the oarsmen. The captain was a famous sea-rover, who had served under Barbarossa and who was known and feared throughout the Eastern Mediterranean under the sobriquet of 'Soleyman of the Islands'.

Piali, as Admiral of the fleet, not to be surpassed by Mustapha Pasha, sailed in a thirty-four-bank galley, 'the largest and most beautiful ship that was ever seen on the

Bosphorus'. Over the carved and gilded poop, an awning of pure silk brocade gave shelter against the Mediterranean sun. Above the High Admiral's stern quarters was set the personal standard of the Grand Turk – a beaten silver plaque, ten feet square, surmounted by the crescent moon and a golden ball from which floated a long horsehair plume. This denoted that Soleyman the Magnificent was represented aboard in the person of his Janissaries. The Sultan was himself an honorary Janissary, holding the courtesy rank of a private. It is said that 'On the day when Soleyman came before the Janissaries to receive his pay as a private, he was accustomed to accept a cup of sorbet from the Aga while he gave this toast, "We shall see each other again at the 'Red Apple'." That succulent red apple was the "Eternal City".' Out of that vast fleet which now creaked and swayed across the tideless sea towards the island, there were many destined to see each other at the Red Apple, but never again the minarets and cypress-green slopes of Constantinople.

Meanwhile Grand Master La Valette completed his preparations. All the buildings which lay outside the walls of Birgu and Senglea were razed to the ground so that they could provide no cover for sharpshooters. Two of the Order's seven galleys were up north in Messina, but out of the five remaining three were put for security in the moat behind St Angelo, and two (the *Saint-Gabriel* and the *Couronne*) were sunk in the waters off Birgu, in such a way that they could be raised again later.

The peasant farmers were ordered to bring all the animals, and every available *ratal* of vegetables and spring crops, within the walls of Birgu and Mdina. Nothing was to be left for the invader. Not wishing to congest Birgu, which he felt certain would bear the brunt of the attack, Valette gave orders for most of the population, incapable of bearing arms, to take refuge within the walls of Mdina. Similar orders were sent to Gozo, and the country people were ordered to shelter in the citadel as soon as the attack started.

It seemed likely to La Valette that he might expect the attack from the south-east, for the large bay of Marsasirocco would provide adequate shelter for the Sultan's fleet through-

out the months of summer. He knew, though, that a prefer-
able anchorage was Marsamuscetto, just to the north of St
Elmo. It might be expected that the Turkish admiral would
try to storm his way into this secure inlet – especially in view
of the fact that Dragut and other Turkish corsairs had been
in the habit of using Marsamuscetto in the past. It was
possible that St Elmo – that new and untried fort – might
have to bear the first onslaught. Whether the Turkish fleet
attempted Grand Harbour or Marsamuscetto, it was St
Elmo which first barred their way. The choice of its garrison
was of the utmost importance.

Luigi Broglia, a Piedmontese Knight, a veteran of over 70,
was the Governor of this key post. Despite his respect for
Broglia's known courage, Valette felt that he should be
assisted by a younger man. He appointed a Spanish Knight,
Juan de Guaras, as second-in-command or 'Captain of
Succours'. The normal garrison of the fort was only six
Knights and 600 men. Valette reinforced them with a further
200 Spanish infantrymen, under the command of Don Juan
de la Cerda. (These Spanish troops had arrived from Sicily
on 13 May and were all that had so far been mustered out of
the Viceroy's promised 1,000.) A further forty-six Knights,
volunteers from each of the seven Langues, were also sent to
St Elmo to strengthen the garrison.

As regards Mdina and the citadel of Gozo, the Grand
Master reinforced them as far as he was able, sending to
Mdina most of the Order's horses and cavalrymen. Although
it had been suggested in Council that these two positions
should be abandoned, and all the forces concentrated in the
keypoints round Grand Harbour, Valette insisted that both
would be worth upholding for their nuisance value. Hoping
that the Turks would make their base in the south of Malta,
Valette saw how important it would be to maintain his communications with the north of the island, with Gozo, and,
thus, with Sicily.

In mid-May, when invasion seemed hourly imminent, the
48th Grand Master of the Noble Order of the Knights of St
John of Jerusalem called together all his Brethren. It was the
last opportunity that he would have to speak to them in

general assembly. No one knew better than he that there were
many present whom he would never address again.

It is the great battle of the Cross and the Koran, which is now
to be fought. A formidable army of infidels are on the point of
investing our island. We, for our part, are the chosen soldiers of the
Cross, and if Heaven requires the sacrifice of our lives, there can
be no better occasion than this. Let us hasten then, my brothers,
to the sacred altar. There we will renew our vows and obtain, by
our Faith in the Sacred Sacraments, that contempt for death
which alone can render us invincible.

The narrow streets of Birgu, hollowed out by cellars, tunnels, and storehouses, echoed and rang as the armoured men
made their procession to the Conventual church. It was
spring, the air warm, the waters of Grand Harbour tranquil,
and the famous honey-bees of Malta busy over the purple
clover. The sun was like butter on the mouldings of the sandstone houses and battlements. Less than three hundred miles
away the Turkish armada was creeping across the still
Ionian Sea.

When the Knights left the church, they were filled with
exultation. '. . . No sooner,' it was said, 'had they partaken
of the bread of life, than every kind of weakness disappeared.
All divisions between them and all private animosities
ceased.'

An equal confidence and certainty prevailed in the
Turkish fleet. Their fighting men were looking to their arms
and armour, while the horses neighed in the stalls and the
slaves bowed over the looms of the oars. Under their silk
awnings the commanders sat eating the sweet grapes of
Trebizond and drinking sorbet. In the cool mornings, at
noon, and in the evening when the sun went down over the
purple sea, the voices of the mullahs exhorted the faithful.
'O true believers,' they cried. 'When we meet the unbelievers coming against you, turn not your back upon them.
Whoever shall turn his back upon them in that day shall
draw upon himself the anger of God, and his abode shall be
in Hell.' They, too, believed in a Paradise reserved for the
faithful.

Chapter 7

The attack begins

The first ships were sighted by the watchmen on the walls of St Elmo and St Angelo on Friday, 18 May. The fleet was about fifteen miles off the island, approaching from east-north-east. As the dawn haze lifted off the water, the sentries saw the ships spread out in a great fan. They came slowly onward, their oars casting ripples in the still sea. The warning guns boomed out from the island.

From St Elmo and St Angelo, three cannon shots were fired. No sooner had their echoes died away on the quiet air than the sound was heard, repeated from the old walled city of Mdina. Soon after, the citadel at Gozo, hearing the signal, and seeing the smoke from Mdina rising against the clear sky, fired a further volley.

At once, the whole countryside was awake. In their square box-like houses, the peasants rose and began to gather in their animals, and to load their horses and donkeys with stores and provisions. Down in the creek between Birgu and Senglea the shipmen and sailors started to get ready a reconnoitring force. Drums began to beat and trumpets to sound from the walled villages and from the stone shoulders of Fort St Angelo. There was a

sounding and beating to arms everywhere. A violent commotion ensued, some labouring with the utmost diligence in polishing and preparing their arms and horses and others loading their beasts of burden and themselves with their household stuff and children, to convey them to a place of security; some gathering together and heaping the crops, already cut in many parts of the country, to transport it into the fortresses.

The warning signal brought not only the Knights of St

John but the whole people of the threatened islands to the alert – just as La Valette had planned.

The only section of the population, of whom there appears to be almost no record throughout the siege, was the Maltese nobility. Maltese folklore abounds with the names of individual soldiers and sailors who are reputed to have done great deeds, and the historians of the Knights have taken care that the Order of St John should be well remembered. Only the old families seem to have ignored the conflict. Almost without exception, they stayed in their houses within the walls of Mdina. It is quite possible that their chief reaction to the Turkish assault was to say of the Knights: 'They have sown the wind, let them reap the whirlwind.' The Turkish attack would never have occurred if the Order of St John had not been based in their island. In any case, the old nobles were not considered eligible for entry into the Order (a fact which, naturally, embittered them), and they had never been consulted as to the defences of Grand Harbour or of Marsamuscetto. They were not seamen, and they had always turned their backs on the world around Birgu and the water.

Four vessels, under Mathurin d'Aux de Lescout-Romegas, were immediately sent out to reconnoitre and to report on the numbers and disposition of the approaching armada. There could be no question of an engagement. Even at this hour, it could be seen that the approaching ships covered the whole horizon to the north-east. There can be no doubt that Chevalier Romegas would have liked to attack had it been at all possible.

Romegas, who at this time was General of the Galleys, was renowned as the finest Christian sailor in the Mediterranean. Like the Grand Master, Romegas had early grown accustomed to the hard and dangerous life of a Knight militant. Pledged by his vows to perpetual war against the infidel, he had taken part in land and sea battles ever since he had joined the Religion as a youth. Natural hazards had also toughened this indomitable sailor. A few years previously he had been one of the only survivors from a galley which had been overturned by a waterspout in Grand Harbour. On that occasion, he had passed the whole night trapped in the upturned ship, 'up to the chin in water, clinging with his hands to the under part of the vessel, with scarcely sufficient air to prevent suffocation . . .'. In the morning, when the rescue parties went out to try and recover the sunken ships, they heard a tapping from inside the hull of the Chevalier Romegas's galley. The Maltese workmen cut a hole in the underside of the hull and, to their surprise, 'the first thing which leapt out was a monkey [then, as now, sailors loved to keep pets aboard] and the second was the Knight Romegas'.

This was the tough veteran whom Valette sent out to reconnoitre and report on the approaching fleet of Sultan Soleyman. But perhaps even this fire-eater was daunted by the number of ships that covered the sea to the east of Malta. In any case, the Turks disdainfully ignored the Maltese galleys and proceeded on their steady course towards the south of the island. Ahead of them went a galliot under Admiral Piali's master pilot. The leadsman was busy in her bows, sounding the way in, as the vast assembly of ships crossed the fifty-fathom line and turned south towards Delimara Point and the harbour of Marsasirocco.

But, as the day wore on, La Valette and his Council were puzzled. The fleet did not attempt to enter Marsasirocco, but kept steadily on, round the southern tip of the island. A light north-easterly wind and swell may have been responsible for this Turkish decision to get right round under the lee of Malta.

As soon as it was clear that the enemy was not immediately bound for the anchorage of Marsasirocco, Grand Marshal Copier, with a detachment of cavalry, was dispatched by Valette to follow the fleet round the coast. Above the rocky cliffs by the fishing village of Zurrieq, the cavalry watched and waited. As dusk fell, they saw the whole Turkish fleet silhouetted against the western sky. They were coasting round and passing between the islet of Filfla and Malta. It was a sight to make even the most hardened member of the Order feel, and fear, the immense power of Islam.

Over 190 ships were counted making their way under sail and oar less than half a mile off the threatened island. In three main divisions, they passed slowly up the coast, like a ceremonial review designed to inspire their enemy with awe. Once under the lee of the steep cliffs, a little north of the village of Mgarr, the fleet began to anchor. Messengers at once spurred back to the Convent at Birgu and told the Grand Master the numbers of the fleet and their place of anchorage.

At that moment La Valette must have wondered whether the enemy did not intend to land in the north. If this were so, the first assault would almost certainly fall on the weak walls of Mdina. Worse than that, if the north of the island were taken and Gozo cut off, it would be easy for the Turks to stop any communication between the besieged garrison and Sicily. A small boat, which had been waiting under the walls of St Angelo, was immediately sent up the east coast of the island. An Italian Knight, Giovanni Castrucco, was in command. His orders were to take the news to Sicily and to Philip II's Viceroy in Messina: 'The Siege has begun. The Turkish fleet is close on 200 ships. We await your help.'

As the night closed down, the peasants were still coming in from the fields, leading their burdened animals, and themselves staggering under sacks of flour and vegetables. Inside the walls of Mdina, Birgu, and Senglea, the bleating of goats and the neighing of horses mingled with the shouts of soldiers and the clang of armourers' anvils. From the cliffs above Ghain Tuffieha, where the enemy lay at anchor, a detachment of cavalry kept watch. Behind them to the south they could see the glow above the old city of Mdina, and at their feet in the dark bay the sparkle of a myriad lamps. Against the silence of the night they could hear all the sounds of a great fleet – innumerable voices, the boomings of gongs, the shrill pipe of overseers' whistles, and the splash and clatter as a straggler dropped anchor and joined the main body.

It was in the small hours of the morning that they first noticed a detachment of over thirty ships beginning to weigh anchor. They watched and saw them turn towards the south. Immediately word was passed along to the next cavalry detachment who, in their turn, began to follow the ships down the rocky western coastline.

In the quiet May night, against the glow of the sky and the phosphorescent movement of the water, they watched the galleys pass. Some of them had large merchantmen in tow. They were making their way back towards the harbour of Marsasirocco. The Grand Master had guessed correctly. The movement of the fleet to the north-west was only a feint – the real attack was to be made from the south.

Chapter 8

The first clash

Acting under La Valette's instructions, detachments of men were busy poisoning the wells in the low-lying land of the Marsa. Hemp, flax, bitter herbs, and ordure were thrown into the water holes and springs. Valette knew that it was here alone that the Turks could hope to water their vast army. It may be that this action contributed to the dysentery which later afflicted the Turkish forces. It certainly never stopped them from using the Marsa's water supply.

Preparations went ahead to receive the imminent assault. The Chevalier Melchior d'Eguaras was dispatched to Mdina with the main body of the cavalry. They were to be used for harassing the Turkish forces and for cutting off foraging parties, but not for action against the mounted Spahis. The guards were now posted on all the defence works. The three French Langues – Provence, Auvergne, and France – held the landward side of Birgu. Aragon (which included Catalonia and Navarre) stood to arms along the westward curtain up to Fort St Angelo. Castile defended the great bastion next to the soldiers of Provence. The Germans held the rest of the line.

The English Langue, that once 'so rich and noble a mainstay' of the Order was represented by only the one Knight, Sir Oliver Starkey, the Grand Master's Latin Secretary. Out of respect for Starkey's abilities and inspired, perhaps, by a nostalgia for the old days when the English had been the spearhead of militant Christendom, Valette assigned to its one remaining member a detachment of various races. He entrusted to 'the English Langue' the defence of the rest of the curtain up to St Angelo.

It was in times of siege that the curious racial grouping of the Order fully justified itself. All were members of the same army but, like soldiers of different regiments, each had its own jealously guarded reputation and tradition. A rivalry, a determination to outshine the deeds of the other Langues, did much to give the Order of St John its fierce and militant zeal.

The small vessels were towed to safe anchorages or dragged ashore, and the galleys were secured in the ditch between St Angelo and Birgu. Once the main assault developed, the Grand Master knew he would be unable to send any shipping out of the harbour. A siege was a man-made hurricane which necessitated everything being battened down.

Across the narrow neck of water between St Angelo and Senglea a great chain was adjusted to bar the entrance against any seaborne attacks. Made of links of hand-forged iron more than 200 metres long, the chain had been specially constructed in the famous smithies of Venice. Every link, it was said, had cost the Order ten gold ducats. On the Senglea side the chain was secured to a huge anchor that had come off the Great Carràck of Rhodes (the Order's flagship). The anchor had been imbedded in the living rock, and then reinforced with stone outworks, so that nothing could move it. At the other end of the chain, on a specially constructed platform at the base of Fort St Angelo, an enormous capstan controlled the chain. In normal times it was eased out and lay partially on the harbour bed, deeper at all points than the draught of any of the vessels that used the creek.

Now, as the last preparations were made, gangs of slaves began to lay their weight against the capstan-bars and raise the chain. As it came taut and broke the surface of the water, Maltese boatmen rowed out dragging wooden pontoons and rafts behind them. The chain was made fast to these at regular intervals, so that it presented an unbroken front against any marauding craft. The pontoons helped to keep it at water level, and prevented any tendency to dip or sag towards the middle. Now, both from land and from sea, the two peninsulas of Birgu and Senglea were sealed off against the invader.

By midday on Saturday the 19th it was known that the

Turks had begun to land in Marsasirocco. The advance guard
which had got under way in the small hours of the morning
had dropped anchor, and the spearhead of the Turkish force
was making an unopposed landing in the south. From the
north, where the main body of the fleet lay at anchor, came
word that this too was beginning to stir and turn southwards.
By midnight on the 19th the whole armada was at sea and
bound for the anchorage of Marsasirocco.

During the day, the ships which had already anchored in
Marsasirocco put ashore some three thousand men, one
thousand of whom were Janissaries. This advance party made
straight inland for the village of Zeitun, about a mile and a
half from the sea. Their orders were to capture whatever
animals and livestock they could, and to prevent the peasants
from destroying or making off with the crops. In this aim they
had been frustrated by La Valette's forethought. They found
the countryside bare, the peasants fled with their animals,
and the crops already harvested. The first clash of the campaign occurred as they were approaching Zeitun.

A cavalry detachment which had been sent by Marshal de
Copier to watch the road between Marsasirocco, Zeitun, and
the north, ran into the advance patrols of the Turks. A Portuguese probationer to the Order, Don Mesquita, the nephew
of the Governor of Mdina, was killed in this first encounter,
while a French Knight Adrien de la Rivière was wounded
and captured. Outnumbered and outflanked by the advancing Janissaries and light infantry, the cavalry patrol
withdrew, leaving behind it the first dead and the first
wounded of the campaign. A Portuguese novice of the Order,
Bartolomeo Faraone, was also captured. Together with De
la Rivière he was taken back to await interrogation by
Mustapha Pasha.

Mustapha, in company with his war council and the main
body of the army, came ashore on the morning of 20 May.
The prisoners were brought before him and he demanded
information about the island's defences. At this moment both
of them must have known that their death was certain, for
they refused to say anything. Mustapha handed them over
to the torturers.

Meanwhile, the advance troops of the army had passed beyond Zeitun and were sacking the next place on their route, the hamlet of Zabbar. Beyond Zabbar there was nothing but barren undulating land as far as the ramparts of Birgu and Senglea, only a mile away.

La Valette completed his preparations while Mustapha and Admiral Piali conferred as to their best approach. The last stores and ammunition had already been sent over to St Elmo, the two peninsular garrisons were ready for action, and the standard of St John was unfurled on the ramparts of St Angelo. Except for a small number, essential for patrolling the ramparts, all available foot-soldiers were ordered down from Mdina to reinforce the garrison at Birgu. Valette already had a good idea of the number of men who were marching against him. Two renegades from the Turkish army had brought him information as to its size and intentions. Their stories confirmed his belief that Mustapha intended to attack the Knights in their strongpoints, and not occupy the north of the island as a preliminary.

Mustapha Pasha was also congratulating himself on having acquired some useful information. Chevalier de la Rivière and his companion Faraone had cried out under torture that the weakest point in the defences was the post of Castile. He decided to make an attempt on it on the following day.

As the Turkish army approached, there was another cavalry action with fairly heavy casualties on both sides, Marshal Copier being compelled to withdraw his troops under cover of the guns of Birgu and Senglea. A Turkish advance party reconnoitring the Marsa, with a view to watering, was set upon by a group of cavalry which sallied down on them from the slopes of Mdina. These early skirmishes gave both sides a chance to test the mettle of the enemy, and to accustom themselves to his tactics and arms. The Turks realized at once that this would be no easy victory. The Knights and their troops met – many of them for the first time – the burning fanaticism of Islam. Other than these clashes between mounted troops, the Turkish army spread unopposed over the whole south of the island.

La Valette's conduct of the initial campaign has puzzled some historians. Why, they have asked, did the Knights of St John fail to confront the enemy from the moment that the landing began? The answer to this involves the whole question of siege and fortress warfare. A fort, by its very nature, is designed to allow a small body of men to withstand the attack of a superior force. In the siege of Malta, Valette could muster no more than 9,000 men against an army of over 30,000. But within a fortification, outnumbered three to one though they might be, the defenders stood a reasonable chance. Their situation was similar to many which had occurred in the Holy Land during the Crusades, and which had led to the evolution of fortress architecture. Outnumbered, in a hostile terrain, and with reinforcements only obtainable across a sea route of thousands of miles, the Christian Military Orders like the Knights of St John had found the only solution to their problems in the fort. Behind their massive walls, bastions, and enceintes, they had been able to hold at bay immensely powerful forces.

It was the same at Malta. If Valette had attempted to oppose the Turkish landings – even though he might have enjoyed some early success – his troops would have quickly been defeated. They would have been outflanked and detachments would have been landed at other points on the coast to take them in rear. In any case, sheer weight of numbers would soon have overwhelmed them. Malta, with no cover, no mountains, and no trees, was not a Crete where a commander could carry out guerilla warfare. Valette had only two options: either oppose the landings from the start; or withdraw within his prepared fortifications. There can be no doubt that he chose the right course.

Three days after the Turkish fleet had been sighted, their army held all the island on a line south of Grand Harbour, and had already occupied the Marsa. Their main body now began to move into position on the low hills that commanded the Harbour from the south. One of the weaknesses in the defences of Birgu and Senglea was the fact that both these fortified villages could be overlooked by the sandstone eminence of Corradino, on the one hand, and high points like Santa Margherita hill behind Kalkara, on the other. In a similar way, Fort St Elmo was overlooked by Mount Scibberas. These natural defects had been pointed out in previous surveys by engineers employed by the Order, but unfortunately neither time nor money had permitted them to be remedied.

As the sentries on the bastions looked south, they could see on the skyline the panoply of the Turk, as he advanced for his first probe against the main defences. Mustapha Pasha had decided, in view of the information extracted from his two captives, to make an attempt on the post of Castile. The low hills were crowned with rich standards, and brilliant with the robes and jewelled turbans of the commanders. The hilts of their scimitars were enamelled and gem-set. Triangular banners of silk floated at the head of the different detachments. The caparison of the horses was almost as colourful as the clothes and armour of their masters. '... The whole, at a distance, seemed an infinite multitude of flowers in a meadow or luxuriant pasture; nor delightful only to the eyes, but also to the ears, from the various instruments, melted down by the air into exquisite harmony.'

Seeing them advance, and remembering Garcia de Toledo's sage advice to husband his own troops, Valette gave orders for all to stay within the walls and hold their fire until the enemy was well within range. He had forgotten, though, the fire and impetuosity of youth – and there were many among his Knights for whom this was their first action. 'It required all his authority to prevent them from opening the gates; and before he had been able to have their shutting compassed, a great crowd of Knights had got out.' Resigning himself to the inevitable, the Grand Master decided to let his young men accustom themselves to this unfamiliar enemy, and 'blood' them early. He sent three divisions from Senglea and Birgu to engage the front ranks of the advancing Turks.

Throughout the six hours in which this first main struggle raged along the land to the south of the fortified positions, Valette stationed himself on the exposed bastion of Provence where it jutted from the main curtain. He watched the fire from the guns sweeping over the dense hordes, while – just

65

below the walls – there resounded the whicker and clash of steel and the crack of musketry as the front ranks engaged. Good though his own arquebusiers were, he noticed that the Turkish sharpshooters were far better. The Janissaries, in particular, were specially trained in accurate fire, and their muskets – which were '7 or 9 palms long' – were more efficient than the European, but they took longer to load. It was while he was standing on the bastion that a soldier next to him fell at his feet, shot dead, while a few paces away his own page was wounded in the neck.

Seeing the weight of Turkish numbers beginning to tell, Valette ordered the signal to retire. The defenders streamed back as the gates were opened, and the gunners held off the advancing Turks. Only twenty-one Christians were killed but several hundred Turks were left dead on the field. There were 150 wounded, though, in this first major clash, and Valette knew that he could permit no further sallies. The action had served to raise the morale of his troops, but from now on his men must be kept back for defence.

A captured Turkish standard was brought forward for his inspection (it was later hung in the Conventual Church). A Knight from Navarre, Jean de Morgut, had killed a richly dressed Turkish officer and now displayed a gold bracelet stripped from the dead man's arm. Someone read out the Arabic inscription engraved on it: 'I do not come to Malta for wealth or honour, but to save my soul.'

As the sun set Mustapha ordered his troops to withdraw. They established themselves in three main divisions; their left wing on the Marsa, their centre against Corradino, and their right wing facing Senglea. It was clear that the post of Castile and, indeed, the whole of the landward defences were strong, well-defended, and protected by a large number of cannon. Losses among the Janissaries had been heavy. The two Christian prisoners had lied when they had said that this was one of the weak points in the defences. Mustapha Pasha gave orders for Chevalier Adrien de la Rivière and his companion, Bartolomeo Faraone, to be bastinadoed to death.

Chapter 9

Objective, St Elmo

After the first assault, Valette and his council may have expected the siege to be opened against Birgu and Senglea. The majority of the Turkish forces were grouped on the hills to the south of them. Any doubts they may have had, were set at rest when, on the evening of 22 May, two Christian renegades (men who had, at some time or other 'turned Turk' to save their skins) made their way to Birgu. They were brought before the Grand Master. One of them had been a personal guard to Mustapha Pasha and had been present that very evening when the Turkish war council had met. Valette learned from him that the decision had been taken to invest Fort St Elmo first of all.

The Turkish council had been divided in its opinions. Mustaphá as general of the army was in favour of occupying the north of the island and Gozo, capturing Mdina and then proceeding to the siege of Birgu and Senglea. St Elmo, he thought, could be safely ignored. He envisaged a part of the fleet blockading Grand Harbour, a part at sea to the north of the archipelago to intercept any reinforcements, and the transports left in their present anchorage at Marsasirocco. It was well for the Knights that his intelligent grasp of strategy was overruled by Admiral Piali. Marsasirocco, he maintained, was entirely unsafe for the maintenance of the supply ships and the large transports. Furthermore, he did not like the prospect of keeping the other ships at sea on the east and north-east coasts of Malta and Gozo.

Piali did not hesitate to point out that he was responsible for almost the whole of the Sultan's fleet – and ships, he may have added, were expensive, whereas men were cheap. He

urged the Commander-in-Chief to ensure a really safe
anchorage for the fleet before engaging in major land
operations. The only safe anchorage – other than Grand
Harbour itself – was Marsamuscetto. Piali's argument as to
the necessity of occupying Marsamuscetto was based on a
false premise: that there was every likelihood of strong winds
or gales from the east and north-east during May and June.
The Gregale, the north-easterly which is the most dangerous
wind in the central Mediterranean, was rightly to be feared
by any seaman. But, where the Turkish admiral was wrong,
was in thinking that a Gregale was likely at that season of
the year. Such gale-force winds rarely blow around Malta
after March, or April at the latest. Marsasirocco would have
served quite adequately for his fleet during a summer
campaign.

His arguments, however, could not be contradicted by
soldiers. His voice carried additional weight because of his
close connexions with the Sultan's family. Reluctantly
Mustapha yielded to this young Admiral whom he had been
told to treat as 'a beloved son'. But to secure Marsamuscetto
as an anchorage for the fleet, St Elmo must first of all be
taken. The fort commanded the entrance, and nothing could
be done until it was in Turkish hands. The Sultan's spies had
earlier reported that the fort was hastily constructed and
weak, so it seemed a matter of no great moment to decide on
its capture. Unlike Birgu and Senglea, it was a fort pure and
simple, with no town behind it from which the defenders
could draw reserves of men, powder and provisions.

The Grand Master was pleased at the news. He knew that,
whatever happened, before the Turks could take the island,
both Birgu and Senglea must fall. Their decision to com-
mence operations against St Elmo meant time gained for
reinforcing and improving the defence of his main citadels.
In the matter of strengthening St Elmo's garrison there was
no time to be lost. Luigi Broglia, Bailiff of St Elmo, was immediately informed that the first blow was to fall on him.
The Grand Master also sent additional reinforcements. A
Provençal Knight, Pierre de Massuez Vercoyran, known
as 'Colonel Mas', had recently arrived from Messina bring-

ing with him 400 enlisted soldiers. Colonel Mas and half of his men, together with sixty-four Knights who volunteered for the post of honour, were at once ferried across Grand Harbour to join the original garrison of St Elmo.

Mustapha's engineers and officers were sent forward to reconnoitre the position and to report on it. 'It is a star-fort,' they said. 'There are four main salients and the front which we shall have to storm is broken into a bastioned form. The cavalier which rises to seaward is separated by a ditch. There is also a small ravelin. Both these outworks are connected to the main fort, the one by a drawbridge and the other a fixed bridge.' It was a classic and somewhat old-fashioned type of fort, and seemed likely to present few difficulties to the sappers, miners and siege artillery of the Turkish army. The greatest difficulty that confronted them, they reported, was the nature of the terrain. Mount Sciberras was a bleak bone of rock, affording no shelter or cover, nor even for that matter any earth in which the troops might entrench.

In the siege of Rhodes, forty-three years before, sapping and mining had played a major part in the Turkish success. In Malta, because of the rocky nature of the island, the Turks had come well prepared for artillery bombardment. Mustapha Pasha now gave orders for the siege guns to be brought up from the transports in Marsasirocco, and positioned on Mount Sciberras. Oxen, captured in some of the villages, galley-slaves from the ships, and even the cattle brought to feed the troops, were yoked to the great guns in their wooden cradles. Slowly over the uneven land and the primitive dirt roads, they began to drag the guns four and a half miles from the anchorage of Marsasirocco to Mount Sciberras.

The weight of Turkish artillery at this period of history far exceeded that of the Christians. The Sultan's artillerymen and engineers, in forty years of land campaigns throughout Europe and the East, had brought bombardment to a fine art. They had learned in siege upon siege the effects of different weapons and the techniques to be applied against varying fortresses. Two 60-pound culverins, ten 80-pounders, and an enormous 'basilisk' firing solid shot weighing 160 pounds were brought up for the attack on St Elmo. With such heavy weapons, the Turkish fire was slower than the Christian. But, when applied at short ranges, the battering power of this heavy iron and stone shot was enormous.

In order to give some protection to their gunners and sharp-shooters the Turks found that they had to bring thousands of sackfuls of earth from the Marsa and nearby country. Until some artificial cover had been constructed, Mustapha had to site the majority of his troops just below the crest of the main ridge. This put them at a disadvantage since the musketeers and arquebusiers could not concentrate their fire on the waters between St Angelo and St Elmo.

On the morning of 24 May, Mustapha Pasha ordered the bombardment of St Elmo to begin. As the cannon and the great 'basilisk' began to boom and thunder, the defenders waited apprehensively. It was not only the weight of the Turkish shot that they feared. Rumour had it that the discharge of such heavy armament would cause the rock cisterns, in which their precious water was kept, to crack. Fortunately the vibration of the guns had been overestimated, but not so their battering power. Within an hour the lime and sandstone blocks with which the fort was built began to powder and flake. Here and there, blocks of stone began to fall away as the heavy shot fell time and again on the same identical places.

The garrison was also seriously harassed by the fire of picked snipers who had established themselves on the Marsamuscetto side of the fort. These troops had managed to erect screens of brushwood, planks, boards and earth, as a cover from which they could enfilade the northern walls of the defences. In some places these snipers were little more than five hundred feet from the ramparts. Being well below the rampart-walk, they could only be fired upon by men who were ready to expose themselves above the parapet. Against the clear blue sky of May, a man's head and shoulders stood out in sharp silhouette. Before long the sentries found it almost impossible to maintain a watch on the northern or Marsamuscetto side. All the time, the yellow dust-clouds of crumpled sandstone marked the slow deterioration of their landward wall.

The Grand Master, on the day when he had reinforced St Elmo, had sent a further dispatch by small boat to the north. With it he had sent a message to the Pope imploring him to secure all possible assistance for Malta. He also wrote a further message to the Priors of the Order in Europe, asking them to exert influence with their rulers to send assistance. The boat's first port of call was Messina, to remind the Viceroy of his promise to bring help before June. These dispatches from the beleaguered garrison passed another small boat at sea which was bringing La Valette the Viceroy's latest message. It arrived on the very day that the siege of St Elmo began.

Garcia de Toledo pointed out that, in view of the numbers of the Turkish forces, he would have to muster a considerable army to effect the relief of Malta. This could not be done quickly or easily. To send over reinforcements in small detachments would only be a waste, as they would be cut to pieces on landing – even if the ships carrying them got through the Malta Channel. The Viceroy asked the Grand Master to endure in patience. Everything that could be done, would be done. In the meantime he asked La Valette to send the remainder of the Order's galleys to Messina.

This request was a typical and sad example of that age-old military problem – the base headquarters asking the impossible of the man on the spot. With Turkish ships at sea off all the coast of Malta, Valette knew that he would only be sending his three galleys to certain destruction if he unmoored them, lowered the great chain across the creek, and ordered them to make for Sicily.

In any case, galleys required slaves to row them, officers to command and navigate them, and soldiers to fight them. Even with reduced crews, three galleys would have depleted Valette's small resources by a thousand men. It was clearly impossible. That night, after he had considered the Viceroy's message, a further small boat was sent out from Grand Harbour. She bore Valette's reply to the Viceroy. He gave his reasons why he could not send the galleys, he gave his estimation of the enemy's numbers and intentions, and he assured His Excellency that 'the morale of the Order, and of all the troops, was high. They would hold out to the end'.

'St Elmo is the key to Malta!' Valette had told Colonel Mas when the latter left to join the garrison at St Elmo. As the bombardment of the second day opened up, he knew that his words were true. So long as the Turkish army and gunners could be induced to wear themselves out, and expend shot and shell on the small fort on that barren peninsula, so much longer had he and the main garrison to strengthen and prepare. The other 200 of Colonel Mas's force were now rowed over to reinforce St Elmo, as well as a labour corps of sixty freed galley-slaves. These were not captured Turks, but Christian convicts who had been serving their time in the galleys.

In order to harass the Turkish gunners on Mount Sciberras, Valette now hastily built an additional rampart on the top of Fort St Angelo. Here he sited two large cannon firing directly across, and almost at a level with, the Turkish emplacements.

On every available occasion, the cavalry from Mdina swept down on the Marsa, cutting off Turkish watering parties and harrying any of their troops whom they came across foraging in the fields. The Knights and their soldiers, and the Maltese irregulars, used every opportunity to harass the enemy. Throughout the whole campaign the presence of De Copier's cavalry in Mdina was to prove a steady drain, like a wound in the side of the Turkish army.

The great advantage which the Moslems always had over Christians was their eastern fatalism, reinforced by the certainty of their warriors that Paradise awaited the Faithful who died in battle. As one historian has put it: 'The disregard of human life among the leaders of the Ottoman Turks at this time was almost incredible; to attain their end in war they sacrificed thousands upon thousands of men with a callous indifference. In no chapter of the bloodstained history of their Empire was this trait more in evidence than it was in the siege of Malta.' This was made

*Jean Parisot de la Valette, Grand Master of the
Order of St John of Jerusalem*

abundantly clear by their ability to construct trenches and ramparts upon the hostile slopes of Mount Sciberras. Under the whip of the overseers, the slaves and labour battalions continued to quarry and dig, to drag up fascines and sacks of earth – all this despite the withering fire of the garrison which left the bodies of the workmen as human mounds to be packed into the growing ramparts.

It was comparatively easy for them to work by night, but even by day the steady lines of men trailed up the slopes (where the modern suburb of Floriana now lies) and dragged their timber and material to the peak of Sciberras. Only two days after the siege of St Elmo had begun, they had erected a formidable parapet on the highest point facing the fort. From here the Turkish gunners could command the ravelin of St Elmo. As the main task of reducing St Elmo went ahead Mustapha began the bombardment of his next objective. He sited a heavy battery in some caves that faced St Angelo.

It was now late May and the summer heats were beginning. At night there would be cool breezes off the sea, but at midday the sun beat down on the small garrison in their menaced fort. Over Sciberras, where the sweating Turkish labour battalion were completing the defence works to shelter fourteen guns, the dust and haze shook like a mirage. The walls of the fort were slowly spilling outward. Fast as the signs of a breach appeared, Luigi Broglia and his troops laboured to build behind it a further walled protection. All the time, like a sand-castle eroded by the sea, the dimensions of the besieged fort were inexorably reduced.

In St Elmo, the difficulty of the defenders' position was increased by the fact that, now the enemy had raised a parapet and a battery on the highest ridge of Mount Sciberras, they were under a direct fire. The haste with which the fort had been built had not allowed for the construction of those underground tunnels and protective ramparts which normally allowed the besieged to move freely about their quarters. From the heart of St Elmo, a man looking to the south west – directly landward down the peninsula – could see the Turkish rampart and the black mouths of the guns. On the evening of 26 May – only two days after the

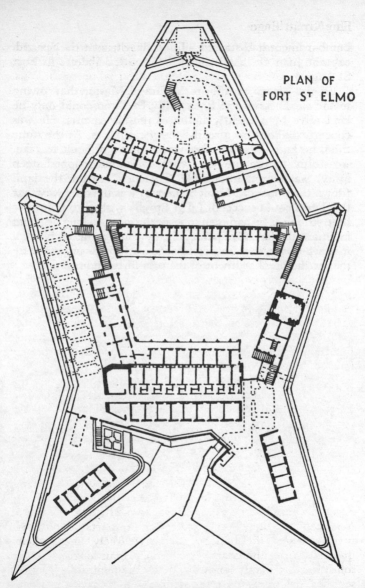

PLAN OF
FORT St ELMO

*Plan of Fort St Elmo as originally designed by the Spanish
engineer Pedro Pardo, in 1552*

bombardment had started – Luigi Broglia sent the Spanish captain Juan de la Cerda by boat to La Valette in Fort St Angelo.

Broglia wished to inform the Grand Master that, owing to the weakness of the fort's walls, St Elmo could only be kept alive by a nightly influx of reinforcements. He was concerned about his already heavy casualties. At the same time, he knew that the fort would prove difficult to take. To storm it from the sea (where the land dropped steep away) was almost impossible. To storm it from the land (down the slopes of Mount Sciberras) was the only way that the Turks could succeed. Luigi Broglia wished to point out that, so long as he had men to serve the guns, so long he could maintain the fort. Unfortunately, he chose as his emissary a man who was either unused to siege warfare, or unnerved by the terrific bombardment of the past forty-eight hours.

Chapter 10

The Janissaries

It was evening and La Valette was in full council surrounded
by the other members of the Sacro Consiglio. The arrival of
de la Cerda from the besieged fortress naturally disturbed
their meeting. All were eager to hear how matters stood in
St Elmo. The Grand Master at once asked the Spanish
Knight to give them his estimation of the position. La
Cerda, who was later described by one historian of the
Order as 'this officer whom fear made eloquent', embarked on a depressing description of the garrison and the
defences. The walls were crumbling, the Knights and
their men were exhausted, against the immense firepower
of the Turks there was no hope – St Elmo, in short, was
doomed.

La Valette's voice was icy. 'How long does the Chevalier
think that the fortress can hold out?'

'About eight days,' replied the Spaniard. 'Eight days at
the most.'

The Grand Master remembered how the embattled
towers and outworks at Rhodes had withstood the enemy
for nearly six months. Perhaps, like many an old soldier, he
felt a disdainful impatience with a younger generation who
seemed to lack the courage of their forebears.

'What exact losses have you suffered?' he asked.

'St Elmo, Seigneur,' replied La Cerda, evading the question, 'is like a sick man worn out and at the end of his
strength. He cannot survive without a doctor's aid and
help.'

'Then I myself will be your doctor!' said the Grand Master. 'I will bring others with me, and if we cannot at any rate

cure your fear, we will at least make sure that the fortress does not fall into the hands of the enemy!'

The manner in which La Cerda had blurted out his ill-considered views in front of the Council enraged La Valette. Instead of Broglia's sensible request for as many reinforcements as could be spared, La Cerda had painted a picture of unrelieved gloom. The Grand Master was determined that, if such was the general mood of the garrison, they should all be relieved. He would cross to St Elmo that night at the head of a band of volunteers and hold the fortress to the end.

Whether it was indeed fear, or just a stupid presentation of Broglia's request for reinforcements, the Spanish Knight now found himself an object of scorn. Several of the Grand Crosses begged La Valette not to trust implicitly to this messenger's opinions. Others pointed out that, whoever went to the relief of St Elmo, the Grand Master must himself stay behind in Birgu to direct the overall campaign. Others again were eagerly volunteering for the relief force.

It is doubtful whether La Valette had any serious intention of leading the relief force to St Elmo.

But, as he was to demonstrate time and again during the siege, he was a master of men's moods. He knew exactly what tone and words were necessary to revive morale. Within seconds of his speech, La Cerda was discredited as a reliable witness, and so many volunteers were applying for the post of danger that it was only a question of making a choice of the most suitable. Finally, fifty Knights together with two hundred Spanish soldiers under the Chevalier de Medran, were selected. They were sent over at once to the embattled fortress.

After these reinforcements had been dispatched, the Grand Master recalled the Council. He knew, he told them, that St Elmo was almost certainly doomed. But the whole campaign hinged upon the length of time which the fort could hold out. The Viceroy of Sicily had promised help but, as they all knew, it would be some time before a large enough force could be mustered and transported across the Malta channel. Every day St Elmo could hold out was vital.

The Council could hear the thunder of the guns of St

Angelo giving covering fire to the relief force as the Grand Master spoke. It was then, perhaps, they really understood for the first time, that under La Valette there would never be any question of surrender. This was a man imbued with all the ancient virtues of courage and self-sacrifice, together with the sure and absolute certainty of his Faith. Beyond Malta there could be no further withdrawal. A sudden silence of the guns told them that the relieving troops had disembarked, and were already making their way up the stony path towards St Elmo.

At dawn next day the Turkish batteries reopened fire on St Elmo. Other heavy guns which had now been transported up the slopes of Sciberras also began to bombard St Angelo. Yellow dust clouds began to lift over the walls of Valette's headquarters. Under cover of this bombardment, the Turkish working parties managed to push forward their trenches and protective screens. Soon the picked sharp-shooters from the Janissaries were able to begin sniping at St Elmo's defenders whenever they showed themselves in the embrasures of the walls. The invaders' morale had also been heartened by the news that El Louck Aly, Governor of Alexandria, had arrived. He brought with him four ships with further ammunition and stores, as well as a corps of Egyptian engineers famous for their skill in siege work.

It was late that afternoon when a dramatic incident occurred. Knight Commander St Aubin, who had been away on a reconnoitering cruise off the Barbary coast, suddenly appeared to the south of the island. He had been warned by La Valette that the Turkish attack might well have started before his return, and had been told to look out for smoke signals from the citadel of Mdina. But St Aubin could have been in no doubt as to the enemy's presence on the island, for the dull rumble of gunfire was audible many miles away. Undeterred, however, he determined to press on towards Grand Harbour, and see whether he could storm through the lines of enemy ships and make for the safety of Birgu and Dockyard Creek.

Admiral Piali, who had been wounded that day by a stone splinter, could hardly believe the report that this insolent single vessel had run up the Cross of St John and was actually daring to attempt to break through his patrolling lines. 'Piali Pasha thought him mad and decided to send out six galleys against this lunatic Christian . . .'

The watchers on St Angelo saw the Maltese galley come on directly towards the entrance of Grand Harbour. Puffs of smoke showed that the first of the Turkish galleys had opened fire. It was seen that St Aubin was replying with his bow-chaser. In the light summer haze that hung over the sea, deepened as it was by cannon smoke, St Aubin had not until now seen how the whole mouth of Grand Harbour was thronged with enemy vessels. Realizing suddenly that he had no hope of running the blockade, he altered course and turned north towards Sicily.

Piali's six galleys immediately gave chase, but were no match for the slim lines of St Aubin's craft. Only one of the Turkish ships managed to hang on his heels. St Aubin, seeing that the other five had dropped away, suddenly reversed his course. It was a classic trick in the naval strategy of the time, and one in which the Knights of Malta had long been practised. The lean, oared galley was suddenly stopped and then, while one side of the galley slaves back-watered, the others pulled their hardest. A Maltese galley could spin round almost within her own length, and the pursuing Turk suddenly found himself faced with no runaway but a vengeful hornet.

Mehemet Bey, in command of the Turkish ship, decided not to face this unexpected opponent. Altering course, he fled back to Grand Harbour with St Aubin's galley hard on his heels. The sick and wounded Admiral Piali, who had watched the whole encounter, was blind with fury. He felt his loss of face deeply before his rival Mustapha and the military leaders. Then as always, there was great competition between the various branches of military service, and Piali felt himself and his navy disgraced by Mehemet Bey's cowardice. When the unfortunate galley captain was brought before his admiral he was publicly degraded. Piali ended his harangue by spitting in his subordinate's face.

St Aubin meanwhile had pursued his course to Sicily.

It was late May and the sun-dried stone of St Elmo was cracking under the incessant fire. Iron, stone, and marble cannon balls were used by the Turks in an almost mathematical system. Selecting one point or salient, they hammered away at it hour after hour. The artillerymen who had subdued half the castles of Europe were not to be deterred by this small fort on a relatively unimportant island. Malta, 'this obscure rock', was not likely to present much difficulty to men who had taken by storm the cities of Persia and the capitals of Eastern Europe.

Valette had seen St Aubin's attempt to break into the harbour and his withdrawal towards Sicily. He knew too that the Governor of Alexandria had arrived to reinforce the besiegers. It was the dark hour when, as he knew well from previous sieges, everything seemed to turn against the defenders. It was with great joy, then, that he heard in the small hours of 29 May the shouts and rattle of musketry as the garrison of St Elmo made a sortie against the Turks. Led by Colonel Mas and the Chevalier de Medran, the besieged dashed out at dawn – the drawbridge having been silently lowered – and captured the advance Turkish trench.

The Turkish labour corps, who had been working throughout the night, were taken by surprise. In the still grey dawn panic spread among the advance-guard of the Moslem troops. The Grand Master and his Council, together with the sentries on the ramparts of St Angelo, watched eagerly as day broke to see what the firing, the calls of trumpets, and the hoarse shouting of engaged troops indicated. They saw the Turkish troops recoil across the bare heights of Sciberras. They knew then that, whatever anxiety they might have felt after La Cerda's unfortunate display, the defenders of St Elmo were still in good heart. They were still capable of taking the offensive against their attackers.

As the island turned pink and gold under the rising sun, it was clear that something approaching a rout was taking place among the enemy. It was at this moment that Mustapha Pasha, coming out from his tent to ascertain the cause of alarm, saw that the time had come for the Janissaries. In assault or in defence, in innumerable campaigns, in many countries, there arose a time when the cry went up: 'Janissaries forward!' It might be to stem a panic, or it might be to turn a wavering victory into a certainty. It was for this critical moment in the fortune of war that this special corps was designed. They were thrown into the balance to make sure that the scales were weighed in favour of the Faithful.

'Janissaries forward!' Mustapha ordered.

As the disorganized labour battalions fled past them, the invincible soldiers came through. The fleeing Turks divided to let them pass – more afraid, perhaps, of the Janissaries than of the Christians who pursued them. In their long flowing robes, with their herons' plumes waving above their heads, their scimitars unsheathed and shining, the Janissaries swept up to meet the Knights and the Spanish troops of Colonel Mas and de Medran. Like the white crest of an ocean roller they burst and fell on the advancing ranks of Christians.

The Janissaries, Yeni-Cheri, or 'New Soldiers' were one of the most extraordinary inventions of the Ottoman Empire. It is fair to call them an 'Invention', for they were unlike any type of soldier known to history, before or since. The most unusual thing about this *corps d'élite* was that none of them were Turkish by birth. All were the children of Christian parents who lived within the confines of the Ottoman Empire. Once every five years a general conscription was made throughout the Empire, and all the sons of Christians who had reached the age of seven were subject to inspection. Those who seemed to show the most promise in physique and intelligence were taken to Constantinople. If they passed a further examination, they were – in the words of W. H. Prescott –

. . . removed to different quarters and placed in seminaries where they might receive such instruction as would fit them for the duties of life. Those giving greatest promise of strength and endurance were sent to places prepared for them in Asia Minor. Here they were subjected to a severe training, to abstinence, to privations of every kind, and to the strictest discipline which should fit them for the profession of soldier. . . . Their whole life may be said to have been passed in war or in the preparation for it. Forbidden to marry, they had no families to engage their affections, which, as with the monks and friars of Christian countries, were concentrated in their own order. . . . Proud of the privileges which distinguished them from the rest of the army, they seemed desirous to prove their title to them, through discipline and by their promptness to execute the most dangerous and difficult services. . . .

Christian by birth, Spartan by upbringing, and fanatical Moslems by conversion, the Janissaries were one of the most amazing military corps in history. It was as if the Turks, remembering over centuries the nature of the men who had defeated their ancestors at Thermopylae, were determined to raise a type of soldier who should combine the most arrogant militarism of the West with the religious fanaticism of the East. These were the men, armed with scimitar, arquebus, and round shield, whom Mustapha Pasha had now sent forward to check the Christian onrush.

Slowly but surely, contesting every inch of the ground, the sortie which had made its way so gallantly out of St Elmo was forced back. Before the Grand Master's eyes, as he stood watching on the top rampart of St Angelo, the white robes spilled onward and downward towards the fort. He could not see the flicker of the Herons' plumes above their heads, but he – who had known a lifetime of campaigning against the Moslem – must surely have known that nobody except the Janissaries went into battle with those high wailing cries, or poured onward like an inexhaustible wave.

Before the advance of these supreme warriors, the defenders fell back, only reaching the safety of the gates in time for the cannon above their heads to open fire on the advancing ranks of their enemies. The smoke lay heavy and thick on the ground. A south-westerly Sirocco, the humid wind that brings all the dampness of the southern Mediterranean with it, was blowing that day. It was not until some time after noon that the watchers on St Angelo and the defenders of St Elmo could see what had happened on the bare slope in front of the beleaguered fort. When they did, they realized that their early success of the morning had been to no avail.

Above a high parapet, formerly in Christian hands – a

parapet that lifted above the outer defence works beyond the ravelin itself – the Turkish crescent flaunted in the southerly breeze. The Janissaries had not only recaptured their own trenches. They had established themselves in a strong position right in the teeth of St Elmo. The men who boasted that 'the body of a Janissary is only a stepping stone for his brethren into the breach itself' had made good their claim.

Chapter 11

The arrival of Dragut

The sound of gunfire at sea brought the defenders of St Elmo, St Angelo, and St Michael out on to their ramparts. High on the walls of Mdina, the sentries stared east as the cannon rumbled. The whole Turkish fleet appeared to be under way!

Admiral Piali was in the van, followed by at least eighty Turkish warships. They came up the coast, passed Gallows' Point at the southern end of Grand Harbour, and then stood close inshore towards St Elmo. As each ship came abreast the smoking fort, it fired a salvo before hauling out again and reforming into line. It was at this moment that the sentries noticed the other ships approaching from the south-east. The word went round: 'It is Dragut!'

It was known, from runaways and captured prisoners, that the great corsair had been expected ever since the beginning of the siege. There could be no doubt that this squadron of fifteen ships approaching from North Africa was Dragut's, the greatest Moslem seaman of his time, and Governor of Tripoli.

Admiral Piali, in order to impress Dragut, had arranged a show of strength off St Elmo before sailing out in formation to meet the famous warrior. Unfortunately for Piali's pride, the gunnery of his fleet left much to be desired. With the exception of a few shots which hit the thick seaward walls of St Elmo, most of the cannon balls passed clean over the fort to fall among the Turkish attackers on the far side. One of Piali's galleys, hit between wind and water by St Elmo's culverin, had to be taken in tow and beached farther up the coast. As a display of naval strength, the evolution had done little or nothing to dishearten the defenders. The arrival of Dragut was another matter altogether.

Dragut Rais, or Torghoud to give him more accurately his Turkish name, was eighty years old when he came to Malta for the Great Siege. Born in 1485, native of Anatolia in Asia Minor, he was the child of poor parents from a village called Charabalac. While he was still a boy, a Turkish Governor who happened to be passing through Charabalac was impressed by Dragut's intelligence and character. He took the boy with him to Egypt and had him educated, with the result that, as a young man, Dragut joined the military corps of the Mamelukes as a bombardier. He became an expert in artillery warfare and later, like many another ambitious young man, turned to the sea to seek his fortune.

Starting as a gunner aboard corsair ships, he finally became owner of a galliot sailing out of Alexandria. From then on, his progress was rapid and assured. The famous corsair Barbarossa took to the young man, and soon Dragut was sailing as one of Barbarossa's lieutenants. Attracted by his intrepidity and cunning, a number of other corsairs joined up with him. Before long, he was in command of his own squadron. On the death of Barbarossa in 1545, he was acknowledged as his natural successor, and the greatest scourge of the Christians in the Mediterranean. His record of success, both by land and sea, was such that he earned from his fellow Moslems the well-deserved title of 'The Drawn Sword of Islam'. The coastal dwellers and sea-captains of Christendom, for their part, were not above saying that Barbarossa's successor was even more audacious than his former master.

The French Admiral, Jurien de la Gravière, assessed him in these terms:

Dragut was superior to Barbarossa. A living chart of the Mediterranean, he combined science with audacity. There was not a creek unknown to him, not a channel that he had not sailed. Ingenious in devising ways and means, when all around him despaired, he excelled above all in escaping by unexpected methods from situations of great peril. An incomparable pilot, he had no equal in sea-warfare except the Chevalier Romegas. On land he was skilful enough to be compared with the finest generals of Charles V and Philip II. He had known the hardship of captivity and he showed himself humane to his own captives. Under every aspect he was a character. No one was more worthy than he, to bear the title of 'King'. . . .

Dragut knew the Maltese archipelago well, for between 1540 and 1565 he had raided the islands no less than six times. On the last of these expeditions he had carried off most of the population of Gozo. It was said that this was his revenge for a previous occasion when Dragut's brother had been killed in Gozo, and the Governor of the citadel had refused him permission to take away the body for burial. But such raids were small episodes in the life of a man who had raided Naples, looted Castellamare, and captured a galley belonging to the Knights with 70,000 ducats aboard. When he had stormed the seaport of Bastia in Corsica he had carried off more than 7,000 captives, and when he took Reggio on the Straits of Messina by storm, the whole population, men, women, and children, had been enslaved. Invested by the great Genoese admiral, Andrea Doria, in the North African island of Djerba, he had escaped by a clever ruse, drawing his ships overland to the far end of the island away from the harbour which Doria was blockading. Escaping by night, he had sailed away and captured a large vessel full of reinforcements bound for the Genoese admiral. His escape had made the great Doria the laughing stock of the Mediterranean – a slight which the Admiral never forgave. It was Dragut who had captured Tripoli from the Knights in 1551.

Like La Valette he had served his time as a galley slave. Despite a period when he had been at variance with the Sultan Soleyman, he had in recent years been confirmed by the Grande Porte in his Governorship of Tripoli. The Sultan as a mark of his favour had also sent the old corsair a gold-encrusted scimitar, and a gem-set copy of the Koran. This was the man whom Soleyman had ordered his two commanders, Mustapha and Piali, to respect in all things and to accept his suggestions and advice.

Dragut brought with him from Tripoli, 1,500 of his picked fighting men, and fifteen ships with siege guns and ammunition. As an old veteran of siege warfare – one who knew Malta better than either of the two commanders – it was fortunate for the Knights and their garrisons that Dragut arrived after the initial plan for the siege had been adopted. He landed in the small bay of St Julian's, a little north of Marsamuscetto. There Piali met him, and the two went ashore to confer with Mustapha Pasha. Meanwhile the fleet, augmented by Dragut's ships from Tripoli, sailed back past St Elmo, and made their way south to the anchorage at Marsasirocco.

The day which had begun with the thunder of guns at sea, the approach of Dragut, and the naval bombardment of St Elmo, was also marked by a cavalry action. Two detachments of Maltese cavalrymen, from Birgu and Mdina, fell upon a body of Turkish troops who had been sent to round up some Maltese living on the west coast of the island near the village of Dingli. (They were mostly peasants, inhabiting some of the old cave-dwellings which honey-combed the rocky western coast.) The Maltese cavalry caught the Turkish foot soldiers on the march. Out of four hundred, half were killed or captured, and the rest put to flight. Once again, Valette's policy of keeping his cavalry for harrying tactics against foot soldiers was well justified.

Dragut, in company with Piali, made his way to the Commander-in-Chief's tent near the Marsa. Mustapha Pasha received him with all the honour due to so famous a man. Having heard the Sultan's official proclamation read aloud – to the effect that Dragut's advice was to be asked for on all major details relating to the siege – the corsair did not mince his words.

'Before attacking any of the main positions, you should have sealed off the island from the north. Why did you not take Gozo first, and then proceed to the capture of Mdina? Both citadels are old and ill-defended. They would have fallen easily. Once they had been captured, it would have been simple to prevent any ships with messengers sailing north to Sicily. The possession of Gozo and the north of

Malta would also have made it difficult for any reinforcements to be landed to aid the Knights. St Elmo – ' he said scornfully. 'It would have fallen of its own accord! You could have ignored it, once you had secured the rest of the island. At your leisure you could then have proceeded to the attack on Birgu and Senglea.'

Dragut saw at once the danger of having the back door to Malta unguarded. The news of that day's cavalry attack (carried out largely from Mdina) reinforced his opinion that the old city should have been taken before any attempt had been made on Grand Harbour. Mustapha, no doubt, felt the weight of his argument. Had he not, himself, suggested that such should be the course of the campaign? Unfortunately, Piali, this young grandson-in-law of the Sultan, had insisted that Marsamuscetto must be taken in order to berth the fleet securely.

Piali repeated that the security of the fleet was all-important. 'Besides,' he added in self-defence, 'the Chief Engineer assured us that St Elmo could not hold out for more than five days.'

Dragut listened with growing impatience while the Chief Engineer defended his views, and while the other authorities presented their side of the case. Dragut, undoubtedly, would have agreed with La Valette that a small Council was more efficient in warfare than a large one. But that was not the way in which things were ordered in the Ottoman Empire. An Eastern respect for lineage, and for pride of place, meant that most Turkish councils were over-large and cumbersome. Dragut realized that it was up to him to assert the authority which the Sultan had vested in him.

'It is a thousand pities that the attack on St Elmo was ever begun.' He said. 'But, now that it has – it would be shameful to give it up.'

Better the loss of many lives, than the loss of irreplaceable morale.

He made immediate arrangements for four heavy culverins to be taken from his galleys and placed on Tigné Point, immediately facing St Elmo from the north. There, at a range of no more than five hundred yards, their steady fire could fall upon the besieged at a point from which – until then – they had been relatively secure. The barren sandstone shelf where this battery was sited bears to this day the name of 'Dragut Point'.

As a master of siege warfare and of artillery work, Dragut knew that it was heavy fire from many points of the compass which finally wore down the defence. He pointed out that the batteries on Sciberras were well enough sited, but that St Elmo was only being engaged from one direction – the landward, or western side.

'These are men who are born and bred to the sound of artillery. The noise will not frighten them. We must use our brains.'

He gave orders for another battery to be quickly transported to Punta delle Forche, (Gallows' Point) – so called because it was here that the Knights hung pirates and other criminals. (The first sight that met the eye on entering Grand Harbour was usually some sun-dried bodies, swaying in their chains, on the spit of land where Fort Ricasoli now stands.) The battery on Mount Sciberras was to be increased by a further fifty guns. An earthwork was to be built from the shore of Grand Harbour to screen this big new battery from the fire of St Angelo, and additional guns were to be placed so as to give cross-fire on the ravelin and the cavalier. St Elmo was to be pounded to pieces from every quarter.

Dragut saw at once what Mustapha and his advisers had apparently failed to notice. St Elmo's strength lay in the fact that La Valette had been able to reinforce its garrison by sending boats over from St Angelo during the night.

'Cut their lines of communication,' he said, 'and the fortress must inevitably fall.'

It was with this in mind that he ordered the battery to be landed on Gallows' Point. But fortunately for the Knights it was Piali who, again unwittingly, acted as their ally. He refused to land the number of guns required from his ships, until Marsamuscetto had been secured. The result was that, although Dragut managed to get a battery established on Gallows' Point, it was not strong enough to ensure that no boats could cross from St Angelo to Fort St Elmo.

It was indicative of Dragut's character that these new dispositions were not conceived in the remoteness of the Grand Council tent. Late though the hour was, he insisted on going over the ground himself and making sure that the information given by the engineers and gunners was correct. He was a man of war, and not an abstract military theorist. At the age of eighty, having been on passage from Tripoli for several days, and having ridden from St Julian's Bay to the conference at the Marsa that morning, he still insisted on going down among the troops. He intended to see the action from the viewpoint of the men who were engaged in it.

'One more thing,' he said in conclusion, 'the ravelin – the outer works of the fort – must be captured at all cost. It is a task for the Janissaries.'

At the news that Dragut was coming to inspect them, the Turkish gunners redoubled their efforts. In the fading light they sent round after round crashing against the walls of St Elmo. The cheers, the thunder of guns, the lights and flares on the slope of Mount Sciberras told the Grand Master and the defenders of St Angelo that someone of importance had arrived upon the scene.

It could only have been Dragut. It could only have been Dragut, who, unlike his Commander-in-Chief or Admiral Piali, refused to return to a silk-lined tent for the evening meal and rest. He took up his quarters in the trenches on Mount Sciberras among the troops. There he stayed. There he had his meals, and there – amid the smoke and thunder of the basilisks – he took his rest.

Chapter 12

'A volcano in eruption . . .'

From the moment that Dragut arrived, it was clear that a coordinating brain had taken charge of the Turkish forces. Within a day, the fire against the fort had doubled. The besieged could also tell, from the activity on Gallows' Point and Tigné, that new batteries would soon be in operation against them. Breaches began to appear in the walls, and fast as the defenders tried to erect counter-walls behind them, so these too were shot away. Before long they could expect a mass assault.

Balbi da Correggio, the Spanish soldier of fortune, who served throughout the siege in the garrison of St Michael's and who left us his eyewitness account, describes St Elmo in these days as being 'like a volcano in eruption, spouting fire and smoke'. Pepe di Ruvo, a Neapolitan Knight who was to die in the fortress, left a note behind him saying that he had counted the number of rounds fired by the Turks. 'On most days, an average of not less than 6,000 to 7,000 shots were discharged at St Elmo.'

It was now the end of May and the temperature was rising to the eighties. The nights were calm and cloudless, and during the day only light airs drifted across the island. Heat and thirst were an added burden to the besieged. The wounded lay in their blood and sweat wherever a little shade could be found. Bread soaked in wine and water was put between their lips. Supply parties made the rounds of the sentry posts and the repair gangs labouring at the walls. They brought them food and water so that no time was wasted on meals. From the ditch beyond St Elmo – where friend and foe lay piled together since the Janissary assault –

the stench of decaying bodies began to mount on the air. The bare slopes of Sciberras were hazy with heat, and beyond Birgu and Senglea the southern ridges shook under the sun.

There was no comfort for besiegers or besieged in the torrid weather. The Turks, no less than the Knights and the Maltese, suffered from the shortage of water. Although they had managed to purify the waterholes and wells of the Marsa, it is probable that the dysentery among their forces stemmed from the water supply. From June onwards they suffered increasingly from disease, so much so that they were forced to erect hundreds of tents in the Marsa to accommodate their sick.

La Valette had no cause to regard the present state of the siege with anything other than pessimism. The day after Dragut had arrived and taken a hand in the attack on St Elmo, a small vessel had managed to run the blockade and put a messenger ashore. It brought the Grand Master the news that there was no hope of an early relief. The Viceroy of Sicily said, in his dispatch, that it was necessary for every fort in the island to hold out as along as possible. Raising reinforcements was proving a difficult and slow business, and Don Garcia was also troubled by a shortage of suitable shipping. He again requested the Grand Master to send up to Sicily the galleys which were lying behind St Angelo and in Dockyard Creek.

It was 31 May, Ascension Day, when La Valette read the dispatch to his Council. There could, of course, be no question of his attempting to send the remaining galleys out of Grand Harbour. He had already pointed out to Don Garcia that he could not afford to man them and, in any case, no galley could have made its way through the blockade. It was a different matter altogether for small sailing boats manned and piloted by Maltese fishermen who knew their own shores, shoals, and creeks, like the palms of their hands.

'We now know,' Valette said, 'that we must not look to others for our deliverance! It is only upon God and our own swords that we may rely! Yet this is no reason why we should be disheartened. Rather the opposite, for it is better to know the truth of one's situation than to be deceived by specious hopes. Our Faith and the Honour of our Order are in our own hands. We shall not fail.'

In his reply to the Viceroy of Sicily, La Valette again pointed out the impossibility of sending the galleys to Messina. He asked rather that the Order's galleys in Messina should be sent to Malta, together with any Knights and men-at-arms who had recently arrived from Europe. He begged Don Garcia to send any men whom he could spare. The losses in St Elmo were mounting daily, and the task of keeping the garrison reinforced was steadily depleting the future defenders of St Angelo, St Michael, and Birgu. Nevertheless, he determined to carry on ferrying in reinforcements as long as it was possible. Every night the wounded of St Elmo were also removed to the security of the Hospital in Birgu.

It was no longer possible to send boats across during daylight. It was not until nightfall that the rowing boats could drop St Angelo point behind them, and make the half-mile crossing to the landing place below St Elmo. Quietly and stealthily though they rowed, the dip of their oars in the flashing phosphorescent midsummer water gave away their movement to the watchful Turks. On one occasion the Turks slipped out in small boats from the creek near Gallows' Point and intercepted the convoy of reinforcements. A miniature sea-battle took place, in the course of which one of the Maltese boats was overwhelmed. In a second attack, it was the Turks who were worsted, losing two of their boats. After that, they contented themselves with bombarding the relief boats with cannon and musket fire.

It was on the morning of 3 June, that day dedicated to St Elmo on the Church calendar, that Dragut's new battery on Tigné Point opened fire on the fortress. St Elmo's patron Saint had long been associated with that phenomenon known as 'St Elmo's fire'. This bluish glow of static electricity – which appears upon masts and yardarms, and whose sibilant fizzing sound can be heard from several yards away – was considered a visible sign that the Saint had taken a ship under his care. On St Elmo's day, it seemed as if the Saint had indeed descended upon the fort that bore his name. The whole star-shaped bastion smoked and crackled, and the fire from the defenders' guns ran like lightning along the walls.

From the captured counterscarp, where the Janissaries had placed their advance guard, the arquebus fire was steady and accurate. Loudly the Janissaries cried to their Lieutenant-Aga that the breaches which were opening in front of them were big enough for them to storm. Dragut, who was awake and in the front ranks at daylight, waited and watched to see how long it would be before an opportunity presented itself for a large-scale attack on the ravelin. As he had told Mustapha Pasha at the first conference, he considered that this outerwork of Fort St Elmo must be captured soon – whatever losses it might entail. He knew that, as soon as the ravelin was in Turkish hands, it could only be a matter of days before the fortress must inevitably be reduced. He saw that the Christians still seemed in good heart and that their return fire was accurate and heavy. The moment that they noticed a concentration of Turkish troops, making ready for a possible attack on the breaches in the walls, their cannon and arquebus fire was instantly directed on to the massing ranks. 'Not yet,' he told himself. He was not willing to hazard the picked troops of the Sultan unless he saw a good chance of success.

It was at this moment of the day, when the morning fires were beginning to smoke among the encampments, that the long-coveted ravelin fell into his hands more by accident than design. A group of Turkish engineers, who had been sent forward to report on the condition of St Elmo's walls, decided to inspect the ravelin. This outerwork, shielding the fort from the north-western corner, had been very badly damaged by Turkish gunfire. They saw that its condition was extremely weak, and close though they came below its walls, no sentry challenged them and no alert arquebusier sent a shot in their direction. It seemed as if the ravelin was deserted. One of the party, standing on the shoulders of a comrade, peered through a low embrasure. He saw nothing but a few exhausted soldiers lying asleep. Silently and swiftly the party slipped back to the Turkish lines and reported to

Dragut and Mustapha Pasha that the ravelin was almost deserted. No sentries seemed to be posted, and it could be easily taken.

Historians have debated the reason why this most important outwork to Fort St Elmo should have been in this condition at the dangerous hour of dawn – the hour when men always stand to the alert in anticipation of attack. Their conjecture is fruitless, for no record has survived to explain what happened. Even Balbi, the most reliable eyewitness of the siege, can only hazard a guess (he himself having been on guard in St Michael's on the other side of Grand Harbour). It is possible that the sentry who should have been patrolling the ravelin walls had fallen asleep. It is more than likely that a stray bullet from one of the Turkish snipers had killed the man at his post, and that his death had gone unnoticed by his sleeping companions.

Within a few minutes of receiving the news, the Janissary advance guard was ordered out from the counterscarp. In the early morning light their white-robed figures slid forward. Their scaling ladders were laid against the ravelin's wall. They burst over the top with a cry that woke the sleeping soldiers and alerted the sentries on St Elmo. It was too late for resistance. Shot down, or hacked to pieces before they could gather their wits, the defenders of the ravelin perished almost to a man.

A plank bridge served as a connecting link between the ravelin and the fort itself, and down this a few survivors now fled to the safety of St Elmo. It was on this bridge that the main fight developed, the Janissaries storming forward from the captured ravelin and trying to burst into the fort before the portcullis could be closed. Lanfreducci, a Pisan Knight, was in command of the two cannon which surmounted the portcullis. As his fellow Christians made for the safety of the fort, he opened fire on the advancing ranks of Janissaries, managing to hold them at bay while the portcullis was raised and the survivors let in.

Still the Turkish troops came on. Some of them stormed right up to the portcullis and began firing through its grille at their enemy within.

'Lions of Islam!' A dervish exhorted them. 'Now let the sword of the Lord separate their souls from their bodies, their trunks from their heads! Liberate spirit from matter!'

Heedless of the gaps torn in their ranks by the cannon, the Janissaries swarmed along the bridge and began to lay their scaling ladders against the fort itself. A lull in the firing, caused by the death of the Knight responsible for the ammunition supply to Lanfreducci's guns, enabled the Turks to get their ladders in place and attempt an escalade. Above their heads the defenders were poised with their muskets in their hands. Now they brought to bear on their attackers all the ingenuity of siege warfare. 'Wildfire and Trumps and firework hoops were loosed upon the white-robed Turks. . . .'

It was for critical moments like this, when the enemy had actually reached the walls, that the ancestor of the modern flame-thrower had been devised. Wildfire, or Greek fire as it was sometimes termed, had been used in warfare since classical times. It was not until the Crusades, however, that the art of making this inflammable mixture had been fully developed. Its exact composition varied according to the gunners or engineers responsible, and many of the formulae were closely guarded secrets of the time. Basically, wildfire was composed of a mixture of saltpetre, pounded sulphur, pitch, unrefined ammoniacal salt, resin, and turpentine. They were packed into thin pots which would break easily (according to the historian Bosio, 'of a size that would fit into a man's hand and could be thrown 20 to 30 yards'). Wildfire when used in this manner was an anti-personnel weapon – a forerunner of the 'Molotov Cocktail' used by the Russians and Partisan Fighters in the last war. The mouths of the pots which held it were narrow, and sealed with linen or thick paper. This was secured by cords soaked in sulphur, four ends of the cords being left free. Just before throwing a pot of wildfire, one or all of the cords were lit, thus making sure that when the pot burst, the lighted fuse would explode it.

Trumps were hollowed-out tubes of wood or metal,

secured to long poles. In the same way as the pots of wild-fire, they were filled with an inflammable mixture, except that it was made more liquid by the addition of linseed oil or turpentine. 'When you light the trump,' wrote one authority, 'it continues a long time snorting and belching vivid, furious flames, and large, and several yards long.' The trump derived its name from the harsh snoring sound it made when alight. A smaller version was attached to the head of a pike. This often had a further ingenious mechanism whereby, when it was almost burnt out, it fired two small cylinders of iron or brass which were loaded with gunpowder and discharged lead bullets.

As the Janissaries attempted to storm the walls of St Elmo, this rain of fire accompanied the arquebus shot and the blocks of stone and cauldrons of boiling pitch, with which the Christians defended themselves. The long loose robes worn by the Turks – suitable though they were for the heat of summer – were the worst possible uniform for men confronted by blazing fire. Like human torches, the escalading soldiers fell back into the ditch below the fort. The sweet, pork-like odour of burning flesh filled the air.

From dawn until shortly after noon, the battle raged around the bridge and the landward walls of St Elmo. Bundles of wool, straw, and earth were thrown by the Turks into the ditch between the ravelin and the fort in order to give easier access to the walls. Soon, all this material was smouldering from the wildfire. The stark ramparts rose out of a mist of flames and smoke.

The Janissaries, who had been waiting for days to prove their prowess, were given their chance that morning. Mustapha Pasha unleashed line upon line of the Sultan's finest troops against the charred and cracked walls of St Elmo. The Turkish losses were heavy, for the defenders behind their parapets made use of every device which the Knights of St John had learned in four centuries of war. Worse even than wildfire or the trump, was the firework hoop – the invention of which was attributed by the historian Vertot to La Valette himself, but by Balbi to a Brother of the Order, Ramon Fortunii.

These hoops,

composed of the lightest wood, were first dipped into brandy, then rubbed with oil, and then covered with wool and cotton which had been soaked in other combustible liquors, as well as mixed with saltpetre and gunpowder. When the preparation was cool, the whole process was repeated several times. On an assault, when the hoops were on fire, they were taken up with tongs and thrown into the midst of the advancing battalions. Two or three soldiers regularly would get entangled with one of these blazing hoops. . . .

Their impact on the Moslems in their loose-flowing light robes was devastating. It was largely owing to these hoops that this first major assault on St Elmo failed.

When Mustapha finally called off his troops, it was estimated that he had lost nearly two thousand, most of them the cream of the Janissary advance guard. The defenders had lost only ten Knights and seventy soldiers. If, on the face of it, the victory might seem to lie with the garrison of St Elmo, the fact remains that the capture of the ravelin alone was worth two thousand men to the Turkish Commander-in-Chief. He was now entrenched within easy distance of the fort, and in a position from which he could bring up cannon and dominate the interior of St Elmo.

Even while the action had been taking place beneath the fortress walls, the Turkish labour corps and slaves from the galleys had begun their task of rendering the ravelin impregnable. Slow trains of oxen and men were already dragging more guns up the slopes of Sciberras. The guns on Gallows' Point and Tigné began to open up again with their unremitting cannonade the minute that the Janissaries were withdrawn.

It was at the close of this day that a Knight of Auvergne, Abel de Bridiers de la Gardampe, was shot and mortally wounded. As his friends ran to help him, he motioned them back with the words: 'Count me no more among the living. Your time will be better spent looking after our other brothers.'

While the cannon thundered, and the fire rained down from the walls, and the Janissaries came on in wave upon shouting wave, La Gardampe dragged himself to the chapel of St Elmo. In the afternoon, when the Knights of the Order made their way to the chapel to give thanks for what seemed almost a victory, they found the Knight of Auvergne stretched dead at the foot of the altar.

Chapter 13

Sentence of death

'Shorn of its outworks the Castle of St Elmo stood like some bare and solitary trunk, exposed to all the fury of the storm. . . .' Now that the Turks had occupied the ravelin, they began to raise behind, and above it, a high mound or cavalier. Once this was completed they would be able to command the whole interior of St Elmo and fire directly at the defenders.

Day by day, as the Turkish fire mounted and as the great ramp rose slowly above the ravelin, so the conditions of the garrison worsened. Marshal Copier, who had been ordered by La Valette to cross over and inspect the fortress, reported that it would be impossible to dislodge the enemy from the ravelin. They were holding the captured position in vast numbers and there was no chance of a sally from St Elmo having any success against them. Marshal Copier also reported that he thought the fort could only hold out if regular reinforcements continued to be sent in every night.

An hour or so before dawn on 4 June, a small boat suddenly emerged from the haze to seaward and pulled rapidly towards St Elmo. As the sentries began to open fire, a figure in the stern-sheets of the boat stood up and called out: 'Salvago! Salvago!'

His voice carried, and the name was recognized. It was a Knight of the Order, Raffael Salvago, in company with a Spanish Captain, de Miranda. The latter was a well-known soldier who had been sent over from Sicily by Don Garcia to examine St Elmo and the defences generally, and to convey the Viceroy's latest message to La Valette. Escorted by the Order's two galleys which had been lying at Messina, they had managed to evade the blockading Turks, and had put off in a small boat when they were within a short distance from St Elmo. The galleys, having seen Salvago and Miranda headed shorewards, had turned back again to Sicily. It was no tribute to the efficiency of Piali's fleet that two galleys should have been able to lie close to the coast at such a moment in the siege.

Landing in a small cove just to the east of the fort, where a flight of steps led up to the heights of St Elmo, Salvago and Miranda told their boatmen to wait while they inspected the defences. Before daylight, they must be on their way across Grand Harbour to give Don Garcia's message to the Grand Master. A swift inspection showed that the state of the garrison was almost hopeless.

... The insupportable fatigues increasing, chiefly the whole night, and the burying in the parapets of bowels and limbs of men all torn to pieces and pounded by the hostile cannon, to such a pass had the hapless besieged been reduced; what with never stirring from their posts, but sleeping there and eating; with all other human functions; in arms always, and prepared for combat; by day exposed to the burning sun, and by night to the cold damp; privation of all kinds, from the blasts of gunpowder, smoke, dust, wildfire, iron, and stones, volleys of musketry, to explosions of enormous batteries, insufficient nutriment or unwholesome, they had got so disfigured that they hardly knew each other any more. Ashamed of retiring for wounds not manifestly quite dangerous and almost mortal, those with the smaller bones dislocated or shattered, and livid faces bruised with frightful sores, or extremely lame and limping woefully; these miserably bandaged round the head, arms in slings, strange contortions – such figures were frequent and nearly general, and to be taken for spectres rather than living forms.

The surface of Grand Harbour was beginning to glow with light, the giant bulk of St Angelo was standing out against the quickening sky, when Salvago and Miranda rejoined their boat and pushed off for Birgu. Fired on by the Turkish gunners and sentries, they managed to reach Birgu with the loss of one sailor. What they had seen at St Elmo convinced them that the fortress had no chance of holding out unless a considerable number of fresh reinforcements was sent over. If that were done, Miranda felt that the fort could probably be held against the Turk for a few days more. There was no hope that it could survive any longer. Miranda – though he knew he was going to his death – volunteered to go over at once and assist the Bailiff de Guaras in the necessary measures for the last stand.

Knight Salvago and Captain de Miranda had other and worse news for the Grand Master. The message they brought from Don Garcia was that he would come to their aid by the end of June – he gave the specific date of the 20th – but only on the condition that the Grand Master sent him the Order's galleys from Malta. Don Garcia has been harshly treated by historians of the Siege for his dilatory behaviour – and not without good reason. In these exchanges with La Valette, he had already been precisely and carefully told why it was impossible to send the galleys north to Sicily. St Aubin (who had tried to break the blockade in his galley) had also told him that it was impossible to get into the harbour. How then could Don Garcia expect the more difficult evolution – taking galleys out – to succeed?

Don Garcia knew exactly how many men La Valette had – a mere 9,000 from the very beginning. He knew too that, even with half-complements, it would have taken several hundred men to crew the galleys, not a single one of whom could be spared from duty in the beleaguered forts. The victor of Peñon de la Gomera, was a very experienced soldier. There can be no doubt that in making his relief of the island conditional on the dispatch of the galleys to Messina, he was doing no more than providing an excuse for his behaviour.

Although no documents have come to light which can explain the Viceroy's actions, there are a number of reasons which could help to explain them. As Governor of Sicily, he was responsible for one of the Emperor Philip II's most important possessions in the Mediterranean. He must have realized that Soleyman's attempt on Malta was probably a preliminary to an attack on Sicily and the Kingdom of Naples. If Don Garcia were to send over a fleet and a relief force of insufficient strength – and if they were destroyed at sea, or defeated ashore – the door to Sicily would be open. Within a matter of hours the Turkish fleet could have put Malta behind them, and begun to land south of Syracuse and in the vicinity of Cape Passaro. If all his available forces and ships had been lost in a hasty attempt to relieve Malta, Sicily would have fallen within a matter of weeks. Don Garcia's reluctance to send a relief force, until he was sure that it was more than adequate, is understandable. The various historians of the Order, from Bosio in the sixteenth century to Taafe in the nineteenth, have been determined to portray the Governor as a villain or coward. He was cautious.

In his reply to this further message from Don Garcia, La Valette stressed that the relief force need be no larger than 15,000 men, and that it could land quite easily in the northwest bays of Malta, either at Mgarr, or Ghain Tuffieha. He pointed out that he was sending anything up to 200 fresh troops into St Elmo every night, and that this drain on the resources of Birgu and Senglea could not continue. He begged Don Garcia to let him have at any rate five hundred men, who could be transported in the two galleys which had just brought down Miranda and the Chevalier Salvago.

It was now 4 June, and if Don Garcia's message was to be believed, the Grand Master had only to hold out a further fourteen days before he would be relieved. Fortunately he was as sceptical as he was clear-sighted.

La Valette accepted de Miranda's offer to return with a relief force to St Elmo. That night, the Spaniard and a number of volunteer Knights were ferried across to the doomed fortress, together with a contingent of a hundred men. St Elmo was being kept alive by this regular blood-transfusion.

The Turkish fire was so heavy that, in the words of a contemporary, it seemed as if 'they were determined to reduce the fortress to powder'. On the northern side, fast as Colonel Mas and his troops laboured to build retrenchments within the shattered walls, so the battery installed by Dragut on Tigné Point pounded them away. On the side facing the ravelin and the main Turkish batteries, the walls were a crumbling heap of ruins, cascading and sliding down to fill the ditch at their feet. Aware of the increasing danger from this point, the defenders had managed to blow up the bridge that connected the ravelin with the fortress. They saw, with increasing despair, that the Turkish labour corps worked continuously through the night to fill the ditch which separated the ravelin from St Elmo.

Behind the make-shift walls, and entrenchments formed of sticks, earth, and bedding, the defenders crept from place to place. It was no longer possible to cross the open ground of the fort in safety. On Thursday, 7 June, with the aid of a bridge made of ships' masts and spars, the Turks attempted another escalade. They preceded their attack by an intense artillery bombardment that left the cavalier so ruined that the defenders could no longer man it. Parts of the walls were also breached on the landward side. During this bombardment, the whole fort shook and trembled like a ship in a storm. To the watchers on St Angelo it seemed as if St Elmo's last hour had surely come. Smoke and dust clouds trembled over the headland; cannon-balls ricocheting off the walls screamed skywards to fall into the sea; vast lumps of masonry detaching themselves from the ramparts, boomed down the steep rock face on the eastern side and crashed into Grand Harbour. It was incredible that anything could live inside such a tempest.

Yet, when the attack came – the Janissaries surging down the ravelin and across the partially-filled ditch – it was met with a hail of bullets and incendiary weapons. The trumps sounded and roared, the fragile pots of wildfire burst among the advancing ranks, and the firework hoops sailed down. They bounded on the ground and, leaping like devilish toys, toppled over, embracing the enemy as they fell.

As the attack began to falter, the signal to withdraw was given. Such a devastating fire was immediately opened upon St Elmo that the defenders could neither man their guns nor take any action against the retreating Turks. It seemed as if every cannon on the slopes of Mount Sciberras fired at the same time, while from Dragut's battery on Tigné

Point the north-western walls were equally battered. The damage caused to the collapsing ramparts by this last bombardment exceeded anything that had gone before. Luigi Broglia, de Guaras, and Miranda, came to the conclusion that there was no longer any hope of holding the fort. In places the breaches were large enough for the enemy to storm. Sapping and mining parties had been at work under cover of the day's attacks and, although frustrated by the solid rock on which St Elmo rested, they had contributed their share of damage. The fort's cavalier was in such a condition that the defenders could no longer make use of it.

After their conference, the senior officers of St Elmo decided to send de Medran over to see the Grand Master that same night. There could be no question of anything said by de Medran being suspect. This gallant soldier had been in the forefront of the battle ever since the siege had opened. (De la Cerda, incidentally, that Knight 'whom fear made eloquent' was now in the dungeons of St Angelo. After his first unfortunate interview with La Valette and the Council, he had returned to St Elmo and been wounded. Ferried out one night together with the other casualties he had been examined on entry into the Hospital, and his wound had been pronounced: 'Only a scratch.' La Valette had immediately ordered him to be confined. In the Great Siege, so long as a man could manage to stand, he was not considered wounded.)

The Chevalier de Medran was received by the Grand Master and the Council with the greatest respect. De Medran's main argument was that the fort was now untenable. He suggested that it was a waste of valuable lives to attempt to hold it any longer. The Knights and soldiers would be of far more use in reinforcing Birgu and Senglea, where the next blow was sure to fall. Furthermore, if an attempt was made to hold St Elmo, this could only be done with the aid of reinforcements – which in itself meant a further drain on the manpower of Birgu. They should evacuate the fortress at once, was his conclusion, blow it up, and add the weight of its defenders to the two main positions.

His argument was reasonable, and the Council was

divided in its views, many of the older members concurring with de Medran's analysis. It was, however, no moment for indecision. It was now that the Grand Master's unique reputation and personality turned the scales. This man of whom it has been said 'His power rested in his superb courage, and in the respect, even fear, he inspired,' remained calm and outwardly unaffected.

For the first time, he told the Council that the Viceroy of Sicily had declared he would not hazard his fleet if St Elmo were lost. He told them also of Don Garcia's most recent message – that he could come to their help by 20 June. This was only the night of Thursday the 7th.

'We swore obedience when we joined the Order,' said La Valette. 'We swore also on the vows of chivalry that our lives would be sacrificed for the Faith whenever, and wherever, the call might come. Our brethren in St Elmo must now accept that sacrifice.'

It requires a higher courage to send your comrades to die than to die yourself. There was not a member of the Council who did not know that La Valette would, if the occasion demanded, go foremost into the breach that very minute. His argument, that every fortress in Malta must, one by one, hold out to the last man and the last tottering wall, was accepted. Only by every defensible position being maintained to the end was there any chance of the Order surviving, and of the Turks being ultimately driven off from the island.

'Noblesse oblige' was a phrase that still held a meaning. If the Knights were aristocratic and privileged, they accepted the fact that the only justification for their special condition arose from their willingness to sacrifice everything if called upon to do so. When he said that there could be no withdrawal, it was a sentence of death that the Grand Master was passing upon Medran and the garrison.

Fifteen volunteer Knights and fifty soldiers from the garrison of Mdina went back with the Chevalier de Medran. They crossed the dark waters of Grand Harbour to Fort St Elmo.

Chapter 14

St Elmo, the Eighth of June

At midnight on 8 June the Grand Master received an unexpected, and unwelcome, messenger. All day the guns had thundered about St Elmo, and in the afternoon he had watched yet another assault made against the valiant fortress. The attack had lasted over six hours, the recall only being made at sunset. St Elmo had once again managed to stagger, like a buoyant ship, over the sea that threatened her. And now, at midnight, came the Italian Knight Vitellino Vitelleschi with a sealed letter from St Elmo's defenders. La Valette opened and read it in the yellow glow of the candles in the council chamber. The light wavered occasionally as St Angelo opened fire against the Turks on Mount Sciberras, or against Dragut's new battery on Gallows' Point.

Most Illustrious and Very Reverend Monseigneur [he read],
When the Turks landed here, Your Highness ordered all of us Knights here present, to come and defend this Fortress. This we did with the greatest of good heart, and up to now all that we could do, has been done. Your Highness knows this, and that we have never spared ourselves fatigue or danger. But now, the enemy has reduced us to such a state that we can neither make any effect on them, nor can we defend ourselves (since they hold the ravelin and the ditch). They have also made a bridge and steps up to our ramparts, and they have mined under the wall so that hourly we expect to be blown up. The ravelin itself they have enlarged so much, that one cannot stand at one's post without being killed. One cannot place sentries to keep an eye on the enemy since – within minutes of being posted – they are shot dead by snipers. We are in such straits that we can no longer use the open space in the centre of the fort. Several of our men have already been killed

there, and we have no shelter except the chapel itself. Our troops are down at heart and even their officers cannot make them any more take up their station on the walls. Convinced that the fort is sure to fall, they are preparing to save themselves by swimming for safety. Since we can no longer efficiently carry out the duties of our Order, we are determined – if Your Highness does not send us boats tonight so that we can withdraw – to sally forth and die as Knights should. Do not send further reinforcements, since they are no more than dead men. This is the most determined resolution of all those, whose signature Your Most Illustrious Highness can read below. We further inform Your Highness that Turkish galliots have been active off the end of the point. And so, with this our intention, we kiss your hands, and of this letter we have taken a copy.

Dated from St Elmo, the eighth of June 1565.

There followed fifty-three signatures.

It was not mutiny, and in no way could the action of these Knights be ascribed to cowardice. Victims of constant bombardment, they had decided that it would be better to die honourably in a last desperate attempt against the enemy rather than remain like sheep, waiting their turn in a slaughterhouse. The signatories belonged to the younger Knights, who had not taken kindly to de Medran's return with the news that there could be no evacuation.

Whether their letter was an attempt to coerce the Grand Master into withdrawing them from St Elmo will never be known. Their names are unrecorded, and it is unlikely that a single one of them survived the siege.

La Valette read the letter and looked up at the Italian Knight.

'Wait!' he said.

He called for three Knights from three different Langues, one a Frenchman, one an Italian, and one a Spaniard. He told them the gist of the message that he had received, and ordered them to cross to St Elmo at once and report on its state.

La Valette had no illusions about the fate of the fort and its garrison. He knew he was demanding almost superhuman qualities from the men under his command. He knew, too, that pride, and fear, and pride again, will make men hold on to positions that are logically untenable. He intended to put steel into the shot-ridden backbone of the garrison. They must stay there and die to the last man, as he himself would in Birgu, when the time came.

'The laws of Honour,' he told Chevalier Vitellino Vitelleschi,

cannot necessarily be satisfied by throwing away one's life when it seems convenient. A soldier's duty is to obey. You will tell your comrades that they are to stay at their posts. They are to remain there, and they are not to sally forth. When my commissioners return, I will decide what action must be taken.

It was in the small hours of the morning when the three Knights selected by La Valette reached St Elmo. They were at once surrounded by the dissident members of the garrison, all eager to point out the impossibility of holding the fortress any longer. Already some of the Knights and their men were preparing for evacuation. They were beginning to destroy arms, ammunition, and stores, so that they could not be used by the Moslems. The scene was one of confusion and near-panic. It was a moment such as occurs prior to any evacuation, when discipline begins to collapse and each man thinks only of his own safety.

Dismayed by the scene, the Commissioners refused to discuss any question of arrangements for withdrawal until they had carefully examined the state of the fort. The older and senior Knights, such as Broglia and de Guaras, and the experienced captains like Miranda and Le Mas, would have no part in any suggestion that the fort should be given up. The rebellion seemed to consist solely of the younger Knights.

After inspecting the fortifications, two of the commissioners, a Castilian, Knight Commander de Medina, and a Provençal, Antoine de la Roche, stated quietly but firmly that they did not regard the situation as quite hopeless. 'The fort,' they said, 'can still be held for a few days more.'

The third Commissioner, a Neapolitan Knight named Castriota, was less tactful. 'It is far from hopeless,' he asserted. 'All that is needed are fresh men and a fresh approach to the problems.' Whether or not he implied that it was lack of courage and ability which had brought St Elmo to its present pass, his words were hotly resented by the young Knights. They were men who had been in the front line, under fire for many days, and here came a staff-officer from 'base head-quarters' to tell them that they were not doing their job properly.

'Just stay with us for a day then!' they cried. 'Let's see your "fresh approach" when the Janissaries come in!'

During the violent argument that broke out, a number of soldiers left their posts to see what their officers, the Knights, were saying. It was then that the practical de Guaras managed to restore order by getting a trumpeter to sound the alarm. At the first high note of the trumpet, Knights and soldiers at once made for their posts. Their well-trained discipline cooled their passions and restored them to order.

On their return to Birgu, the Commissioners went straight to La Valette. They found the Grand Master waiting for their report. Old men need little sleep. Time and again during these long months, at whatever hour of the day or night it might be, the Grand Master was always ready and alert. Later, during the siege of Birgu and Senglea, he seems hardly to have slept at all. Whenever danger threatened he was present, yet at the same time he was constantly busy with Council matters, or occupied in devising new methods of defence.

The Castilian and the Provençal Knight stated at once that they considered the position practically hopeless. Castriota, on the other hand, indignantly maintained that, with a fresh infusion of troops and with a new outlook on the question of retrenchments and defence, St Elmo could be held for some time. He volunteered to lead a party to St Elmo, and to make good his words. He would, he said, with the Grand Master's permission, go straight out into Birgu and find enough volunteers to replace the existing garrison.

La Valette gave Castriota his permission, and within an hour (before the Turkish guns had begun their routine morning bombardment of the fort) the Neapolitan had mustered six hundred men who were prepared to go to St Elmo's relief. It is doubtful whether La Valette ever intended that anything like so many useful troops should be dispatched to a place whose loss he knew was imminent. He was using his knowledge of the Knights' psychology to bring them to a burning point of pride where they would die rather than be relieved.

A message was sent across to St Elmo in the evening of that same day. It completed the shame of the rebellious Knights. They had already been informed of Castriota's volunteer corps. Their friends in their various Langues had also sent over messages, pointing out that they were dishonouring their nations as well as the Order. The fifty-three Knights were appalled at the position in which they found themselves. Accused of betraying the honour of the Order and of their Langues, they longed only to prove that such had never been their intention.

A volunteer force has been raised [La Valette wrote] under the command of Chevalier Costantino Castriota. Your petition to leave St Elmo for the safety of Birgu is now granted. This evening, as soon as the relieving force has landed, you may take the boats back. Return, my Brethren, to the Convent and to Birgu, where you will be in more security. For my part, I shall feel more confident when I know that the fort – upon which the safety of the island so greatly depends – is held by men whom I can trust implicitly.

His sarcasm burned them more than any angry words could have done. At a blow they saw themselves stripped of honour, and defamed before the Order and all the nobility of Europe. For the rest of their lives, they would be branded as the men who had saved their skins but lost St Elmo.

Within minutes of the Grand Master's letter being read out, the revolt was over. La Valette had succeeded in his object. He had put such steel into the defenders of the garrison that nothing could ever again shake their morale.

A Maltese swimmer (some say the almost legendary Toni Bajada, whose saga is still told in the island) volunteered to take a letter across to Birgu. In it, the Knights begged the Grand Master not to relieve them. They assured him of their devotion to the Order and of their steadfast obedience to all

his commands in the future. They would not sally forth
against the enemy. They would stay and die in St Elmo,
rather than return to Birgu.

La Valette at once cancelled the orders for Castriota's
relief force, and sent in their stead only fifteen Knights and
less than a hundred soldiers. It was now early morning on
the tenth of June. Whatever he expected of the garrison,
he could hardly have dreamed that they would hold out
for more than three or four days.

Chapter 15

Embattled fortress

From every aspect, the Turkish High Command felt that the campaign was going not only slowly, but badly. A raiding party under Marshal Copier had succeeded in destroying Dragut's new battery on Gallows' Point. It was now twenty-three days since the invasion had begun. Long ago, by all calculations, the fort of St Elmo should have been taken, and the assault directed against the main positions of Birgu and Senglea. Mustapha Pasha began to worry about the possibility of a relief force landing in the north and suddenly taking them in the rear. On the morning of 10 June his fears were confirmed. Two Maltese galleys suddenly appeared off the north of Gozo.

Under the command of St Aubin and a nephew of La Valette's, these galleys had at last been sent over with about 500 troops in response to the Grand Master's request for some reinforcements. The galleys, having backed and filled off Gozo throughout the day, were compelled to withdraw to Sicily by Piali's fleet. Dragut, suspecting that the ships might be no more than the advance guard of a large force, suggested that the watch on Malta Channel should be intensified. From then on, a hundred galleys were stationed to the north of Gozo. At dusk they rowed out in formation and made their way north towards Sicily. At dawn they turned and made the other leg of their patrol back towards Gozo.

Dragut was determined that no relief force should be able to sneak up and make a surprise landing. At the same time, realizing even more clearly what he had pointed out in his first conference with Piali and Mustapha Pasha – that it was the nightly reinforcement of St Elmo which was enabling the fortress to hold out – he decided to re-establish the battery on Gallows' Point. This time, it was no half-hearted affair. Dragut's men landed in force on the rocky spit and established strong guards on the landward side, so that there could be no more question of Marshal Copier's cavalry surprising their gunners. They at once set about establishing a really powerful battery on the point. Several of the heaviest guns were brought ashore from the ships, and labour corps troops began to erect ramps and defensive palisades. This battery would be able to command the sea-approaches between St Angelo and St Elmo. They would attack St Elmo's strongest wall, on the side of Grand Harbour, and in due course they would be able to turn the weight of their fire-power upon St Angelo.

It was on 10 June that the first great night attack of the siege took place. All day the bombardment had kept up without respite and Mustapha decided that, as soon as it was dark, his fresh troops would have every chance of catching the worn-out defenders off their guard. The Lieutenant Aga of the Janissaries addressed his men before sending them into action. To them, he said, fell the honour of capturing the fortress and slaughtering the infidel. To them – troops who had never turned their back upon an enemy – fell the honour of being the first into the breach and the masters of this strong-point upon which the island of Malta depended.

Directed at the south-western corner of the fort where a large breach had begun to open in the walls, the attack was made by the light of torches and the vivid brilliance of fireworks and flames. This time it was not only the defenders who used artificial fire and fire bombs. The advancing ranks of Janissaries threw ahead of them *Sachetti* or fire-grenades, somewhat similar to those which the Christians hurled down upon them. The Ottomans had perfected a type of incendiary which when it burst clung to the armour or the body. Time and again, the Knights who stood in the breach were only saved from being roasted alive in their mail by leaping into great barrels of water that had been placed in position along the defences. So great was the glare during this attack that Balbi, watching from the walls of St Michael's, remembered how:

> The darkness of the night then became bright as day, due to the vast quantity of artificial fires. So bright was it, indeed, that we could see St Elmo quite clearly. The gunners of St Angelo, for their part, were able to lay and train their pieces upon the advancing Turks, who were picked out in the light of the fires.

The smoke from the torches, the trumps, and the incendiary grenades hung in a dense cloud over Grand Harbour. Time and again the attackers stormed across the ditch in front of the fort. Time and again they were beaten back. When dawn broke and the recall was sounded, it was estimated that 1,500 of the Sultan's finest troops lay dead or dying in that no-man's-land between the ravelin and the fort. The defenders' losses totalled sixty.

The only desertion to the enemy from Fort St Elmo during the siege occurred on 13 June; a Spanish fifer slipped out and crossed the ditch to the captured ravelin. Brought before Mustapha Pasha, he assured him that the garrison was at its last gasp. 'If only the ravelin were raised a little higher, you would,' he said, 'be able to demoralize them by preventing any movement in the fort at all.'

'If you lie,' said Mustapha, 'we will find an interesting way to kill you. It will be neither the rope, nor the bastinado – both are too good for cowards and common men.'

Nevertheless he proceeded to act upon the deserter's advice. The latter, for his part, managed to escape from his new masters. The threat of what lay in store for him if the Turkish attacks failed, made him wish that he had never deserted. The Turks were notorious for their skill in torture. If the bastinado, which had been applied to a noble prisoner of war like the French Knight Adrien de la Rivière, was considered too good for a deserter, the fifer may well have trembled. (In the bastinado the soles of the feet, and then the belly, were beaten with bamboo rods until every nerve became a screaming torment. Death from internal haemorrhage usually released the sufferer.) Bosio records that the fifer slipped out of the Turkish lines and made his way to

Mdina, where he reported himself a Christian slave who had escaped from the Turkish army. He was recognized, however, by a genuine Turkish renegade (an Italian who had decided to desert the Christian side). 'Tied to a horse's tail, the fifer was stoned and then put to death at the hands of the mob.'

One of the most remarkable things in the whole course of the siege is the fact that, although there were a number of cases of desertion from Birgu and Senglea, there was never a single instance of a Maltese crossing over to the enemy. These native islanders who had little cause to love the Knights or the Order, displayed an extraordinary devotion and courage throughout the whole campaign. From childhood they had grown inured to the terrible toll which the Moslem corsairs yearly exacted from their small islands. It may well have been a determination to take their revenge which helped to ensure their steadfastness. The Maltese can also claim to be of the oldest Christian peoples in the world (their conversion dating from St Paul's landing upon the island in A.D. 60) and they no doubt drew great strength from the ancestry of their Faith. Even Bosio, that historian of the Order who is mainly concerned with demonstrating the unshakeable courage of the Knights and the 'Religion', is forced to comment: 'During the Great Siege, some there were from almost every Nation who fled over to the Infidels. But of the native-born Maltese, there was never a single one.'

Unfortunately, except in legend, the names of the many Maltese heroes have gone unrecorded. The deeds of individual Knights and even of the Turkish enemy were chronicled, but the heroism of the islanders has been passed down only by word of mouth. Men like Luqa Briffa, the great Maltese horseman, and Toni Bajada, swimmer, horseman, and something of a Mediterranean Robin Hood, remain in folklore, but not in documents. That they, and many like them, existed there can be no doubt. The Knights were the steel spine of the defence and there could have been no resistance without them. But it was on the five or six thousand Maltese men of military age, that the main defence of Malta rested. Until some local historian rescues from song and legend the names and exploits of his forebears, the historian can do no more than record the few names which occur in contemporary documents. What must never be overlooked in the story of the Great Siege, is that it was not only the noblest names of Europe who defied the Turkish invaders. Alongside them stood the dark, short-legged, barrel-chested men of Malta. A sturdy race of islanders, descendants perhaps of the Phoenicians, they proved – as their ancestors had done so many centuries before in the siege of Carthage – that they could endure almost unbelievable hardships.

'No war is more cruel and bloody than siege warfare . . .' The truth of this statement was to be proved over and over again during the next few months. The Turks were now so enraged by the Christians, that any instinct of chivalry which might once have animated their commanders had long since disappeared. Mustapha and Piali both felt equally at fault for the long delay in front of St Elmo – this small and relatively unimportant fort should have fallen long ago. Dragut, resigned to a long-drawn-out affair by the initial bungling of the Sultan's commanders, had now become as adamant as the Admiral and the Commander-in-Chief that the siege of St Elmo should never be abandoned.

On the night of 14 June a Turkish spokesman was sent out into the ditch between the ravelin and the fort, to call on the defenders, and tell them that Mustapha promised a safe passage to any who wished to leave that night. By his beard, and by the tombs of his ancestors, the Turkish Commander-in-Chief had sworn that any who wished to retire might now leave the fortress unmolested. It is just conceivable that, had the offer been made a few days earlier, there were those among the younger Knights and the troops who would have accepted. But, by now, they had all resolved to die where they stood. Furthermore, although they knew they could not hold out for much longer, their successes had been so great that their morale was high. Merely by looking down at the mounds of corpses which fringed their beleaguered garrison they could see what their defence was costing the Turks. Mustapha's spokesman was forced to retire under a hail of arquebus shot. There would be no more deserters from St Elmo!

Throughout the following day the increased bombardment showed that another attack was impending. From Mount Sciberras, from Tigné and from the re-established heavy batteries on Gallows' Point the fire never ceased. Deafened, stunned, and tired almost beyond caring, the defenders prepared themselves for the inevitable assault. If the bombardment was intended to demoralize them, it did not succeed. It merely served to put them on their guard, and to make them all the more ready for the attack when it came. The night of 15th to 16th was also broken by minor raids. The enemy had clearly grown confident and was beginning to feel that the prize lay within his hand.

La Valette, listening and watching from across the water, must have felt that the end was near. St Elmo had already held out beyond any reasonable expectation. It might be tomorrow, or it might be the day after, but it was inconceivable that the garrison could survive much longer.

The attack began at dawn, on Saturday 16 June. The island was still damp from the night air and the headland was scented with the sea, when the flares ran like fuses along the ramparts of St Elmo. The defenders had noticed the enemy troops massing. They had heard the high voices of the mullahs calling upon the Faithful to die for Paradise.

> *One of the saintly murderous brood*
> *To carnage and the Koran given ...*

stood on the high ravelin and cried out that in the Holy War between True Believer and Christian all who fell with their face towards the enemy would inherit that perfect world promised by the Prophet. There in that Paradise were wells of clear spring-water. The date-palms were shady in an eternal afternoon, and the juice of the grape (forbidden to the Faithful in this mortal life) would refresh them. There divinely beautiful houris would welcome such warriors in their arms, and the climax of love would last a full ten thousand years.

Vowed and devoted to their other heaven, the Christians

awaited them. They heard the dull booming of tambours and the brassy call of trumpets. They looked seaward and saw that the whole Turkish fleet had crept up during the summer night and now lay like a ring around the point. At such a moment even the bravest felt fear stick dry as a crust in their throats.

Nearly 4,000 arquebusiers spread themselves in a great curve from the water on Marsamuscetto, across the dip below Mount Sciberras, over towards Grand Harbour. They opened a devastating fire on the embrasures of the fort. Ladders, scaling irons, and improvised bridges made of masts and spars, were dragged down into that ditch where the bodies of so many of the flower of the Sultan's army were already black and bursting from the summer heat. Piali's fleet opened fire as the light spread over the water. The sun, rising behind the ships, cast the shadow of their hulls and sails across the sea. Within minutes of this naval bombardment, Mustapha's gunners on Sciberras opened up with their 60-, 80-, and 160-lb. shot. North and south the batteries on Tigné and Gallows' Point began their cross-fire against St Elmo.

Huddling against the walls, taking shelter behind improvised barricades, the defenders awaited the onslaught. They had fire hoops and incendiary grenades, boiling cauldrons and trumps piled ready by the embrasures and behind the threatened breach on the south-west wall. Only two nights before, La Valette had managed to reinforce them with a convoy of these incendiary fireworks. He had also sent further supplies of wine and bread, for St Elmo's bakery had been destroyed and their water was running short.

For this attack – the attack which Mustapha felt sure would deliver the fortress to him – the Janissaries were held back in reserve. In their place, and for the first mad assault wave, he sent in the Iayalars. They were a fanatical corps, without the Janissaries' iron training as soldiers, but with a complete disregard for their own life or any other. Maddened by hashish, the Iayalars were a fervid sect of Moslems, deriving their blind courage from a blend of Religion and Hemp. Like the Berserkers of the North, the Iayalars induced a deliberate frenzy which made them oblivious to everything but the lust to kill. They were 'picked men, clothed with the skins of wild beasts, and having as head covering gilded steel helmets. The surface of their skin-tunics was enriched with varying designs and characters in silver. They were armed with the round shield and scimitar. . . .'

In a frenzied wave – seeing only the line of the battlements before them and Paradise beyond – the Iayalars came down for the first assault. The pupils of their eyes were like needles, their salivaed lips held only the one word 'Allah!'

On the lips of the Maltese was also the word 'Alla', for in their language the Christian God was called the same. Behind the ramparts, and in the breach on the south-western side, the Knights, the Spanish soldiers, and the Maltese waited.

In many, nay, in most campaigns, personal feeling enters but little into the contest. . . . At Malta the element of actual personal individual hatred was the mainspring by which the combatants on both sides were moved: each regarded the other as an infidel, the slaying of whom was the sacrifice most acceptable to the God they worshipped.

If the concept of a *Jehad*, or Holy War, had originated with the Moslems, it was something which the Christians had also adopted many centuries before. The horror and the implacable nature of the Wars of Religion was not only that the soldiers on each side believed Heaven awaited them if they fell in battle, they also believed that they owed it to their adversaries to send them to hell.

Beaten back by the defenders' fire, the Iayalars retired leaving the ditch filled with their bodies. They were followed by a horde of Dervishes. Mustapha was keeping back his crack trained troops until 'the Religious' had laid a gangway to St Elmo with their corpses. At the last, he looked towards the Janissaries and gave the order for the pride of Islam to advance. It was two days since the Lieutenant-Aga, the General of their Corps, had been killed by a cannon-ball fired from St Angelo. Now was the time for the 'invincible ones' to redeem his death with Christian blood. Sons of Greeks, Bulgarians, Roumanians, Austrians, and Slavs, these converts to Islam swept forward, and on – and up to the breached walls. Time and again though they charged, they too faltered and broke before the defenders' fire.

The deadliest toll was taken by a small battery on the southern side of the fort. From this angle the gunners were able to enfilade the advancing enemy. Despite the Turkish shot directed against them, they maintained their murderous rate of fire all the day long. St Angelo, too, aided the defenders. The gunners on the high cavalier of the fortress kept sweeping the ranks of the Moslems with a long traversing fire. The cannon blew great black holes in the white surge of the advancing enemy.

Throughout the action both Dragut and Mustapha Pasha stood in full view on the ravelin, and supervised the attacks. Dragut was busy everywhere. With his own hands the old corsair laid the guns, advised the master gunners, and directed the bombardment. While Janissary or Iayalar attacked in one section, Dragut made sure that – in the area where there were no Moslem troops – the shot fell thick and fast. The minute an assault weakened, and the troops withdrew, he shifted target and kept up an unrelenting bombardment against the weak positions. St Elmo was like a rock lashed by a hurricane.

It was not until night fell that the attack was called off. It seemed incredible to Turk and Christian alike that so small a fort could have resisted so long. One hundred and fifty of the garrison were dead and many more were wounded, but the Moslem casualties littered the whole ground in front of the scarred and tottering walls. A roll-call made this same night showed that the Sultan's forces had lost over 4,000 men in the past three weeks – nearly one thousand of them in that one day's attack.

The gallant de Medran was among the dead of St Elmo. Pepe di Ruvo (the Knight who had calculated the number of shots fired against the fort during the siege) was also killed. Miranda had been seriously wounded. If 16 June was a victory it was a Pyrrhic one. Small though the losses of the defenders were, they could not afford them. The time was not far distant when Dragut's battery on Gallows' Point would prevent any reinforcements reaching them. The moment that happened, all was lost.

For the first time since the beginning of the siege, La Valette refused to order any more men or Knights to reinforce St Elmo. He called for volunteers. Thirty Knights, and three hundred soldiers and Maltese from Birgu, came forward. They offered themselves for the post of certain death.

Chapter 16

The territory of the Knights

The day after the assault the Turkish Commanders held a further conference to decide what other means they could use to subdue the fortress. Seeing the havoc wrought in their own ranks by the concealed battery on the southern corner of St Elmo, they made arrangements to bring two heavy guns into action against it. The reason for their failure still lay, as Dragut was not slow to point out, in the fact that a transfusion of troops, stores, and ammunition was pouring nightly across Grand Harbour from Birgu.

'Until the garrison is completely cut off from any outside help, it will continue to resist us.'

He proposed that all available labour should at once be set to erecting a wall of stones, earth, and brushwood, to screen the Turkish troops from the guns of St Angelo. Constructed along the eastern flank of Mount Sciberras and continuing right down to the waters of Grand Harbour itself, this protective wall would enable the Turks to deploy their troops without their movements being observed. It would also give them a safely-screened vantage point overlooking the harbour. From here they would be able to maintain a heavy arquebus fire against any boatloads of reinforcements which tried to land.

It was the last counsel and assistance the old corsair was to give. On 18 June, while engaged with Mustapha in supervising the erection of the new battery and the protective screen, Dragut was struck to the ground. A cannon shot, fired from St Angelo's cavalier, fell near the party of dignitaries. It is likely that the gunner concerned had deliberately aimed at them, for both Dragut and Mustapha scorned to shelter from the Christian fire, and their brilliant clothes and those of their entourage were enough to indicate their importance. As the cannon-ball crashed into the hard earth and ricocheted overhead, it threw up great splinters of rock. One of these struck Dragut above his right ear and would have killed him on the spot had it not been for his thick turban. He fell to the ground, the blood gushing from his nose and ears.

Mustapha Pasha at once assumed that the old warrior was dead. He ordered one of his staff to cover the body quickly with a cloak and have it carried secretly to the headquarters at the Marsa. So great was Dragut's name and reputation that he feared the troops would be demoralized if they learned of his death. A few minutes later, a second shot landing in almost the same place killed the Aga of the Janissaries. Mustapha, however, refused to move, and carried on his consultation with the gunners and engineers. While the decision was confirmed to extend the screen right down to the water's edge, as Dragut had advised, the apparently lifeless body of 'The Drawn Sword of Islam' was carried back to his tent on the Marsa. Many years before, during his campaign against Gozo, in 1544, at the time when his brother had been killed, Dragut had had a premonition of his fate. 'I have felt in this island the shadow of the wing of death!' he had said. 'One of these days it is written that I, too, shall die in the territory of the Knights.'

That evening a deserter from the Turkish army brought the news to the Grand Master in Birgu that their great enemy was dead. His information was premature, for Dragut lingered on for several days. He never left his tent again, or assisted any further in the campaign. Since he had been the one man able to coordinate the operation of army and navy, and it was only he whose advice was observed by both Piali and Mustapha Pasha, his loss was a disaster for the Turks.

On the following day their morale was further weakened when Antonio Grugno, the Knight in command of St Elmo's cavalier, directed a cannon against a group of Turkish officers and managed to drop a shot right into the middle of them. Among those killed was the Master General of the

Turkish Ordnance, who ranked second only to Mustapha himself in the army. The news of Dragut's injury and the death of the Aga of the Janissaries had – despite Mustapha's attempts at secrecy – become known to his troops. The death of yet another senior officer added to their dismay. Antonio Grugno, for his part, did not long enjoy his success. Seriously wounded a few minutes later by a sniper's bullet, he had to be relieved of his post and ferried over to the hospital.

So, with the death and disablement of brave men on both sides increasing daily, the siege of St Elmo entered its twenty-seventh day. The first batteries on Mount Sciberras had opened fire on 24 May and it was now 19 June. Yet still, this small, old-fashioned star-shaped fort, which the Sultan's spies had told him should 'fall within four or five days', held out into a second month.

It was on the nineteenth, that the sudden roar of an explosion in St Angelo made the besieging Turks turn their eyes towards the fortress on the far side of Grand Harbour. A cloud of dust, smoke, and flame lifted above the battlements. They knew at once that nothing short of a magazine going up could have caused such an explosion. It was, so Balbi tells us, a small powder mill which blew up, taking eight men with it and blowing the roof off a part of the fortress.

And I could hardly tell you what a great cheer the Turks raised, with their bestial voices, thinking that the damage was much more. But the Grand Master immediately ordered a half-dozen cannon shots into the Turkish ranks to give them something else to think about. . . .

By midnight on the nineteenth, it was clear that nothing could save the fort. A message from Miranda informed the Grand Master that 'the loss of St Elmo may be expected from hour to hour'. An attempt to break down the Turkish bridge, which had been built across the ditch, had failed. In some places the ditch was almost completely filled by stone blocks from the ramparts, while in others little more than a low wall of broken masonry protected the defenders. A further message from Miranda on the evening of the twentieth stated that 'every new reinforcement sent into the fort is lost. It is cruelty, therefore, to send any more men to die here.' The investment of the fort was now complete.

The battery which Dragut had been installing at the moment when he was struck down, already dominated the eastern side of the fort. It also commanded the place where reinforcements had been able to land. The screening wall, and the covered way leading down to the water's edge, were completed and the Turkish snipers could now pick off any troops being ferried across. La Valette realized the hopelessness of the position when he sent across a single boat with the Chevalier de Boisberton aboard it to confer with Miranda. The waters of Grand Harbour were splintered by a hail of cannon shot and arquebus fire as the boat ran the gauntlet. Riddled with bullets, it only just managed to complete its mission. One man had his head taken off by a cannon ball on the outward passage, and another was shot dead on the return.

Boisberton brought back to La Valette the message that Miranda and the other senior Knights thought that they might be able to withstand one more Turkish attack. After that, he said, there could be nothing for them but to retire to Birgu.

La Valette's 'noble features, which usually wore a tinge of melancholy, were clouded with a deeper sadness, as he felt that he must now abandon his brave comrades to their fate.' He knew, what they, perhaps, had not yet realized, that there could no longer be any question of evacuating St Elmo. The Turkish engineers and labour corps, acting on the last advice of Dragut, had sealed off the garrison from the outside world. St Elmo was now finally and completely alone.

Chapter 17

The fall of St Elmo

Through the narrow streets of Birgu, the Order of the Knights Hospitallers of St John of Jerusalem went in solemn procession to the Conventual Church of St Lawrence. It was Thursday, 21 June 1565, the Feast of Corpus Christi – an occasion that, throughout all the centuries since their foundation, the Knights had never failed to honour. At this dark moment of the Great Siege, with the fall of St Elmo hourly expected, they maintained this tradition, and put aside their arms and armour. Dressed in the formal dark robes of the Order, with the white eight-pointed Cross embroidered upon it,

The Grand Master and all the available Knights . . . participated with lay and ecclesiastical dignitaries in escorting the Holy Host through streets lined by a devout population, the route chosen being that considered the safest from the Turkish artillery, and on the procession returning to St Lawrence's they all knelt down and implored the Lord of Mercies not to allow their brothers in St Elmo to perish utterly by the merciless sword of the Infidel.

It was during this day that the cavalier of St Elmo, long battered by the guns sited by Dragut on Tigné point, finally became untenable. Janissaries, who had slipped along the shore of Marsamuscetto, crept up the slopes and occupied this outer defence of the fort. The garrison's first indication that the cavalier now lay in hand of the enemy, was when the Janissary snipers began firing on them from the rear. By directing a cannon on this Janissary advance guard, they managed to dislodge them for the moment. But, as soon as night fell, the Sultan's picked corps of arquebusiers came back again – and this time in strength. Now, both the ravelin and the cavalier, the two outer defences of St Elmo, were held by the Turks.

The bombardment never ceased. From first light, right through the midday heat of late June, until the sun set behind the low western ridges of the island, the siege guns, the ships' cannons, and the giant basilisks, kept up their ceaseless thunder. The temperature at noon was now in the nineties, the small untended fields were cracking under the heat, the irrigation ditches ran no more, and the few forgotten crops that burst through the dried soil, withered and died. In the Marsa, the tents of the Turkish sick and wounded spread wider across the low land. The casualties of fire and sword from St Elmo lay side by side with the victims of enteric, malaria, and dysentery. Dragut heard, in the intervals of unconsciousness and delirium, the steady boom of the guns. He no longer knew whether it was a summer storm, or whether it was the man-made thunder with which his life had been filled.

In Birgu and Senglea the garrisons looked to their final preparations. They tensed themselves like sailors who can tell, by the ever-growing swell, that a hurricane is nearly upon them. 'As for food, they had seven or eight thousand Salmes (bushels) of wheat, not counting the barley which had been cut at the beginning of the harvest, and of which they had about three thousand Salmes.' They had also, according to Vendôme, 40,000 casks of water, apart from the water of the spring in Birgu. The food stocks in Birgu and Senglea were adequate for a long siege. There were quantities of salted meat, cheese, butter, olive oil, sardines, tunny, and dried cod. Ammunition supplies were also plentiful but, 'As regard these,' he wrote, 'I can give no figures for these are things that are always kept secret.' The Viceroy of Sicily had said that he would come to the island's relief by 20 June, and it was now the 21st. Contemplating all the preparations that he had made for a long siege, La Valette can only have felt glad that he had learned to mistrust promises while still a young man. If he had relied upon help from outside, the island would have fallen already.

The Great Siege

On Friday the 22nd, it seemed almost certain that the fortress had been taken. The bombardment began at dawn, and the assault by the troops soon afterwards. As in the previous attack, the Turkish fleet had moved up over night and formed a semicircle to seaward. From all four compass points the fort was under concentrated fire, and it seemed incredible that anything could exist in that smoking ruin. Yet the very fact that the fort still flamed back with guns, fire-hoops, trumps, and incendiaries, showed that the defenders still held the walls.

The movements of the Turkish troops were now largely hidden from the gunners of St Angelo, and it was not until they emerged from behind their screening wall for the final charge that they exposed themselves to fire. By this time, they were too close to the walls and the defenders for St Angelo's gunners to risk firing on them. (On an earlier occasion a mis-directed shot from St Angelo had killed eight of St Elmo's garrison.) The concealed battery on the southern side of St Elmo, which had played so large a part in repulsing previous attacks, had been destroyed by Turkish gunfire.

Time and again, the Turks burst across the ditch. They came hand-to-hand with the defenders lining their breached walls. Yet still St Elmo held out. Still, as the Iayalars and the Janissaries scrambled up the slippery ditch, they found the steel-clad men waiting for them in the breach. It was now, when incendiaries and arquebus shot had failed, that men fell back on the simple weapons that had been evolved in earlier wars. Some of the men-at-arms wielded partisans – long-handled wooden spears – while the Janissaries favoured the scimitar and shield. A Knight lifted high above his head a long two-handed sword, while his adversary thrust at him with a stabbing sword. Pikes and glaives (like a pike but with a curved cutting edge), battleaxes, and even daggers, came into action, as attacker met defender on the crumbling edges of the walls. Men locked together in mortal combat rolled down into the ditch where the sandstone had long since grown dark and foul.

At one moment it seemed as if the Moslems had burst through the breached wall, at the point where the fighting

had been thickest all morning. A group of Janissaries succeeded in reaching the top and closed with the Knights and
soldiers. The small group fell into the ditch, as part of the wall
gave way beneath their feet. For a moment it seemed that
the breach was clear of defenders, and another rush of
Janissaries made for the open space. While they were still
struggling up the incline, reinforcements moved over from
left and right of the breached wall, and presented once more
that line of steel which had come to seem almost part of St
Elmo's natural fortifications. It was just at this moment that
the Janissary snipers, who had reoccupied the cavalier over
night, opened fire. Struck down by bullets from the rear, and
attacked from the front, the defenders wavered and began
to crumple. Another band of Turkish troops swept over the
ditch and started to escalade.

The position was only saved by the Chevalier Melchior de
Monserrat, a Knight of Aragon who had become Governor
of St Elmo after Luigi Broglia had been incapacitated by
wounds. De Monserrat, identifying the cause of the trouble,
immediately brought a gun into action against the cavalier,
and blew the Janissary sharpshooters off their vantage
point. But for his swift action, the wild onrush of the Turks
might well have swept them through the breach and into the
fort itself. Only a few minutes later, de Monserrat was killed
by a musket shot.

For six hours the Turks attacked, hurling themselves
regardless of losses against the thin line of defenders. For
six hours the battle swayed back and forth, trembling sometimes in the balance, but always – as the smoke and dust
clouds cleared away – revealing the besieged still active with
arquebus, cold steel, or artificial fire. Two thousand Turkish
troops are believed to have lost their lives on this grim
Friday, and Mustapha, finally acknowledging that St Elmo
could not be taken within that day, ordered the recall. The
Grand Master and the other watchers on St Angelo's cavalier
suddenly heard a burst of cheering from their brothers in
St Elmo, whom they had already given up for lost. The
defenders were proving to La Valette, to the Order, and
indeed to all of Europe, that if they were destined to die, at

least they counted that day another victory. They had lost two hundred men in the battle, and they knew that the end must soon come, for there would be no more reinforcements.

La Valette did make one last attempt to relieve the garrison. Even this unemotional man was moved to pity that evening. A Maltese soldier dived from the rocks below St Elmo and managed, by swimming for long periods under water, to escape the enemy's fire and reach St Angelo. He brought the last message from the garrison. He described the day's fighting and told how nearly all who survived were wounded. De Guaras, Miranda, and le Mas, three who had endured the whole siege, still lived, but each was desperately wounded – one with sword cuts, one with a musket shot, and the other terribly burned by wildfire. Yet still, the messenger said, the garrison's discipline held and their morale was high. Every man had his task and would do it to the last. Even those who were too enfeebled to bear arms, were playing their part 'by carrying about large deep plates, with wedges of bread steeped in wine and water, to refresh and invigorate the combatants without their having to move from their places.'

It is recorded that, on hearing this recital of his brothers' bravery and suffering, 'La Valette was moved to tears.' On an impulse, he agreed to the suggestion that a last volunteer force should try and reach the fort. That great seaman, the Chevalier de Romegas, led the expedition and five open boats were immediately crowded with volunteers. Fifteen Knights and many soldiers and Maltese from Birgu willingly came forward and, as one historian adds, 'what is astonishing, two Jews volunteered to go and die with them.' That two members of a race so persecuted and despised by sixteenth-century Christians, should have elected to die with the Order in Fort St Elmo, is evidence of the strange power that heroism has to inspire other men.

La Valette's action, based for once on emotion rather than calculation, was doomed from the beginning. No sooner did the Turkish lookouts see the boats sliding across Grand Harbour than every available gun and arquebus was trained upon them. At the same time, a number of open boats which Piali had sent into the mouth of Grand Harbour expressly to stop any such action, made for the landing place below St Elmo. The dark waters of the harbour erupted in fountains as shot and shell poured across from Gallows' Point, and from the snipers established at the end of the covering wall near the water's edge. Nothing could pass through that curtain of fire and live. Beyond it, Romegas saw the flickering shapes of the Turkish boats waiting to cut them off, if ever they succeeded in nearing the other side. Having nearly lost his own boat, he ordered the relief force to retire. The survivors in St Elmo watched them pull rapidly back to St Angelo, and into the sheltering waters of the creek. They made themselves ready for death.

The two chaplains who had stayed with the defenders throughout the siege confessed the remaining Knights and soldiers. 'They received the Holy Sacrament, they embraced one another, and they encouraged each other with such words of consolation as only brave men about to die can use. . . .' Pierre Vigneron, the French chaplain, and Alonso de Zambrana, a Spanish chaplain from the Langue of Castile, were both to die with them in the ruins of St Elmo.

Later that night, the Knights and the chaplains hid the precious objects of the Faith beneath the stone floors of the chapel. They dragged the tapestries, pictures, and wooden furniture, outside and set them on fire. They were determined that the Mohammedans should have no Christian relics to mock or desecrate. As a last gesture, and as a signal to their friends and brethren in St Angelo, Birgu, and Senglea, that they had made their peace and were ready for the end, they began ringing the bell of the small chapel.

The Turks, seeing the fire and hearing the sound of the bell, smiled, thinking that the garrison was making a last appeal to their brothers to come and save them. Their own dead lay thick on this sandstone hump of land, but tomorrow they would take their revenge.

> *From the lands where the elephants are to the forts of Merou and Balghar,*
> *Our steel we have brought and our star to shine on the ruins of Rum . . .*
> *For the coward was drowned with the brave when our battle sheered up*
> *   like a wave,*
> *And the dead to the desert we gave, and the glory to God in our song.*

The Great Siege

In St Angelo and Senglea, the lookouts saw the glow of the fire and heard the clangour of St Elmo's chapel bell. They and their officers looked across the water and knew that it was their comrades' last message. 'And that same night,' wrote Francisco Balbi, 'the poor ones of St Elmo, having seen that our attempt to send them help had failed, prepared themselves to die in the service of Jesus Christ . . .'

On 23 June, with the first light that precedes the sunrise, the grey shapes of Piali's ships closed in for the kill. Aware that the cavalier was now in Turkish hands, some of them even darted between St Elmo Point and Tigné. They were the first of the Turkish fleet to gain the harbour of Marsamuscetto – that harbour for which the past month's battle had been waged. As the light quickened, the galleys came slowly in, crossing the five-fathom line, and pointed their lean bows at the ruined fort. Their bowchasers opened up. At almost the same moment the first massed charge was made by Janissary, Spahi, Iayalar, and the Levies. Today there were no special storming parties formed of élite troops. Today, the whole army fell on St Elmo in a great torrent. No losses could check their advance, and the failing volleys and few incendiary grenades and hoops could not stem this relentless tide.

To the astonishment of Mustapha and his council, Fort St Elmo held out for over an hour. Less than a hundred men were left in the garrison after that first onslaught, yet few though they were, they forced the Ottoman army to draw back and reform.

De Guaras and Miranda, both too wounded to be able to stand, had themselves placed in chairs in the breach. They crouched there, each with his large two-handed sword by his side.

This time, there was something about the battle cries of the Turks that told the garrisons of Birgu and Senglea that all was over. The white-robed troops poured down the slopes, hesitated like a curling roller above the wall, and then burst across the fort. From the north-eastern walls of Birgu, the soldiers and the Maltese could see the Turks pouring like a sea over St Elmo.

De Guaras, hurled from his chair in the onslaught, picked himself up and seizing a pike attempted to stem the enemy's advance. His head was struck from his shoulders by a scimitar. The gallant le Mas was torn to pieces. Paolo Avogardo of the Italian Langue was cut down at the door of the chapel, where he stood sword in hand fighting off the Janissary spearhead. One by one the defenders perished, some quickly and mercifully, others dying of wounds among the bodies of their friends. The Italian Knight, Francisco Lanfreducci, acting on orders received before the battle began, crossed to the wall opposite Bighi Bay and lit the signal fire. As its smoke curled up and eddied in the clear blue sky La Valette knew that the heroic garrison, and the fort they had defended to the end, were lost.

It was now that Mustapha Pasha, impatient to view his conquest, crossed the ditch. Followed by his staff, he stepped through the breach into St Elmo. Behind him a standard-bearer carried the banner of Sultan Soleyman the Magnificent, Conqueror of the East and West. The flag of St John, which for so long had mocked the Turkish Commander, was hauled to the ground and a Janissary officer flung it in the dust at Mustapha's feet. A soldier made fast to the stained and sun-bleached halyard of the flagstaff the Crescent flag of Turkey and Islam.

Standing on the ruins of St Elmo's walls, the conqueror looked across the bright still waters of Grand Harbour. Behind him rose the crackle of flames, and the cries of the wounded. In his nostrils was the sweet sickly smell of blood. He heard the boom of gongs and the brassy note of trumpets as the triumphant fleet swept in to drop anchor in Marsamuscetto. In his moment of triumph he did not forget the man who had in so many respects been the author of it – the dying Dragut. A messenger was at once dispatched to the corsair's tent in the Marsa to give him the news. 'He manifested his joy by several signs and, raising his eyes to heaven as if in thankfulness for its mercies, immediately expired: a captain of rare valour and even abundantly more humane than are ordinarily these corsairs.'

But Mustapha Pasha, looking over the ruins of St Elmo,

felt little cause for joy. He gazed at the frowning bulk of St Angelo across the water.

'Allah!' he cried. 'If so small a son has cost us so dear, what price shall we have to pay for so large a father?'

Chapter 18

Bodies in the water

St Elmo fell on 23 June. For three days it had been completely cut off from all outside help. It had held out for thirty-one days of continuous siege and its defence was to prove, in retrospect, the keystone of the whole campaign. This small fort, which logically should have been stormed or forced to surrender within a week, was a disaster for the Turkish army. Accounts vary as to the Turkish losses during the siege of St Elmo, but an average of the commentators and historians puts the figure at about 8,000. This was nearly a quarter of the force which had embarked from Constantinople. The defenders lost about 1,500 men – a ratio of nearly one Christian dead for every six Moslems. The majority of those killed were either Spanish, Maltese, or other foreign troops. One hundred and twenty Knights and Servants-at-arms were lost, the highest number, thirty-one, being from Italy. The rest were almost equally divided between Aragon, Auvergne, France, and Provence. The German Langue lost five of its members.

In the slaughter that followed the final storming of the fort, there would have been no survivors at all had it not been for some of Dragut's corsairs. They were men to whom a hostage was worth more than a dead body, and they managed to take nine Knights as prisoners of war. Balbi records their names – five Spaniards; Lorenzo de Guzman, Juan de Aragon, Francisque Vique, Fernandez de Mesa, Velasquez d'Argote; three Italians; Pedro Guadani, Francisco Lanfreducci, Bachio Craducci; and one French Knight, Antoine de Molubech. There seems to be no record of any of these Knights having been ransomed (as the Corsairs naturally hoped). Perhaps they died of wounds, or remained galley slaves for the rest of their lives. A few Maltese soldiers managed to escape from the ruins of the fortress. Five of them, we are told leaped from the rocks at the foot of St Elmo and swam across Grand Harbour to Birgu. It was from the reports of these Maltese that Balbi gathered the material for his story of the last three days of St Elmo.

If Mustapha Pasha had had his way, there would have been no survivors. The Turkish Commander-in-Chief had always a reputation for ruthlessness, but the long resistance of St Elmo had infuriated him. Historians of the Order have been prompt to condemn Mustapha for his orders 'No Quarter', but, in doing so, they have forgotten the curious 'rules' that governed warfare at that time. Siege warfare was normally conducted to a code of rules. It was generally recognized that, once a large breach had been made, it was up to the defenders to surrender. If they did so, they were entitled to the normal courtesies and might even be allowed to go free or, at any rate, be liberated by ransom money. If, on the other hand, the defenders of a besieged fortress refused to surrender but remained defiant to the very end they were not entitled to any quarter. They might either be enslaved, or put to the sword.

Mustapha Pasha, then, was within his rights when he said that no prisoners should be taken. In any case it would have been difficult, or impossible even, for him to have controlled his troops. Their losses had been so immense that they were determined on vengeance. Except for the nine Knights and the few Maltese who escaped across Grand Harbour, there were no survivors from the garrison.

Mustapha's determination to take no prisoners is understandable. His other actions bear the mark of that ruthlessness which he had shown on many other fields of battle. He was a man who believed that the enemy may often be cowed by offensive acts of cruelty. He ordered the bodies of the Knights to be set apart from the common soldiers. He then had the principal Knights identified. The heads of le Mas, Miranda and de Guaras were struck from their bodies. They were fixed on stakes overlooking Grand Harbour, and were turned to face the fortress of St Angelo.

It was not difficult to identify the Knights. No one else bore such elaborate arms and armour. Mustapha had some of them stripped of their mail. The bodies were decapitated and the headless trunks were nailed to cross-beams of wood in mockery of the crucifixion. (Some commentators say that the sign of the cross was cut in their breasts while they were still alive, and their hearts were ripped from their bodies before their heads were cut off.) One thing is certain, a number of these headless trunks were launched on to the waters of Grand Harbour on the night after St Elmo fell.

It was the eve of the Feast of St John, the patron Saint of the Order, and despite the loss of St Elmo, the Grand Master gave orders for the normal celebrations to take place. No powder or incendiary material could be spared for elaborate flares or fireworks, but bonfires were lit throughout Birgu and Senglea and the church bells pealed out. The Turks, noting these signs of apparent celebration in the Christian camp, lit 'an infinity of fires in the Marsa', wrote Balbi, 'not because they held the feast of St John, but because of their capture of St Elmo. . . . It grieved us greatly to see them, because this was a celebration the Knights always held in honour of their patron saint.'

On the morning of Sunday, 24 June, the gentle current which sweeps through the entrance of Grand Harbour in summer, and which washes the shores of the creeks on the south-eastern side, bore with it a sinister cargo. Floating on their wooden crucifixes, the headless bodies of four Knights were washed up to the base of St Angelo.

La Valette was immediately informed of what had happened. He came down to the shore with his Latin Secretary, Sir Oliver Starkey, and the other members of the Council. Only two of the bodies could be identified, those of Jacomo Martelli and Alessandro San Giorgio, both Knights of the Italian Langue. They were each recognized by their own brothers who were among the defenders of St Angelo.

La Valette, who had realized from the outset that the siege of Malta was a *guerre à outrance*, did not hesitate. He would impress upon his followers as well as the Turks, that there could be no question of honourable surrender. He gave orders for all Turkish prisoners to be executed. There were many of them in Birgu who had been captured in Marshal Copier's cavalry raids. They were at once taken before the executioners. Their heads were struck off and their bodies thrown into the sea.

While Mustapha's army was collecting the captured cannon in St Elmo and making them ready for dispatch to Constantinople as trophies of war, they were disturbed by the boom of cannon. The large guns on the cavalier of Fort St Angelo were firing at them. They were firing the heads of the Turkish prisoners.

Even some of those historians who have been determined to find no fault in this extraordinary man, have been hard put to justify the Grand Master's action. W. H. Prescott wrote: 'He commanded the heads of his Turkish prisoners to be struck off and shot from the large guns into the enemy lines – by way of teaching the Moslem,' as the chronicler tells us, 'a lesson in humanity.' A Victorian writer, General Whitworth Porter, commented:

It would have been well for the reputation of La Valette, had he restrained the feelings of indignation which this disgraceful event (the decapitation of the Knights) had most naturally evoked within reasonable bonds; but unfortunately the chronicler is compelled to record that his retaliation was as savage, and as unworthy a Christian soldier, as was the original deed; nay, more so, for Mustapha had contented himself with mangling the insensible corpses of his foe, whilst La Valette, in the angry excitement of the moment, caused all his Turkish prisoners to be decapitated, and their heads to be fired from the guns of St Angelo into the Ottoman camp. Brutal as was this act, and repulsive as it seems to the notions of the modern warrior, it was, alas! too much in accordance with the practice of the age to have been regarded with feelings of disapprobation, or even wonderment, by the chroniclers of those times. Still, the event casts a shadow over the fair fame of otherwise so illustrious a hero, which history regrets to record.

The Grand Master, by his immediate and ruthless reply showed once and for all that this was a siege in which no quarter was to be expected. When he ordered the heads of his prisoners to be fired at the Turkish lines, he was, in effect, saying to all the garrison and the people of Malta:

'There is no turning back. It is better to die in battle than to die like this.'

Chapter 19

The Little Relief

The Grand Council met that same morning and the last dispositions were made. Five companies of soldiers were ordered down from Mdina to reinforce Birgu and Senglea. The last stocks of private food belonging to merchants and householders were bought in for the general store. (It is indicative of La Valette's character that he paid a fair market price for the provisions, where many another commander of a besieged city would have confiscated them.) All the dogs in Birgu and Senglea were ordered to be destroyed, because '. . . they disturbed the garrisons by night, and ate their provisions by day'. La Valette, like most of the nobility of his time, was a great lover of the chase, but he made no exceptions to his rule. His own hunting dogs were destroyed, together with the dogs of the householders.

La Valette was well aware that it is not only planning and organization that wins wars, but also morale.

'What could a true Knight desire more ardently than to die in arms?' He said to the Council.

And what could be more fitting for a member of the Order of St John than to lay down his life in the defence of his Faith? We should not be dismayed because the Moslem has at last succeeded in planting his accursed standard on the ruined battlements of St Elmo. Our brothers – who have died for us – have taught him a lesson which must strike dismay throughout his whole army. If poor, weak, insignificant St Elmo was able to withstand his most powerful efforts for upwards of a month, how can he expect to succeed against the stronger and more numerous garrison of Birgu? With us, must be the victory.

He pointed out that the Turks – as they knew from their

spies and from deserters – were being decimated by disease. Their stores were running short, and 'their ships sent to Africa, Greece, and the Archipelago to bring back more provisions were not returning.'

It was a century when the nobility did not condescend to explain the reasons for their actions to the soldiers and men-at-arms who served under them, yet even in this the Grand Master proved his astute knowledge of psychology. He remembered that at Rhodes there had been trouble among some of the townfolk – trouble which might perhaps have been averted had the native inhabitants felt more clearly that their lot was cast in with the Order. Accordingly, after the Council had dissolved, he went out and addressed the Maltese what their condition would be if the Turks succeeded in taking the island. Had they not for centuries suffered from the annual depredations of the Moslem pirates? For good or ill the Maltese were committed to fight to the end.

He reminded the soldiers: 'We are all soldiers of Our Lord, like you, my brothers. And if by ill-chance you lose us and all your officers, I am quite sure that you will not fight with any the less resolution.' The defenders of Mdina were also committed to fight to the death. La Valette gave them the same order that he had already promulgated in the Grand Harbour garrisons: 'No prisoners.' Every morning, until the end of the siege, '. . . they hanged one Turkish prisoner upon the walls of Mdina'.

Although the Turks, immediately after the fall of St Elmo, began to train their guns upon St Angelo, it took them several days to prepare for the investment of the two main positions. Nearly all the guns and weapons which had been so laboriously transported up Mount Sciberras had to be dismantled and moved round by way of the Marsa to the land at the back of the two peninsulas. New entrenchments and emplacements had to be dug, and engineers had to make a survey to ensure that the best use was made of the natural lie of the land.

It was while the Turkish army was slowly moving round and preparing for the major action that La Valette received some welcome help. Unknown to him, on the very day that St Elmo was in its death throes, a small relief force had arrived off the north of Gozo. Consisting of four galleys (two belonging to the Order and two to Don Garcia de Toledo) they had sailed down from Messina and were waiting a favourable moment to land their troops. They had aboard 42 Knights, 20 'gentlemen volunteers' from Italy, 3 from Germany, and 2 from England. They had also 56 trained gunners and a detachment of 600 Imperial Infantry (Spanish troops raised from the garrisons in Sicily and Southern Italy).

Under the command of the Chevalier de Robles, a distinguished member of the Order and a famous soldier, this 'small Relief Force' – the *Piccolo Soccorso* as it came to be known – had been sent to Malta with the express orders that it was not to land if St Elmo had fallen. The Spanish naval commander, Don Juan de Cardona, had received explicit instructions from the Viceroy that if the garrison was in Turkish hands he should return at once to Sicily.

Fortunately for the defence of Malta, the fate of St Elmo never became known to Cardona until it was too late. Coming to anchor in the north-west of the island, he immediately sent one of the Knights ashore to discover the state of affairs. His emissary quickly learned that St Elmo had fallen, but returned to the ship and concealed the news from Cardona, only informing the Chevalier de Robles, who decided to slip through the Turkish lines overnight and reinforce Birgu. Having received permission to land, de Robles took all his troops ashore. Keeping to the western side of the island, he managed to evade the Turkish patrols. The relief force passed well to the south of the large enemy camp on the Marsa, circled round the new lines which were being established off Birgu and Senglea, and came down to the waters of Grand Harbour near the place where the fishing village of Kalkara now stands. Messengers had been sent ahead to acquaint La Valette with the news that there were close on seven hundred reinforcements making their way to the creek. Don Cardona, meanwhile, returned with his four galleys to Sicily, unaware that he had been deceived.

It was the night of 29 June when de Robles led the 'Little Relief' through the occupied island and round to Kalkara. By an unusual stroke of fortune, the Sirocco was blowing. This warm southerly wind is rare in June, a month when the north-west wind, bringing clear skies, usually prevails. But the moist and humid Sirocco, which has blown across the sea from Africa, is often accompanied by a dense sea mist. It brings to Malta the nearest approach to a northern fog that the island ever knows. That night the mist lay thick in the stony valleys and narrow lanes down which the troops made their way. The bare paths and the rough country walls sweated with damp. The olives and the untended vines glistened and dripped. The Turks hunched themselves round their campfires and waited for the dawn. In safety, without the loss of a single man, de Robles reached the shore of Kalkara Creek. He found that La Valette had boats already waiting. Silently they slid across the cable-wide stretch of water. (The head of the creek was occupied by Turkish patrols.) But no one challenged, and no shot rang out in the white mist. In safety the 'Little Relief' gained the shores of Birgu. It was a triumph. At such a moment in the siege, the arrival of seven hundred trained and untired men was to prove an invaluable asset.

Next morning the Turks learned what had happened. The Christians did not trouble to conceal their joy, and derided the enemy with the banners of their new comrades-in-arms. This may well have been the reason why Mustapha Pasha decided at this point, to attempt a negotiation. Despite La Valette's action against the Turkish prisoners, and despite every evidence that 'these sons of dogs' had no intention of surrendering, Mustapha wondered whether he might not achieve the same result as at Rhodes. His losses at St Elmo had been out of all proportion to the size of the fort. He would offer La Valette the same terms that Grand Master de l'Isle Adam had accepted forty-three years before – a safe passage for himself and all his followers, conditional on surrender of the island. They might retire from Malta to Sicily with the normal honours of war.

A messenger was accordingly dispatched under a flag of

truce to the Grand Master in Birgu. Admitted through the landward gate, the messenger's eyes were immediately blindfolded. The man whom Mustapha Pasha had chosen for the mission was an old Greek, a slave who had been taken captive by the Turks while still a boy. Chosen perhaps because he could speak French or Italian, or perhaps because Mustapha felt that a Christian slave would be treated gently, the old man was led in front of La Valette. The latter listened to the Turkish proposals 'without deigning to reply,' then:

'Take him away and hang him,' he said.

The messenger fell at his feet and begged for his life. It was not his fault, he cried, that he had been made the Pasha's messenger, nor was it his fault that he had been captured and enslaved in Greece those many years ago.

It is unlikely that La Valette had any intention of carrying out his threat. But he was adamant that, whatever story got back to the Turkish Commander-in-Chief, Mustapha would clearly understand that the Grand Master was inflexible in his determination never to yield.

'Bandage his eyes again,' he ordered.

The slave was led out from the Council chamber 'and they took him out by the gate of Provence and set him between the bastions of Provence and Auvergne. And when he was in the middle of them, they uncovered his eyes and let him see the depth of the ditch before him and the height of the wall above. . . .'

'What do you think?' they asked. The old man looked at the thickness of the walls, at their height, and at the ditch beneath him.

'The Turks will never take this place.' He answered. Then La Valette gave him his reply to Mustapha's offer.

'Tell your master that this is the only territory that I will give him.' He pointed to the ditch. 'There lies the land which he may have for his own – provided only that he fills it with the bodies of his Janissaries.'

They led Mustapha's messenger back between drawn-up ranks of soldiers, and blindfolded him again. So frightening had been his experience, so awe-inspiring the guns, the battlements and the defences, so grim the silent ranks of armoured men, that – as the chronicler tells us – '. . . he dirtied his breeches'.

Mustapha's reaction to La Valette's reply was one of blind fury. He had offered the best of terms to this Christian madman and the only reply he got was an insult. The conqueror of St Elmo, the victor of a hundred battlefields from Austria to Persia, was not to be treated in this way by a Christian pirate, the leader of a handful of fanatics. He would take Birgu and Senglea, he swore, and he would put every member of the accursed Order to the sword.

Now that the fleet lay safely at anchor in Marsamuscetto, the problem of transporting guns and siege weapons was much easier. The head of Marsamuscetto was less than two miles by land from the Knights' fortresses. Mustapha decided to bring round for the investment of Birgu and Senglea not only the guns that had been used against St Elmo, but every other available weapon. By cattle, oxen, mule, and slave, he would drag them all to Corradino and the land behind the strongpoints. From Mount Sciberras and the heights of Corradino he would open a crossfire on the Spur bastion at the end of Senglea and blow it into the sea. With his main force he would attack the fortress St Michael on Senglea. After St Elmo, it was the weakest point in the defences. Once St Michael had been reduced and its defenders put to the sword, he would devote the entire strength of his army and Piali's fleet to the reduction of Birgu and St Angelo. No more reinforcements should ever reach them by land. No more should ever reach them by sea. The last home of the Knights of St John was completely surrounded. They, and their ships, and their flag should never again trouble the subjects of the Sultan.

Chapter 20

The attack on Senglea

There were strange sounds in the island. In the summer
night, whips cracked, wood creaked and groaned, and men
shouted. At the landward end of Mount Sciberras, where
the gaunt slopes tumble down towards the Marsa, the
darkness was broken by flares. Under their wavering light
the naked figures of men were revealed, the sweat-stained
sides of oxen, and long lines of ropes and chains. Then,
lifting suddenly out of the darkness, the high prows of ships
emerged. The source of the noise was now revealed. It was
the sound of ships being dragged on wooden rollers from
Marsamuscetto creek across into Grand Harbour, by way
of half a mile of rocky land.

Mustapha had hit upon a master stroke. The Knights
thought that nothing could pass the heavy guns of St Angelo?
They thought that they had only to reckon with an enemy
attacking from the landward side to the south? Now they
would find that the waters of Grand Harbour, which they
had looked upon as their own safe and secure preserve, were
suddenly full of enemy shipping. They had no ships afloat
to deal with this menace and – besieged on both sides – they
would surely not be able to hold out for long.

Within a few days the galley slaves of the fleet had trans-
ported eighty ships, across the neck of land that divides
Grand Harbour from Marsamuscetto. The Grand Master
and his Council watched with dismay as the vessels loomed
over the ridge and began their gradual descent to the Marsa.
It was clear at once where the first attack would develop.
The ships could not penetrate the creek between Birgu and
Senglea, because of the chain defence. They would be unable

to sail up Grand Harbour and attack Birgu from the north because of the guns on St Angelo. The Turkish ships were designed to attack Senglea along its southern side.

Mustapha Pasha has generally been given the credit for this ingenious scheme, yet it seems far more likely that the inspiration for it had come from Dragut. It was by this very same trick (dragging his ships overland from the harbour of Djerba to the far side of the island) that Dragut had made his famous escape from Admiral Doria.

La Valette's estimation that the first attack was destined to fall on Senglea was confirmed in a remarkable way. A Knight called Zanoguerra, who was on watch at the spur bastion at the end of Senglea, suddenly noticed a man waving to him from the shore below Sciberras. He immediately informed the Grand Master that there seemed to be a Turkish deserter trying to contact them. To judge from his appearance, the man was no slave but someone of importance. La Valette ordered a boat to be sent across to collect the deserter. Just as it was being launched, the Turks themselves saw their renegade, and a body of them began to run down the slopes of Sciberras to cut him off. Realizing his fate if captured, the Turk – although unable to swim – threw himself into the water. Seeing him struggling, and on the point of drowning, three sailors in the garrison of Senglea dived into Grand Harbour and swam out to him. They managed to keep him afloat until the boat reached them. Balbi records the rescuers' names – Ciano, a Syracusan; Piron, a Provençal; and a Maltese called Giulio.

This Turkish officer was, indeed, no common deserter but a Greek from the ancient and noble family of Lascaris, a family which numbered among its ancestors three Byzantine Emperors. Captured when a young man, Lascaris had risen to high rank in the Turkish army. He was familiar with all its techniques in warfare, as well as the particular plans which Mustapha and his Council had devised for the present siege. The reasons he gave for his sudden decision to throw in his lot with the Knights are recorded by Vertot: 'The heroic courage which the Knights showed every day in abundance had excited his compassion; he reproached himself for fighting in company with barbarians, with men who had caused the death of most of the Princes of his own family and forced the others – ever since the capture of Constantinople – to seek exile in far-off lands.'

Brought before the Grand Master, Lascaris lamented the years that he had spent fighting on the side of their common enemy and freely proceeded to give all the information to which he had had access. Throughout the weeks that followed, Lascaris proved invaluable in his advice and a brave soldier into the bargain. He told La Valette that it was of immediate importance to strengthen the defences on the southern side of Senglea. As soon as all eighty boats were afloat in Grand Harbour, Mustapha intended to attack the peninsula in force, both by land and sea. While the bulk of the army was thrown against the fort of St Michael, the ships were to land troops all along Senglea – from the spur, right down to the head of the creek.

The first of the siege guns had already been transported on to the heights of Corradino overlooking Senglea, and skilled arquebusiers were repeating their technique used so efficiently at St Elmo. The moment that a man showed his head in the embrasures he was liable to lose his life. La Valette decided to build a palisade, or 'stoccado', along the shore, strong enough to prevent the Turks beaching their boats and dense enough to hinder their soldiers from swimming ashore. Working steadily for nine nights, and compelled to retire at dawn every day, Maltese workmen and sailors from the galleys managed to complete the task in time.

The palisade stretched all the way from the point of Senglea to the end of the fortifications. It was a masterpiece of improvisation, formed by driving stakes into the sea. These stakes were bound at the top with iron hoops, through which a long chain was passed. In some places, where the water was too deep or the bottom too hard to admit stakes, long sail-yards and masts of ships were nailed together. Not content with this defence alone, and aware that the Turkish fleet might even make an attempt through the mouth of Grand Harbour to storm the northern walls of Birgu, La Valette had a somewhat similar palisade erected in Kalkara

Creek. This was sited along the three main garrisons of Birgu, the posts of Castile, Germany, and England. (The post of England, which up to then had been held by Sir Oliver Starkey's mixed corps of foreign soldiers, had received two English volunteers in the relief force led by the Chevalier de Robles. Balbi records their names – Juan Smilt (John Smith?) and Eduardo Stamle (Edward Stanley). These two soldiers of fortune were probably Catholic exiles, a number of whom had taken up residence in Rome rather than return to the England of Queen Elizabeth.)

At the end of the first week of July, large-scale bombardment started. Some sixty to seventy guns, sited on Mount Sciberras, Gallows' Point, Mount Salvatore, and the heights of Corradino, opened a heavy crossfire on St Angelo, St Michael, and the villages of Birgu and Senglea. The heaviest fire fell upon St Michael's fort and Senglea, just before Mustapha prepared to launch his ships into Grand Harbour. Seeing the palisades that had been erected along the shore off Senglea, he gave orders to break them down in advance of the attack.

A party of Turks, specially selected for their swimming abilities, was brought down to the shore below Corradino. The palisade was their objective. Armed with axes and hatchets they swam the four or five hundred feet across the creek and, before the garrison of Senglea realized what was happening, began to destroy the new seaward defence. Admiral de Monte, the Commander of Senglea, informed of what was happening, immediately called for volunteers to repel them. It was an age when few men, even sailors, were swimmers, but the Maltese were then, as now, native to the water from children. They climbed the walls, ran down the bare rocks at the water's edge and, throwing themselves naked into the sea, set out for the palisade.

Under the bright morning sun, in the still waters of French Creek, one of the strangest battles of the siege took place. The Maltese had swum out with knives and short stabbing swords between their teeth. The Turks were armed with the weapons with which they had been cutting down the stakes. Around the cable and the wood of the defence works, plunging out into deeper water or standing on the palisade itself, Turkish and Maltese swimmers met in hand-to-hand combat. The Maltese, more skilful swimmers and inflamed by the desire to get at the invaders of their island, were more than a match for the enemy. One Turk was killed in the first few minutes and several others were wounded. Leaving the waters of the creek stained with their blood, the Turks retreated as the victors began to make good the damage. Balbi records the names of four of these Maltese heroes – Pedro Bola, Martin, Juan del Pont, and Francisco Saltaron. They do not sound much like Maltese names, having no doubt been translated by Balbi into their nearest Spanish equivalents. Of the battle itself, he has this to say: 'They attacked the Turks with such spirit that I do not say, for Maltese, but for men of any other nation, it would have been impossible to be more courageous.'

On the following morning, Mustapha ordered more troops to cross in boats and to secure ships' cables to the stakes, and masts. As soon as this was done, the ends of the cables were taken back to capstans on the shore of Corradino. Gangs of slaves began to lay their weight into the capstan bars. As the cables rose dripping from the water, so they began to drag out large sections of the defence work. Once again the Maltese rushed down from Senglea and swam to the defence of the palisade. Reaching it, they hauled themselves on to the chain and, sitting astride it, began to cut off the Turkish hawsers. This second attempt to destroy the barricade failed as had the first.

Mustapha Pasha decided to delay no longer. He had been joined a few days before by Hassem, son-in-law of Dragut, and Viceroy of Algiers. Hassem, landing to inspect the captured fort of St Elmo, had irritated his Commander-in-Chief with the tactless remark that 'He could not understand how it could possibly have held out for so long.' He indicated that he thought the attacks had lacked the necessary dash and fire. He volunteered to lead the first assault against Senglea. His lieutenant, Candêlissa, would, he said, lead the seaborne attack while he himself led his Algerians against St Michael from the land.

Mustapha was happy to teach this young fire-eater a lesson, and to let him learn how fierce was the resistance offered by the Knights and their troops. Just after dawn, on the morning of 15 July, he gave the signal for the first major attack. From the summit of Corradino he watched the ships under Candêlissa creep up the Marsa, while Hassem plunged in at the head of his troops against the landward wall and the fort of St Michael. The sun had just risen when the attack began, and even the defenders on their threatened walls had to admit that the advance of the Moslems was a magnificent sight. Balbi, whose post was on the bastion at the end of Senglea, watched the whole invasion – the ships coming up Grand Harbour from the south, and innumerable small boats loaded with troops putting off from the shores opposite. '. . . It was a sight truly most beautiful – if it had not been so dangerous.'

Ahead of the invasion fleet went three boats containing Imams. They were clad in dark robes, and they were pronouncing to the Faithful that this was a *Jehad*, a Holy War. Behind them again, came boatloads of Moslem chiefs, Turks, and Algerians, dressed in rich silks, ornamented with gold, silver and jewels. They wore elaborate gem-set turbans on their heads and in their hands were 'scimitars of Alexandria and Damascus. Their fine muskets from Fez were as decorative as they were deadly.'

As the first wave of boats approached the palisade, the oarsmen redoubled their efforts. They ploughed at full speed into the line of stakes and chain. But the workmen had done their job too well. Laden with their soldiers, the boats hung motionless against the defences. Now the musketeers on the walls of Senglea had them within range, and began to open up a deadly fire. Candêlissa, who was in the van, motioned his troops to follow him and threw himself into the water. Soon the attackers were swimming and wading to the shore, holding their shields above their heads to protect themselves against the bullets and incendiaries. Now was the time when two mortars, which were mounted on the rampart, should have been turned on the Turkish troops to check their advance. Either through the death or disablement of the gunners, they failed to open fire. The Turks, leaving the bodies of their comrades lolling behind them in the shallow waters, rushed the shore and prepared to escalade the walls.

At the same moment that the landing parties touched down on the beach below the walls of Senglea, Hassem and his Algerians attacked the landward walls. Determined to prove to Mustapha that the men of the Barbary coast were more warlike and courageous than the Turks, the Algerians were heedless of their lives. Without waiting for breaches to open in the walls, they came on in a wild screaming rush, and attempted to lay their ladders against the strong post of Senglea. The massacre wrought in their ranks was indescribable. Time and again the cannon blew great holes in the advancing troops. 'But still they charged forward with such ardour and resolution that soon one saw their banners waving along the parapets.' The Chevalier de Robles, who had led the relief force through to Birgu, had been made commander of this strong point. It was he who, directing the fire himself, caused the greatest havoc in the Algerian ranks. Yet, even so, a number of them managed to reach the parapets and hung there – Moslem and Christian locked together – like bees swarming. Every now and then, one of these groups would give a curious convulsive shudder and plunge downward into the ditch below.

The seaborne attack, meanwhile, showed every sign of succeeding. A powder magazine situated near the spur at the seaward end of Senglea suddenly blew up due to a spark falling into it. In the roar, smoke, and confusion, as the defenders staggered back to safety, a part of the wall was breached and slid down into the water. Candêlissa's troops did not neglect their opportunity. They took the smoking slope at a run and, as the dust cleared away, the Christians were horrified to see the Turkish banners lifting above the breach. Zanoguerra, the commander of the point, immediately led a counter-attack. At his side, cross in one hand and sword in the other, was the redoubtable Fra Roberto. He was a Brother of the Order and, therefore, technically forbidden to carry arms. With his robe hitched up round his waist, he flew at the enemy, calling upon the defenders 'to die like men, and to perish for their Faith'.

Where warfare was so personal – where a single man could act as a rallying point – the example of a Commander like Zanoguerra, or an ecclesiastic like Fra Roberto, was often capable of turning the scales. Zanoguerra, a tall man in gleaming armour, was like the point of a spear. The invaders began to retreat and the mood of the battle changed. But then (and this was the almost inevitable reverse side of the coin) Zanoguerra was shot dead by a musketeer. His death caused a near panic. The Turks at once set up a cheer and counter-attacked.

It was at this moment, when the action hung in the balance, that La Valette's foresight bore fruit. Aware that the garrison and defences of Senglea were not as strong as Birgu and St Angelo, he had had a bridge of boats built across between the two peninsulas so that they could be reinforced, one from the other, at a minute's notice. Seeing the enemy standards planted along the far walls of Senglea, he at once dispatched a strong reinforcement to the threatened position. The soldiers of Senglea saw their comrades coming at the run across the bridge of boats, and took heart once more. With the help of the new arrivals the position was soon stabilized.

Just as La Valette sent his reinforcements to threatened Senglea, Mustapha Pasha, watching the ebb and flow of battle from Corradino, decided that now was the time for his master-stroke. He had kept back ten large boats, with a thousand Janissaries aboard, ready to throw them in whenever, and wherever, the battle seemed critical. Now was such a time. He could feel victory within his grasp.

He gave the order. An officer on the staff signalled Mount Sciberras. The ten boats were waiting at the water's edge with the Janissaries already aboard and, the second that the signal was received, they pushed off and made straight for Senglea. It was Mustapha's intention that, while the defenders were all engaged on the southern wall, these thousand men should land just round the northern tip of Senglea – a little way above the great chain that barred the entrance to the creek. He watched them cross Grand Harbour. He saw the leading boat begin to disappear behind the tip of Senglea, and smiled in anticipation.

Unknown to Mustapha, another observer had been keeping his eye on the boatloads of Janissaries. The Chevalier de Guiral was in charge of a five-gun battery sited almost at water-level below St Angelo. (This concealed battery, which had escaped the notice of the Turkish gunners and engineers, was designed to stop ships trying to storm the creek.) Scarcely able to believe that these Turks were really going to try and land right under the muzzles of his guns, de Guiral gave orders to load.

It was only 200 yards from de Guiral's battery to the northern side of Senglea. Slowly the boats came on, and the Chevalier realized that there could be no doubt – they were going to attempt a landing right opposite him. When the boats were all grouped directly in line with his guns, he gave the order to fire.

Ball and shrapnel stormed across the water. Before the Janissaries had time to realize that they were under fire, they were blown to pieces. At so short a range, the crowded boats had no chance. Nine out of the ten boats were hit in that first salvo. The second salvo completed their ruin. Amid the roar and thunder of cannon, the water burst into pillars of foam. The torn white waves showed where chain-shot and shrapnel lashed around the boats. Within seconds Mustapha's master plan, designed to prove the turning point of the day, turned to disaster. Nine boats were sunk, and eight hundred men were hurled into the water. The tenth boat-load of Janissaries just managed to struggle back across the harbour to the slopes below Mount Sciberras.

. . . This day [wrote Balbi] the battery of Commander Guiral was, in the judgement of all, the salvation of the Island [Senglea]. There is no doubt that, if these boats had managed to land their troops, we should not have been able to hold out any longer.

The wounded and dying Turks were drowned in their hundreds in the narrow stretch of water between St Angelo and the spur of Senglea. Those who managed to reach the shore did not survive. Remembering the treatment that had been accorded the Knights and the soldiers of St Elmo, the Maltese inhabitants of Senglea took no prisoners. Hence there arose the expression (used in Malta to this day) 'St Elmo's pay', for any action in which no mercy is given.

Mustapha was not immediately aware how great the disaster had been. For some time yet the action went on. The attackers poured across by boat from Corradino, and stumbled up the rocks to Senglea's walls. Hassem's Algerians continued to hurl themselves at St Michael, and hand-to-hand fighting took place along the walls.

A Turk seeing the carnage that the Chevalier de Quinay was making of his comrades, rushed at him – ready to die if only he could kill him – and shot him through the head at point blank range. At the very same moment, another Knight ran the Turk through with his sword, stretching him dead alongside his victim. ... Meanwhile the Maltese inhabitants, both women and children, hurled stones and artificial fire down upon their attackers and upended over them great cauldrons of boiling water.

The attack went on for over five hours. Not even the scorching heat of midday checked the eternal assaults by land and sea upon the battered peninsula. It was not until Hassem had suffered such heavy losses that he could hardly get his men to attack again, that the assault was called off. Compared with 250 Christian dead, the Turkish losses were nearly 3,000.

Many notable men fell in this day's action, among them Frederic de Toledo, the son of the Viceroy of Sicily – the 'promising youth who took the habit', and who had been left behind in Malta as an earnest of his father's promise to come to the island's relief. He had been under the Grand Master's special care, but, during the relief of Senglea when the reinforcements were rushing across the pontoon, he had slipped away and joined them. He was struck down by a cannon shot while on the ramparts of Senglea, a splinter from his steel cuirass killing a companion who was at his side. In this same action, Simon de Sousa, a famous Portuguese Knight, 'whilst, regardless of his own safety, being busy repairing the breach, was killed by a cannon-ball which took off his head.'

As the Algerians fell back in disorder from the walls of St Michael, the Knights opened the gate. The garrison rushed out in a body and pursued the fleeing enemy. Hassem realized that his earlier arrogance had been ill-justified. He had learned, at bitter cost, what Mustapha had already learned at St Elmo – this was no ordinary enemy. Hassem had commanded in the great Moslem sieges of Oran and Mers-el-Kebir, but never before had he encountered such resistance among the besieged, or such determination to die rather than to yield. His lieutenant, Candêlissa, only just escaped with his life. When the order to retreat was given, Candêlissa and his men stumbled out through the shallows to reach their waiting boats. The bodies of men were thick in the water: Algerian, Turk, French, Italian, and Maltese. Looking back, he saw that some of his men, unable to reach the boats, were endeavouring to surrender.

'No quarter!' cried the inhabitants of Senglea, and 'Remember St Elmo!' As Candêlissa and his defeated troops made their way back to Corradino and the Marsa, the cannon again began the bombardment of the blood-soaked walls. Enraged by his failure, Mustapha made sure that the defenders should have no chance to rest.

That same evening, bands of Maltese swimmers were busy in the waters on either side of the peninsula. They were dragging ashore the bodies of richly dressed Turks, and seizing their jewels and rings, their ornamented daggers and purses of money. '. . . And for days after, the bodies of the killed floated on the water. They were seized by the expert Maltese swimmers who reaped a rich harvest.'

Chapter 21

Arms and the men

By midday in July the temperature was in the nineties. Although the Knights, the Maltese, and their soldiers, were used to the summer sun as well as the Turks and Algerians, the conditions under which they fought were very different. The Christians were constricted to small fortresses where every ounce of bread and every jar of water had to be carefully husbanded. The Moslems were able to retire at night to the safety of their tents, to reasonable provisions, and adequate water.

In one respect the invaders were certainly better equipped for the summer heat than were the Knights of St John. They wore loose robes, and little armour. Their robes were a disadvantage when it came to attacking a rampart where the defenders were using incendiary weapons yet, under ordinary conditions, they were cool and protected their wearers from the sun. It is difficult, on the other hand, to imagine how the Knights can have endured the weight and the heat of their elaborate armour. Under the July sun in Malta even the sandstone becomes hot to the touch.

It is one of the mysteries in the history of armour [wrote C. J. Ffoulkes] how the crusaders can have fought under the scorching sun of the east in thick quilted garments covered with excessively heavy chain mail, for this equipment was so cumbersome to take on and off that it must have been worn frequently by night and day. . . .

By the time of the Great Siege of Malta, the Knights were no longer encumbered with the chain mail of the predecessors. It is still fantastic that they could have sustained long hours of battle in midsummer Malta – only a fraction less hot than Palestine and Syria. It is possible that plate armour may have been a little cooler than mail, yet the fact remains that beneath it, the Knights wore a long jerkin of leather or quilted fabric. This was designed to protect their bodies from the bruising that would otherwise have resulted whenever they were hit.

The island of Malta lies south of the Tunisian and Moroccan coastline, south, indeed, of many cities that are renowned for their high midsummer heat. (Both Algiers and Oran are north of Malta.) In June – at the time when the main Turkish attack started against Senglea and Birgu – it is common for the midday temperature to reach over 90 degrees, and this is often coupled with a humidity as high as 72 degrees. (In this heat, metal is almost unbearable to the touch.) It gives some indication of the endurance and stamina of these men, that they could fight a six-hour battle – in armour – under these conditions. Heat stroke, of course, was not unknown. An early illustration of this is the case of the Knight Nicholas Upton, an Englishman and the head of his Langue. In 1551, on one of the occasions when Dragut was attacking the island, Upton succumbed to the heat and fell dead off his horse with a heart attack. He was, the chronicler tells us, 'a large and very corpulent man'.

The type of armour worn by the Knights of St John during the siege varied greatly for, by the middle of the sixteenth century, the armourer's craft had become very elaborate. It had, in fact, passed its peak and now tended towards a certain exaggeration of design akin to the baroque in painting and architecture. There had been some improvements on earlier work. A new type of helmet had become fashionable, the *armet* or close-helm, which was a fine defence for the head, being provided with a movable visor that could be locked or opened by the wearer whenever required. Some Knights and soldiers, too, wore the open type of helmet, the *salade*. This, although it had been evolved nearly a century before, was cooler and more suitable to a hot climate. The *salade*, however, left the face bare, and its other disadvantage was the fact that, in hand-to-hand fighting it could be easily knocked from the head. (In appearance it was not so unlike the modern American Army helmet.) The Venetian *salade*, which was quite different, was based on the helmet once worn by the soldiers of classical Greece. It protected the nose and also the cheeks.

The weight of the armour, which at first would seem to have been its greatest inconvenience, was not nearly so hard to bear as the heat. A well-fitted suit of armour – and the Knights of St John went to their armourers as a modern rich man goes to his tailor – was constructed so that its weight was distributed evenly over his body. 'It has been found that if all the joints of the movable parts of the suits, such as elbows and knees, are measured exactly to the wearer, there is little inconvenience experienced in the actual weight of the metal, but this is so well distributed that a comparatively heavy suit can be worn without much discomfort.' Except for the greater slowness of his movements, he was hardly aware of the weight he carried. Yet, even so, it is worth remembering that they may have been wearing anything up to 100 lb. of armour. (A sixteenth-century suit of armour in the Palace of Valetta has a total weight of 110 lb. and the backplate is 22½ lb. The helmet alone weighs 25 lb.) A special, ball-proof, reinforced breastplate might weigh as much as 18 lb. These were tested for musket shot, but were not necessarily proof against it. We are told that Zanoguerra was wearing one when he was shot dead in the battle for Senglea.

While the Knights, for reasons of tradition and convention, went armoured into battle, their soldiers were more lightly clad. Leather jerkins or jackets of mail were considered adequate protection against sword or pike thrust. A type of jacket popular at this time was the so-called Brigantine jacket. (There is one in the Armoury at Valetta, reputed to have belonged to Dragut.) These jackets consisted of small iron plates attached by brass rivets, and strung together on a linen or leather base.

A light and elegant type of armour worn by some of the Knights during the siege was called the 'Maximilian', after the Emperor Maximilian of Germany. It had been made for him by his armourer Seusenhofer, after the Emperor had protested at the weight of the armour which was then fashionable, saying: 'You shall arm me accordingly as I wish, for it is I and not you who have to fight. . . .' The Maximilian style had become popular during the sixteenth century, since its fluted method of construction made it lighter than plate armour. The flutes meant that the armour had a glancing surface, with the result that any blow was deflected up or down the grooved channels, and away from the wearer.

Whatever its disadvantages in a hot climate, armour meant that a man had a better chance of survival in hand-to-hand fighting than his unarmoured adversary. The comparatively small casualties of the Knights during the great siege were not entirely due to the fact that they were fighting behind fortified positions. The armourers of Germany, Italy, Spain, and England must take some credit for the Knights' ability to expose themselves, time and again, in the positions of greatest danger and still survive musket-shot, sword, and pike thrust.

The Great Siege of Malta marked one of the transition periods in the history of warfare. It occurred at the time when the common soldier, with his musket or arquebus, was beginning to achieve supremacy over the armoured nobility of the past. 'The Turks,' wrote Jurien de la Gravière, 'at the time of the siege of Rhodes were not yet used to the arquebus. They grew familiar with this weapon – to our distress – from the wars in Hungary onwards . . .' The greatest firearm-makers of the period were undoubtedly the Germans, and it was from them, and from weapons captured in the Hungarian war, that the Turks developed their own efficient small-arms manufacture.

During the siege of Malta it was noticed that the Turkish musketeers were much more efficient than were the Christians. Although slower to load than the European, the Turkish musket 'of 7 to 9 palms long' was a precision instrument. It was one which accounted for a great number of the casualties among the defenders.

In the attacks on St Elmo, Senglea, and Birgu, the weapons – other than firearms – were practically unchanged from those that had existed for centuries. The sword, the axe, the pike, the halberd (a combined spear and battle axe), and the mace, were still to be found in both armies. Warfare was personal, and it was all the more horrible for that fact. Except for artillery bombardment, men only engaged with one another at close quarters. They struggled hand-to-hand together, with weapons that were little more sophisticated than those used for thousands of years. In Malta, the Wars of Religion reached their climax. If both sides believed that they saw Paradise in the bright sky above them, they had a close and very intimate knowledge of Hell.

Chapter 22

Death in the Marsa

After the first great assault on Senglea, Mustapha proceeded with more caution. He decided to use the same technique as at St Elmo, reducing the walls, and sapping the morale of the defenders by incessant bombardment. Then, as soon as his engineers considered that the positions were breached, he would throw the whole weight of the army against both points at the same time. In this way he would be able to prevent La Valette from reinforcing either side with detachments of fresh troops. Both garrisons would be exhausted by fatigue, worn out by bombardment, and compelled to man their defences at the same time.

It was true that the reduction of St Elmo had taken over a month, and that Senglea and Birgu – the latter in particular – were much stronger. But Mustapha felt reasonably confident that he had little to worry about large-scale reinforcements reaching the island from Sicily. Piali's ships were on guard to the north of Gozo, and were ready to prevent any major relief force getting through.

It was a different matter altogether with individual ships, or small squadrons, and Mustapha was still worried by the ease with which de Robles's seven hundred men had been able to get into Birgu. He made sure that no more small detachments could creep through his lines and cross by Kalkara creek. Only this one small headland was unoccupied by the Turkish army. From the south, Senglea was cut off by the bulk of Corradino : and Sciberras, and the entrance to Grand Harbour, had long been in Turkish hands. Mustapha now instructed his engineers to complete entrenchments from Mount Salvatore right down to Kalkara Creek.

At the same time, he strengthened the battery on Salvatore with sixteen guns, among them two enormous basilisks firing stone shot weighing 300 lb.

Remembering how the fall of Rhodes had been facilitated by mutinies and dissensions within the garrison, Mustapha did not neglect the importance of psychological warfare. Realizing that the Maltese might have little love for these Knights who had brought such ruin on their island, he tried to suborn them by pointing out how ill-treated they were under their present masters. The Maltese language is very similar to Arabic, and it was not difficult to suggest that they were more akin to the Moslems than they were to this European nobility who not only despised them, but did not condescend to speak their language. The Maltese were promised freedom and fair treatment if they would give up the struggle.

It was correct that there was an affinity of blood and language between the Maltese and the Arabs. The islands had been under Arabic domination for over two hundred years (until brought back into the European confederacy by Count Roger the Norman in 1090). But Malta's devotion to the Church was the rock upon which Mustapha's hopes were wrecked. To suggestions that they should desert, or lay down their arms, he received the reply that 'The Maltese would rather be the slaves of Saint John, than the companions of the Grande Turke.'

During the whole of the siege of Senglea and Birgu only one man is known to have been prepared to accept the terms offered by the enemy. He was an Italian private soldier who had joined the garrison with de Robles's relief force. At the time when Mustapha's emissary came to La Valette, and the news was broadcast what terms were offered, this unfortunate man was rash enough to say that he thought there was no hope, and that the terms should be accepted. Knowing how quickly the contagion of cowardice spreads, the Commander of the garrison had him taken out upon the ramparts and hanged.

Piali was now put in charge of the operations against Birgu. Mustapha Pasha directed the attacks on Senglea and St

Michael. Candêlissa, the lieutenant of the discredited Hassem, was given command of the fleet which night and day cruised off the entrance to Grand Harbour. Among his other new dispositions, Mustapha sited a further large battery in Bighi, the short stubby peninsula to the north of Birgu. From north and south, and from the landward side to the east, the fortresses were played upon by an immense weight of fire. 'A storm of marble and metal fell upon the houses and, though they were built of stone, soon reduced them to ruins. . . .' The post of Castile, the large bastion facing the land at the end of Birgu, bore the brunt of this bombardment. During the last week of July the Turkish gunners gave the besieged no respite. 'All day and all night even,' wrote Balbi 'the enemy never ceased their fire . . .'

To protect the inhabitants of Birgu, La Valette ordered great barriers of solid stonework to be built across the streets. Thinking, perhaps, that the Turks would spare their fellow Moslems, he ordered the slaves to carry out this work. But if the Grand Master had been prepared to sacrifice his own brethren in St Elmo, the Turk was no less ruthless. As soon as the gangs of slaves set about constructing these new barriers, they came under a vicious fire. Driven to their work by the overseer's lash, they fell in their hundreds. Even members of the garrison were moved by their plight. Balbi records that over five hundred were killed in this work, and refers to them as 'these poor creatures'. Some of them, who attempted to mutiny against their task, were put to death. 'It was only by the most severe, indeed cruel treatment,' wrote W. H. Prescott, 'that these unfortunate beings could be made to resume their labours.' Any who showed a disinclination to work had their ears cut off.

Anticipating that Birgu might also be attacked from the sea, La Valette redoubled the defences along the rocks that fringed the village in Kalkara Creek. As at Senglea, he determined to make the enemy's passage to the walls as difficult as possible. Barges laden with stone were sunk off shore, and grappled together with heavy chain taken from the Order's galleys.

It was now the first day of August. There was still no sign

of the major relief force promised for over a month ago. It was clear that, long before any help could reach them, the Turks would have time to throw the full weight of their army into the attack. Already the conditions of Birgu and Senglea were such that the Grand Master expected a large scale assault at any hour.

It came on 2 August. Just before dawn, the enemy began to move forward and at first light the preliminary bombardment began. Every battery opened up at once, and the encircling hills and ridges behind the garrisons spouted flame. 'So great was the noise that in Syracuse and Catania, the one 70 and the other 100 miles from Malta, the inhabitants heard the sound – like the distant rumble of thunder.' From Mount Salvatore alone, 38 guns opened fire, 26 of them directed at the bastion of Castile, 8 against the posts of Auvergne and Germany, and 4 against St Angelo. The latter was also under fire from batteries on Gallows' Point, Mount Sciberras, and captured St Elmo. From the heights of Corradino, an equal number of guns opened up against Senglea and its fortress, St Michael. 'It seemed as if the two peninsulas had risen from the sea like two new smoking volcanoes, the one a Vesuvius, and the other an Aetna.'

It was by far the heaviest bombardment that had yet occurred in the siege, and it must have seemed to the Turkish Commander-in-Chief that no man could live, let alone fight, in those two crumbling ruins on the headlands. The day was brilliant, the sky cloudless, and the whole island shook under the sun. From every ridge and slope the Turks swept like a hurricane against the walls of the two garrisons. Yet still, after six hours continuous assault, the Christians held out. Five times the Turks were driven back from the bastion of St Michael's. On more than one occasion they had actually established themselves in a breach of the walls, only to be hurled down again by savage counter-attack. Reluctantly, in the early afternoon, the Pasha ordered his troops to withdraw.

For hours the smoke hung over the creeks in the languid summer air. It was not until a faint sea-breeze drew onshore towards sundown, that Mustapha saw again the ramparts of his enemy. Above shell-torn Senglea and Birgu the banner of St John still flaunted. Casualties among the attackers had been heavy. He decided to give his two targets a further five days continuous bombardment.

During those days there was no room in the garrisons for a single useless hand. Men, women, and children worked side by side, repairing the breaches, rebuilding the barriers in the streets, manufacturing incendiaries, and making good the damage to guns and weapons. In this brief lull between one attack and another, La Valette managed to send a further message to the Viceroy in Sicily. Despite the encirclement of the two peninsulas, it is a tribute to the Maltese who were used as messengers that reports still got through. Acquainted from birth with every nook and cranny of their small island the Maltese messengers invariably managed to pass through the enemy's lines to Mdina. From there the message was relayed to the north of the island and to Gozo, where fishermen from small villages like Marsalforn took it over. Embarking at night in their small open boats, they crept out to the east so as to avoid Piali's patrolling squadrons, then, altering course after daybreak, the boats gradually made their way under sail and oar to Cape Passaro at the southern end of Sicily. The seamanship and courage shown by these men was superb. Every one of them knew that if he was caught by the Turks he would die under torture or – at the best – go straight to the galley bench. Yet there is no record, throughout the whole siege, of any messages dispatched by La Valette failing to reach their objective.

On 7 August, after a further five days of intensive bombardment, the assault was renewed. As day broke, even the bravest of the defenders might have felt his spirits sink. From whatever bastion or embrasure that man looked, they could see nothing but the enemy and the standards of the Grande Turke. They were ringed in by cannon, and under fire from every point of the compass. As the thunder of the guns ceased, the attack fell on Birgu and Senglea simultaneously. Piali's troops swept over the ditch in front of the ramparts of Castile, half-filled as it was with the rubble from the walls. They burst into a yawning breach where whole sections of the main wall had given way. Impatient of victory, they surged forward into what appeared to be the undefended space – only to find themselves confronted by a further interior wall. Built under La Valette's supervision, these inner walls had been run all round the landward side of Birgu, so that even when the main wall was breached the enemy only found himself in a trap. The troops who had poured in through the outer breach now came under a withering fire from the garrison. Caught in that narrow corridor between one wall and another, and unable to turn back because the weight of numbers relentlessly pressed them forward, they were slaughtered in their hundreds.

The defenders waited until they saw that the attackers were beginning to waver and then they, in their turn, took the offensive. With swords in hand, they leaped from their retrenchments and turned the Turkish indecision into a rout. The enemy had suffered heavily from cannon fire on their first charge towards the breach, and they had been decimated by musket and incendiary once within the wall. They were now hacked down as they turned to flee over the ground slippery with the blood of their comrades.

The assault on Birgu, which at first sight had looked as if it might be victorious, turned into a disaster. Bitterly Piali watched his troops stagger back from the walls and run for the safety of their lines. The Knights and their troops did not make the mistake of following up the attack. They withdrew at once and, together with the rest of the garrison, set about repairing the breach.

In the meantime Mustapha's forces, who were attacking St Michael's on Senglea, had stormed one part of the wall and had a footing in the citadel. Gradually their weight of numbers began to tell. This was the moment when Mustapha's policy of attacking both garrisons at the same time, seemed as if it might prove successful. The Grand Master could only look in dismay at the wavering line of Turkish pennants along the ramparts of St Michael. He could not withdraw a single man from his own hard-pressed garrison to send to their rescue.

The Turkish Commander-in-Chief was another of those

incredible old warriors like Dragut and La Valette. Seeing that the moment had come for a decisive action, he came down at the head of his own bodyguard, seventy years old though he was: 'He himself was to be seen everywhere, sword in hand, cheering on his followers with promises of reward and booty . . .' Under the Pasha's eye, the Janissaries now came in for the final onslaught.

The garrison of St Michael were steadily forced backwards. They looked hopelessly across the water to see if help was on its way. At that moment the men of Birgu were completely occupied in driving back the enemy from their own breached wall. They had no chance to give a thought to their brethren on the other side of the creek. Victory for Mustapha seemed imminent.

Suddenly the unbelievable happened. Clear above the noise of battle, the Turks heard the signal to retreat. Their officers and under-officers passed on the order 'Retire! Retire!' The Janissaries were as hard to call off as a pack of wolf-hounds. Senglea was within their grasp. It was very reluctantly, and only at the command of their new Aga, that they gave up the conquered ground. The wall, where only a few minutes before the Moslem banners had waved, was suddenly deserted. To the stupefaction of the Christians, the enemy began to withdraw at the very moment when they had felt unable to resist any longer. La Valette, who had been on the point of sending a handful of his own troops over from Birgu was as astonished as the rest. What could have caused Mustapha to call off his troops at such a time? And why were they all streaming away, past the end of French Creek, past Corradino, in the direction of the Marsa? For a moment the Grand Master and many others must have thought that the unbelievable had happened – that Don Garcia de Toledo had managed to land with a large relief force.

That, in fact, was the very message which Mustapha had received. A horseman had spurred up from the Turkish camp at the Marsa reporting that a large Christian force had fallen upon the encampment and was putting every man to the sword. There was no large Christian force in Malta, except for the beleaguered garrisons. Mustapha's natural assumption was that the relief from Sicily had taken him in the rear. Alarmed at the prospect of losing his base and of having his lines of communications cut, he had at once given the order to retire.

When he reached the Marsa, it was a grim and bloody sight that met his eyes. Dead and dying lay in heaps among cut-down tents, mutilated horses, and burning piles of stores. The vast camp, full of Turkish sick and wounded, had been set upon and practically destroyed. In the absence of all the other troops engaged at Senglea and Birgu, they had been unable to offer any resistance. There lay the dead, and there the ruined camp, but of a large Christian force there was absolutely no sign.

When Mustapha Pasha learned the truth, his rage was uncontrolled. He forgot the dead at his feet and thought only of the victory that had been snatched from his hands.

What had happened was this. Early that morning, the Chevalier Mesquita, Governor of Mdina, hearing the fury of bombardment, had conjectured that this could only mean another major assault against the two garrisons. Guessing – correctly as it proved – that the Turkish camp would only be lightly guarded, he had dispatched his whole cavalry force to the Marsa under the command of the Chevalier de Lugny. He had taken his troops down from the rocky heights of Mdina, watching all the time how the smoke and cloud hung over Grand Harbour, and trusting that on a day like this he would meet with no Turkish patrols. He had ridden round until he was south-west of the Marsa and had then sent forward his scouts. They had reported that the Turkish camp was unguarded save for a few sentries. De Lugny formed up his cavalry.

They came down off the slopes above the Marsa like demons of vengeance. In the first charge they overwhelmed the sentries. Then the cavalry were among the tents occupied only by the sick, the wounded, and the few slaves who tended them. The guy-ropes to the tents were cut, and their silk and canvas was set afire. Provisions and stores were destroyed. The grazing horses were killed, ham-strung, or taken back to Mdina. The Turks were slaughtered as they lay defenceless in their ruined camp. It was a massacre.

As his troops streamed back to take up their positions once more on the lines behind the fortresses, Mustapha Pasha had time to look round his camp and contemplate the bodies of his dead. He tore his beard and swore to have vengeance.

'By the bones of my fathers – may Allah brighten their tombs! – I swear that when I take these citadels I will spare no man. All, shall I put to the sword. Only their Grand Master will I take alive. Him alone I will lead in chains – to kneel at the feet of the Sultan!'

Chapter 23

The great decision

Deep within the walls of Fort St Angelo, the Grand Master was in conference with Sir Oliver Starkey. Outside, the cannonade continued ceaselessly. A fine drift of sandstone powdered down from the ceiling as the guns on St Angelo's cavalier fired back. La Valette had just received the reply to his last message from Garcia de Toledo.

Sir Oliver was constantly at La Valette's side in these grim days. The Grand Master derived great strength from his companionship with this last of the English Langue. As his Latin secretary, Starkey was responsible for the wording of his dispatches, and for advice on his speeches in the Grand Council. He and the Grand Master were now considering what action should be taken in view of the Viceroy's latest message. It was brief and to the point. Before the end of August, Don Garcia promised that he would come to Malta's relief, with a force of 16,000 men.

'We can rely no more upon his promises,' said La Valette. 'When the Council meets tonight they must be told that there is no more hope of a relief force. Only we ourselves can save ourselves.'

It was several days since the last combined attack on Birgu and Senglea, and there had been no more Turkish attempts by land. It was clear that Mustapha had decided to soften up the defences even more, before attempting any further mass attacks. His own losses had been tremendous, something over 10,000 men already killed or incapacitated since the first landing – and nothing to show for it but the small, ruined fort of St Elmo.

Within the garrisons the situation was no less desperate.

The Great Siege

The great Hospital was full to overflowing. There was hardly a man, woman or child who did not bear some wound or injury. While the Turkish army could revive their strength and morale in the comparative security of their trenches, the defenders never had a moment's respite. Within their tottering walls, and amid the ruins of their houses, they worked day and night to try and maintain the slowly disintegrating fabric of their fortress. Only their courage and their Faith sustained them.

That night the Sacro Consiglio assembled. They knew that a messenger had come in with a dispatch from Sicily and they hoped for some good news. The Grand Master did not waste time, nor mince his words.

'I will tell you now openly, my brethren,' he said, 'that there is no hope to be looked for except in the succour of Almighty God – the only true help. He who has up to now looked after us, will not forsake us, nor will he deliver us into the hands of the enemies of the Holy Faith.'

The Priors and the Conventual Bailiffs, the Knights Grand Cross and the Piliers of the Langues bowed their heads. They knew now that Don Garcia had abandoned them.

'My brothers,' went on La Valette, 'we are all servants of our Lord, and I know well that if I and all those in command should fall, you will still fight on for liberty, for the honour of our Order, and for our Holy Church. We are soldiers and we shall die fighting. And if, by any evil chance, the enemy should prevail – ', he paused – 'we can expect no better treatment than our brethren who were in St Elmo.'

His last words contained the essence of what he had to say: 'Let no man think that there can be any question of receiving honourable treatment, or of escaping with his life. If we are beaten we shall all be killed. It would be better to die in battle than terribly and ignominiously at the hands of the conqueror.'

When the Council had dispersed, the Grand Master took care that his speech should be made known to all the troops in the two garrisons. 'And from that moment forward,' wrote Balbi (who heard the Grand Master's words as he stood among the defenders of St Michael), 'there was no more talk of relief forces. From then on every man determined to die rather than fall alive into the hands of the Turk. We would sell our lives as dearly as possible.'

La Valette now made use of a weapon which he was convinced would strengthen not only the morale of the Order, but also of the Maltese. Pope Pius IV, Giovanni Angelo Medici, had recently promulgated a Bull which granted plenary indulgence to all who fell in the war against the Moslems. This Great Siege was just such an occasion, when any man or woman might be truly considered to have died for their Faith. They were therefore entitled to a complete remission of all their sins. When this was made known 'there was no man or woman who had reached the age of discretion who did not at once appreciate what it meant. With the greatest devotion, with the firmest hope and faith that they would be received into glory, they resolved to die for their cause.'

While the Grand Master had explicitly said that he had no hope of any relief force coming from Sicily, he cannot have known how nearly accurate his statement was. He must still have believed that his ambassadors in Messina and the other Knights in Europe, as well as the politic sense of Don Garcia, would not allow Malta to fall. Yet the fact is that, during the discussions which were taking place at that time in the Viceroy's court, it was being seriously suggested that Malta should be abandoned. 'The Knights were not subjects of Philip II. At the time of Rhodes, no European monarch had gone to their aid, why should the Spanish Emperor do so now?'

To counter these arguments, the party supporting the Order were quick to remind Don Garcia that Malta had been a Spanish gift to the Knights, and that they had never failed to acknowledge their feudatory obligations. 'Besides, as a matter of practical common sense, what would happen to Sicily if Malta fell? How long could the Viceroy defend his own shores if the whole of the Turkish fleet were to be based in those inestimable harbours that lay on either side of ruined St Elmo? When the flag of the Grande Turke flew over Malta, it would not be long before his ships were blockading Sicily and Southern Italy. Had there ever been an occasion', they asked the waverers, 'when the Sultan had been content with the extent of his possessions? He menaced them from the north, where Belgrade and Budapest were in his hands. He had also concluded a defensive alliance with their enemies, the French. If he held Malta, could it be expected for a moment that that "barren rock" would be the limit of his territorial demands? Malta was only a stepping stone.'

It was fortunate that in the end the logic of this argument prevailed. The hesitant policy of Don Garcia, naturally apprehensive lest he lose a fleet and an army in defending a territory that did not technically belong to his master, was swayed finally towards a realization that something must be done quickly. He had delayed and delayed, hoping that somehow the situation would resolve itself. He had sent one small reinforcement which had got through – despite his express orders that it was not to land if St Elmo had fallen. He had sent another small force in two galleys which had failed to get ashore. Now, if the island was to be saved and with it his own charge, Sicily, he must strain every nerve to send help within the month. But it was already the second week of August, and a dilatory policy could not be reversed so quickly. La Valette had not been so far wrong in his assumption that if the Order was to be saved, it could only be through its own exertions.

It was in these desperate days that the providence and forethought of the Grand Master, his secretary, and the Council, paid dividends. The organization of stores, water and supplies, which had been determined upon long before the Turk ever set foot on Malta, proved excellent. At no time – although food was short – was there any question of starvation, that determining factor in so many other sieges. At no time, in an island always notoriously short of water, did the defenders find themselves reduced by the worst of all enemies, thirst. The fireworks, the incendiary grenades and hoops, the ammunition for the guns – all were adequate. Even minor points had been carefully thought out. Tubs filled with seawater were stationed all along the ramparts, so that men burned by wildfire could immediately soak themselves. Jars of watered wine, and panniers of bread were kept constantly ready in the main defence points, so that the soldiers could get food and drink without having to leave their guard posts.

To maintain this steady supply of provisions, as well as arms and ammunition, the women and children of Birgu worked night and day. If they could not bear arms, they could still act as a supply corps. In the heavy attacks, while the soldiers manned the guns, the Maltese inhabitants reinforced them on the ramparts – hurling rocks at the attackers and upending cauldrons of boiling water over the escalading Turks. The defence of the two garrisons, if it was a miracle of courage, was also evidence of La Valette's careful preparations. 'If all these sensible precautions had not been taken,' wrote Balbi, 'there would have been no possibility of so small a garrison as ours withstanding such a furious and persistent attack by so great an army'.

The Grand Master did not delay in sending back a reply to Don Garcia de Toledo. 'The fortifications of the island,' he wrote,

are in a state of complete ruin. I have lost the flower and the élite of my Knights in many attacks. Of those who remain, most are injured or are in the Hospital. Send me at least those two galleys of the Order which are now in Messina, together with any of the other Knights from the more distant nations who have now arrived to help us. It would not be right for one particular section of the Order to be spared, when the whole body is exposed to almost inevitable loss.

He had in mind, perhaps, those members of the German Langue who, because their estates were farther from Malta, had not been able to come in such great numbers for the initial defence. It was, in fact, the French, the Italians, and the Spanish – in that order – who formed the major part of the Knights engaged in the siege.

It was upon the Spanish-held bastion of Castile that Mustapha's next blow was to fall.

Chapter 24

Into the breach

For the first time in the siege the Turks were driving mines beneath the defences. At St Elmo they had been unable to do so because of the hard rock on which the fort was built. They had now found out that it was just possible to sink a mine on the landward side of the ditch of Birgu. Trained teams of sappers were busy night and day, and the defenders of Birgu could hear – if they kneeled and put their ears to the ground – the sinister tap-tap-tap of the Turkish mine-head probing towards them. It was by mining, more than artillery fire, that the Turks had won Rhodes. They now attempted to repeat their success.

In that scorching summer, in that dry sandstone which seems in August to glow with heat, the naked labour gangs toiled with pick and shovel – sinking their tunnel below the ditch, aiming to lay their charges right beneath the bastion of Castile. It was a task of incredible difficulty and even the specially trained Egyptian engineers found themselves faced with an almost insuperable problem. The soil of Malta is at the most about six feet deep. Below that lies sand and limestone, material that, when quarried, can be cut quite easily. It is difficult to tunnel through at short notice.

While the sappers worked below ground, the batteries on Mount Salvatore and the far side of Kalkara Creek continued to play without ceasing about the threatened position. Even at night, as the sentries bent to try and catch the sound of the miners at work, they were deafened by the eternal rumble and thud of solid stone and iron shot flailing their weakening walls.

Mustapha's plan was to explode the mine beneath the

bastion of Castile at the same moment as launching a large assault on Senglea. Before setting off his mine, he intended to leave Castile itself unattacked, hoping that the garrison would think that only Senglea was in danger. If his ruse succeeded, part of the garrison would have crossed the bridge pontoon to reinforce their comrades in threatened Senglea. When the mine went up, he intended to rush the bastion of Castile and catch the garrison unprepared. While waiting for the completion of this mining operation, Mustapha had a large siege engine made – a type of tower carrying aboard it a heavy drawbridge. Engines of this type were commonly used in sieges, their purpose being to allow the attackers to get right up to the walls, mount the tower, lower the drawbridge and swarm in over the walls. Mustapha intended to use this against Castile immediately after the mine had been sprung. While his men poured through the expected breach in the wall, from another quarter the tower would discharge its load of attackers on to what remained of the parapet.

During this period of the siege Balbi's diary records with grim monotony '. . . and all day and all night the enemy's guns did not cease'. It was the immense weight of the Turkish fire-power that made the siege of Malta memorable above all others. When they had invested Rhodes the Turks had brought an even larger army against the Knights, nearly 100,000 men. But, as the Knight Anne de Montmorency was later to remark in a conversation with Charles X and Catherine de Medici, '. . . Their artillery was far greater at Malta than at Rhodes, where they used mining operations more than gunfire. In Malta over 70,000 cannon shots were fired during the course of the siege.'

It was on this occasion that Catherine de Medici asked 'Was it really the greatest siege? Greater even than Rhodes?'

She was answered by Knight Commander de la Roche, of the French Langue: 'Yes, Madame, greater even than Rhodes. It was the greatest siege in history.'

On 18 August all was ready for Mustapha's next co-ordinated attack. His engineers reported to him that the head of the mine was now under the bastion of Castile, and that its explosion should be sufficient to bring the ramparts crashing down. Piali, as before, was put in command of the attack to be made on Castile, while Mustapha directed the assault on Senglea. It was during this day that a Turkish runaway slave brought the news to Birgu that Mustapha had sworn to put all to the sword, with the exception only of the Grand Master. At that night's council meeting, one of the Knight Commanders reported what he had heard. La Valette gazed round at the members of the Council. 'I shall surely prevent him,' he said, 'and even if this siege, contrary to my expectation, should end in a victory for the enemy, I declare to you all, that I have resolved that no one in Constantinople shall ever see a Grand Master of our Holy Order led there in chains. If, indeed, the very worst should happen and all be lost, then I intend to put on the uniform of a common soldier and throw myself, sword in hand, into the thick of the enemy – and perish there with my children and my brothers.'

On the morning of the 18th the excessively heavy bombardment of Senglea warned them that an attack was imminent. It was not slow to develop. The moment that the rumble of the guns died down, the Iayalars and Janissaries were seen streaming forward across the no-man's-land to the south. The attack developed in the same way as on previous occasions, with a mass assault on the bastion of St Michael. Piali, meanwhile, held back his troops from Birgu according to plan. Mustapha waited anxiously to see if the Grand Master was to be lured into sending some of his garrison across the bridge to reinforce hard-pressed Senglea.

La Valette clearly expected some trick, and was not to be caught. At last, having failed to draw off the Christians as he had hoped, Mustapha gave his engineers the order to spring the mine under Castile.

Although La Valette had known that the Turks were mining towards his walls he had been unable to discover the exact position. The blow, when it fell, was not unexpected but it was none the less devastating in its effect. With a gigantic rumbling crash the mine went up, and a great section of the main wall of the bastion fell with it. The dust cloud was still spilling outwards into the ditch, when Piali's troops poured forward *en masse*.

For a moment panic ensued among the defenders. The wounded staggered back from the breach and in the general confusion it seemed as if the position was surely lost. Hardly had the smoke cleared away, than the first wave of Turks were over the ditch and had gained a foothold. Their banners were planted on the torn and tottering rampart. Their spearhead began to drive forward into the very town itself. The bell of the Conventual Church was rung – a prearranged signal that the enemy was within the fortifications. A Chaplain of the Order, Brother Guillaume, seeing the Turkish standards waving over Castile rushed to the Grand Master.

'All is lost,' he cried, 'we must retreat to St Angelo.' It was a moment when a flicker of indecision would have spelled ruin. La Vallette, who was in his command post in the small square of Birgu, did not hesitate. '. . . This intrepid old man, placing only a light morion on his head and without waiting to put on even his cuirass, rushed boldly to meet the infidels.' Seizing a pike from a soldier standing nearby, he called on his staff to follow him and led the way towards the bastion of Castile.

Seeing the Grand Master at the head of a small group of Knights running towards the point of danger, the Maltese inhabitants swarmed round to lend help. The waverers and the disheartened, hearing that the Grand Master himself was leading the counter-attack, forgot their moment of fear. 'Accompanied by the Knights who were immediately about his person, the Grand Master led so impetuous a charge that the tide was turned.' Up the scarred and still smoking slopes where the mine had breached the wall, La Valette led his band of Knights and townsfolk. A grenade burst alongside him and he was wounded in the leg by splinters. The cry went up, 'The Grand Master! The Grand Master is in danger!' From every side Knights and soldiers came rushing to the attack. The Turkish vanguard staggered back and began to yield.

'Withdraw, Sire! Withdraw to a place of safety,' urged one of Valette's staff. 'The enemy are in retreat.'

The Great Siege

It was true that the first impetus of the Turkish assault had spent itself. The position, though, was still far from secure. A group of their soldiers occupied the breach. Their pennants still lifted above the bastion. La Valette knew that it was his presence which had put new heart into the garrison. It was no time for him to withdraw. Limping, he went forward up the slope.

'I will not withdraw,' he said to the Knight beside him, 'so long as those banners still wave in the wind.'

Knights, soldiers, and Maltese from Birgu now surged forward and began to hurl the enemy down into the ditch. Within a few minutes the wall was cleared and the enemy routed. To further protestations from his staff that he should now retire, the Grand Master only replied: 'I am seventy-one. And how is it possible for a man of my age to die more gloriously than in the midst of my friends and brothers, in the service of God?' Not until he had seen the whole bastion reoccupied, and the defences re-manned, did La Valette withdraw to have the wound in his leg dressed.

Just off the western coast of Gozo, there is a small bay known as Cala Dueira, whose mouth is almost closed by a curiously shaped and almost inaccessible islet, Fungus Rock. On it grows a 'strange and repellent-looking black plant', a kind of fungus from which the rock takes its name. Known to the Maltese for centuries as a sovereign cure for wounds and haemorrhages, the fungus is an astringent and a styptic. It was no doubt with this that La Valette's wound was dressed. As soon as his leg had been bandaged, he insisted on returning to the bastion of Castile. As he was on his way there, some Knights brought before him the Turkish flags captured in the action. He ordered them to be hung with the other trophies in the Conventual church, then made his way back to the bastion.

The Grand Master knew that, after breaching the wall so successfully, the enemy was almost certain to attack again – possibly that very night. He was proved right in his conjecture. Mustapha and Piali, having called off their attacks on the two garrisons during the afternoon, renewed the offensive soon after sunset.

It was a night without darkness. From the mouth of Grand Harbour where the ships under Candêlissa had begun to close in towards Bighi Bay, came the rippling flash of gunfire. From all the ridges and hills around Senglea and Birgu, the rumble of the cannon was like a summer thunderstorm. Soon the enemy brought up incendiary flares, and the ground below the walls became as bright as day. Wildfire poured down from the ramparts of Castile and St Michael. Incendiary grenades burst with a smoke and flare among attackers and defenders alike. Silhouetted in the breach, the figure of the Grand Master was a rallying point for his men – a rallying point like a rock round which the storm rages. But when the dawn came and the Turks withdrew, the two fortresses were still in the hands of the defenders.

Their condition was critical. Their losses during the night and the previous day had been heavy. There were no longer any reinforcements to call upon. For the first time, even the ammunition was running low, and fresh supplies had to be hastily brought up from the underground powder mills of St Angelo. Every bed in the great Hospital was full, and there were 'none considered wounded in those days if he could but walk'. The garrison could expect no rest that day. The Turks, having so nearly succeeded during the past twenty-four hours, would not allow the defenders any time to recoup their strength. Mustapha was going to make full use of his manpower.

That day, 19 August, was the worst so far in the siege. Even La Valette felt at times that the end was near. Among those killed in the fighting below the bastion of Castile was his own nephew, Henri de la Valette. In company with a companion, the Knight Polastron, the young Valette had attempted to destroy the great siege tower which the Turks had brought up. Both he and Polastron were cut down by the Turkish crew of the tower. A furious battle then raged around their bodies, the Turks bent on capturing the valuable armour of the two Knights while the Christian soldiers were equally determined to drag their dead leaders back within the walls.

The disadvantages of armour are clearly shown by this

episode. As Balbi remarked of the young Valette. 'It was because he was dressed in rich and gilded armour that all of the Turks opened fire upon him.' When his body was finally brought back within the walls they carried it to La Valette. The Grand Master gazed long on the face of his dead nephew. Some of the Knights who were standing nearby condoled with him on his loss. He quietly reproved them.

'All the Knights are equally dear to me. I look upon all of them as my children. The death of Polastron moves me as much as that of my nephew. These two young men have only gone before the rest of us by but a few days. For, if the relief from Sicily does not come, and we cannot save Malta, we must all die. To the very last man – we must bury ourselves beneath these ruins.'

It was the first and only time in the course of the siege that the Grand Master allowed a note of hopelessness to sound in his words.

Chapter 25

'... The world was coming to an end'

The state of Birgu was now almost as bad as that of Senglea. Strong though Birgu and St Angelo were, they had endured constant bombardment for nearly two months. From 23 June, when St Elmo had fallen, the weight of the Turkish batteries had been largely directed against them. Nearly every house within the walls was ruined, and the walls themselves were collapsing. Mustapha's mine under the bastion of Castile had made a breach which no amount of labour was likely to be able to repair. 'The breach, the very fort itself, seemed to be all on fire. The tumult of the combatants, the noise of arms, the cries of soldiers, the groans of wounded men and women, made a spectacle that was both terrible and moving.'

After the young Valette's desperate sally against the Turkish tower, the Grand Master himself took a hand in compassing its destruction. The tower, protected against incendiaries by great sheets of leather which were kept constantly soaked with water, was now so close to the wall that from its top platform Janissary snipers were beginning to pick off the defenders within Birgu itself. La Valette ordered a band of Maltese workmen to make a hole through the base of the wall just opposite the tower. A large cannon was wheeled into place, so that, the moment the workmen had breached the wall from the inside, it could open fire against the siege engine. Meanwhile the Grand Master was conspicuous on the danger point, the shattered bastion of Castile. 'Of his own safety he was still more careless than that of others. . . .' At a given moment when all was ready, he ordered the workmen to knock down the outer blocks in the tunnel.

The Turks aloft in their high tower, concentrating entirely on that part of Birgu which they could see, had not been able to observe what was happening in the wall immediately below them. Suddenly, with a rumble and a cloud of dust, a narrow opening gaped beneath their feet. The dark muzzle of a cannon was run out. Within seconds, before the slaves and labour gangs could begin to move the tower to safety, the cannon had opened fire. La Valette had taken the advice of a Maltese carpenter who had pointed out that the weakness of the tower lay in its lower section. With this in mind, he had given orders for the cannon to fire chain-shot. This consisted of two large cannon balls or half-cannon balls fastened together by chain. Immediately on leaving the cannon's mouth, chain-shot whirled round and round in a parabola, acting like a giant scythe. The Knights and their gunners were skilled in its use. Chain-shot was a standard weapon in sea actions, where it served to cut down the enemy's mast and rigging.

Within a few minutes of the tunnel in the wall being opened, the cannon had done its work. The tower began to totter and fall. With every shot its main supports were cut away. At point-blank range, the whirling chain sliced, pulped, and pounded into the wooden structure. The Turks, called up to withdraw the tower to a place of safety, were shot down by musketeers on the walls. The Janissaries in the top storey of the tower began to desert, leaping to the ground as the whole vast erection sagged and buckled. Finally, with a thunderous crash – spilling men, arms, ammunition, pitchers of water, and incendiary grenades, it collapsed, taking dozens of its crew down in its ruins. The defenders set up a cheer. The cannon was run back inside the fortress. Immediately the Maltese working party set about restoring the wall.

While this action was taking place opposite Birgu, Mustapha had attacked Senglea again. He had great hopes for 'an infernal machine' with which he intended to make a breach in the bastion of St Michael.

This machine had been invented by one of his engineers. It was shaped like a long barrel, encircled and bound with iron hoops, and filled with gunpowder, iron chains, nails, and all sorts of grape-shot. A slow match was fastened to this machine, which passed through the whole of it. . . .

Under cover of a violent frontal assault, a gang of Turks managed to drag it up the battered walls and let it fall into the middle of the Knights and soldiers who were grouped on the far side. Then, on a prearranged signal, they all with-drew, and waited for the explosion. They massed on the far side of the ditch, ready to attack the moment that the machine had blown a breach in the wall.

There now occurred one of those incidents from which derives the phrase 'Hoist with his own petard'. The fusing on the Turkish bomb was too slow, and the Knights and soldiers among whom it had fallen at once started to roll it back up the ramp. With its slow-match spluttering and flaring, the long-barrel-shaped object was hoisted back to the top of the wall. A moment later, and it was hurled down into the ditch. It bounced, rolled, bounced again – and then went off. It exploded right in the face of the Turks who were waiting for the assault. The vast weight of gunpowder, let alone the shrapnel with which it had been filled, wrought havoc in the Turkish ranks. Without waiting for an order, driven by a swift impulse to make use of the occasion, the defenders streamed down the slope of their ruined wall and fell upon the enemy. The Turkish troops broke and ran.

The day which had begun so badly for the defenders ended in something like a victory. The giant tower, whose remains littered the ground outside the bastion of Castile, was set on fire. The failure of this engine-of-war, as well as of Mustapha's 'infernal machine' had caused great despondency among the Moslem troops. Their officers were reporting to Mustapha that, as day succeeded day, it was becoming ever more difficult to induce them to attack. Sickness was steadily increasing. Apart from dysentery and fever, there was every chance of plague breaking out in the island. Under the harsh sun, with a daily heat between eighty and ninety, hundreds of bodies lay stinking and putrefying from Corradino to Kalkara Creek.

Even ammunition and provisions were beginning to run short. Ships sent south to Tripoli were slow in returning, or failed to return altogether. Unknown to Mustapha, Christian galleys and corsairs out of Sicily had been sailing south of Malta and intercepting his supply line. Here, as in so much else, it was a failure on the part of the Turkish fleet and its admiral which crippled the prosecution of the siege.

It was now the third week of August and Malta was still uncaptured. Within a few weeks it would be necessary for Mustapha and Piali to think about weather conditions in the Mediterranean. They were nearly a thousand miles by sea from Constantinople. With the autumn the Sirocco might be expected to blow, and this southerly wind was likely to disrupt their communications with Africa even further. If Malta did not fall before mid September, the army would either have to withdraw, or winter in the island. Mustapha, seeing it was possible that he would not take Birgu and Senglea within the next three weeks, was in favour of spending the winter in Malta. However difficult his own supply problem, he knew that the stores and provisions in the two beleaguered garrisons could not hold out indefinitely. Provided that no relief force reached them, they would be almost certain to fall into his hands before the spring.

It was Admiral Piali who again blocked his project. The fleet and its safety, he maintained, were more important than anything else. He had no intention of hazarding his ships throughout a winter in Malta. Marsamuscetto might have been suitable as a summer anchorage but it would not do for the Sultan's ships throughout the winter months. Besides, there were no facilities for repair or maintenance. At the first hint of winter, he and his fleet would leave. If Mustapha Pasha decided to quarter his army in Malta, that was his own affair and responsibility.

The animosity which had long smouldered between the two commanders now burst into flame. Only Dragut, while he was alive, had been able by virtue of his great reputation to heal the breach between the army's Commander-in-Chief and the Admiral. The division of the command, which had been Sultan Soleyman's own design, now revealed its inherent weakness.

But if the Turkish commanders and their troops were disheartened, it seemed to the two garrisons 'as if the world was coming to an end'. The conditions of their ramparts and fortifications were like those of St Elmo in its last hours. Bodies lay unburied in the streets, there being no time between the successive attacks to spare a single man for burial duties. Women and children lay dead beside Knight, soldier, and sailor. There were not enough men to spare to look after the wounded in the Hospital. The Maltese women now proved themselves a mainstay of the defence. They not only took over the duties of nurses to the sick and cooks to the garrison, but they also carried ammunition, and worked at repairing the fortifications. When the Turkish attacks came, they manned the walls with the soldiers. Hard centuries of life in an infertile island, perpetually threatened with the raids of Barbary corsairs, had produced a staunch and enduring race.

One hundred and fifty miles to the north, in Messina, the preparations for the relief were gathering momentum. Determined at long last not to be put to shame by the indomitable heroism of Malta, Don Garcia de Toledo was making every effort to comply with his last promise to La Valette. 'Before the end of August I will sail with some two dozen galleys and as near 14,000 men as possible, and come to the island's relief.'

Every day Knights of the Order were arriving from their estates in northern Europe. The party which had supported a non-intervention policy towards Malta had long since been discredited. It was clear, from every report reaching Messina, that La Valette – whatever the precedent of his illustrious predecessor Villiers de l'Isle Adam – had no intention of treating with the Turk. Even those who had little use for the Order, men who perhaps disliked it for its disdainful manner, and for the rigidly aristocratic selection of its members, were compelled to an unwilling admiration.

It was just over three months since the élite of the Turkish army and the whole of the Sultan's fleet had sailed against the island. Less than 9,000 men, commanded by as many hundred Knights of St John, had held out through the whole long summer.

The heroic defence had aroused the admiration of all Europe. Even that great Protestant Queen, Elizabeth I of England, whose country was only represented by Sir Oliver Starkey and those two gentlemen adventurers 'Mr John Evan Smith and Mr Edward Stanley', was moved by this siege. It recalled the great days of medieval chivalry. Queen Elizabeth was too astute a ruler not to be aware of what might happen if the island were conquered. '. . . If the Turks,' she wrote, 'should prevail against the Isle of Malta, it is uncertain what further peril might follow to the rest of Christendom.'

Chapter 26

No withdrawal

A Grand Council meeting was held on 23 August. One and all, the Knights Grand Cross, proposed to La Valette that the time had come to abandon Birgu. 'Birgu,' they said, 'is mined on all sides. Its defences are ruined. The enemy is master of the landward ditch. The breach caused by the great mine is irreparable.' The Turkish sappers had not remained content with their one success. As one of the Knights pointed out: 'The whole ground near the ruined walls is so honey-combed with the enemy's mines, and our counter-mines, that one seems to be treading on the crust of a volcano.'

'Abandon Birgu!' They urged. 'St Angelo is the strongest of all the defences. There we can hold out. We will be able to do so better in the fort, than spread out as we are along the perimeter of this place.'

There was not a single dissentient voice to this plan to withdraw within St Angelo – except the Grand Master's. Having heard the opinions of all his senior Knights, La Valette rose to his feet.

'I respect your advice, my brethren – but I shall not take it. And these are my reasons. If we abandon Birgu we lose Senglea, for the garrison there cannot hold out on its own. The fortress of St Angelo is too small to hold all the population as well as ourselves and our men. And I have no intention of abandoning the loyal Maltese, their wives, and their children, to the enemy. St Angelo's water supply, even supposing that we can get all the people within its walls, will not be adequate. With the Turks masters of Senglea, and occupying the ruins of Birgu, it will only be a matter of time before even

the strong walls of St Angelo will fall before their concentrated
fire. At the moment, they are forced to divert their energies
and fire-power. Such will not be the case if we and all our
men are locked within St Angelo. No, my brothers, this and
this only is the place where we must stand and fight. Here
we must all perish together, or finally, with the help of God,
succeed in driving off our enemy.'

The Grand Crosses accepted his decision. But to make
quite certain that there could never be any question of retreat
to St Angelo, La Valette now burnt his boats. He summoned
nearly all the garrison from St Angelo, leaving behind only a
limited number to man the guns, and brought them into
Birgu. He now gave orders for the drawbridge, which
communicated between St Angelo and Birgu, to be blown
up. St Angelo was now on its own, and so was Birgu. The
Grand Master's action impressed the defenders more than
any words could ever have done. 'The moment that it became
known, every man realized that he must stand and die in the
post which he now held.'

The wisdom of La Valette's action cannot be questioned.
Had he followed the advice of his Council and retreated to
St Angelo, it could only have been a matter of a week or so
before the island would have fallen. With Mount Sciberras
and St Elmo in their hands, with Senglea and Birgu also
occupied, the entire weight of the Turkish fire would have
been directed at the one fort. Nothing could have withstood
it. Piali's fleet would have been able to bombard from the sea,
while the garrison was completely engaged on the landward
side. The Grand Master's view, that only by keeping
Mustapha's army and gunners divided between the two
positions could Malta be held, was as correct in theory as it
proved in fact. Defence in depth was something that was
little understood in the military theory of that time. La
Valette's genius in the hard trade of war is proved by his
ability to make a correct assessment and act upon it without
hesitation.

On 20 August, only three days before this all-important
Council meeting, a mass attack led by the Turkish Commander-in-Chief had failed dismally before the ruined

walls of St Michael's. Eight thousand troops, all protected
by a new type of light morion to shield their heads and
shoulders against the defenders' wildfire and incendiaries,
had come in to the assault. At the head of the advancing
Janissaries had been a famous old soldier, the Sanjak
Cheder, who had sworn either to take St Michael's or die in
the attempt. Carrying his own personal standard, Cheder
was followed by a bodyguard who had dedicated themselves
to conquer or die at the side of their master. Recognized by
the brilliance of his clothes, his jewelled turban, his enamelled
and gem-set scimitar, the Sanjak became an immediate
target for the Christian musketeers. The Chevalier Pessoa,
one of La Valette's pages, is credited with having killed this
old veteran. A violent struggle took place round the Sanjak's
body. It was during this fight that the Spanish captain Juan
de la Cerda wiped out for ever the stain of cowardice which
had rested upon him since his first report on the state of St
Elmo. Leading a furious counter-attack against the Sanjak's
Janissaries, La Cerda was cut down and his body buried
beneath a wave of enemy. '. . . He had boldly sought his
death in many different engagements, and at last died
bravely in the breach on this memorable day.'

It was on the 20th that the Turks had also brought up another siege engine against the breached bastion of Castile.
Manned by Janissary snipers, the base of the tower had been
reinforced with earth and stonework so that La Valette's
previous ruse with the cannon could not be effective. Soon
after daybreak, the snipers on this tower began to pick off
everyone on the other side of the ruined walls. Within a few
hours the situation was becoming desperate for the defenders.
La Valette realized that if the tower were to remain there,
keeping the garrison pinned down unable to move, a further
frontal assault on Castile would almost certainly succeed.

As before, he ordered the Maltese workmen to open a way
through the wall at the base, at a point where they could not
be seen by the Janissary snipers. Then, at a given moment, he
sent a raiding party into this tunnel. The moment that the
last stone blocks fell away, two Knights – Knight Commander
Claramont of the Langue of Aragon, and a Castilian,

Guevarez de Pereira – led out their men. They made straight for the tower. Never expecting that the defenders would venture outside the walls – and prepared for cannon shot only – the Turks were taken completely by surprise. Clara- mont and Pereira, at the head of their soldiers, clambered up the tower, the stone base giving them easy access to the lower reaches. Within a few minutes they had swept up the laddered floors and killed the Janissaries.

The siege engine, which had seemed as if it might prove the death of Birgu, was now made to serve another purpose. A picked troop of gunners with two cannon were established in it, protected by a band of Knights and men-at-arms. The Turkish tower was now turned into a subsidiary bastion of Castile, and the new vantage point gave them increased fire power against enemy attacks. That a small handful of men should have been able to capture and hold the tower is significant of the declining morale of the Turkish troops. They were still in their thousands, while the defenders were in their hundreds, and nearly all of them wounded or exhausted. Yet it was the invincible morale of the Christians, animated by the superb example of the Grand Master, which gave them their superiority.

On that same day, 20 August, a spy in the Turkish army had shot into Birgu an arrow bearing one word 'Thursday'. La Valette had at once told the defenders that so long as a man could stand he must be at his post. When the attack had come on Thursday the 23rd, 'Even the seriously wounded from the infirmary dragged themselves to the walls.' There were no more reserves to call upon.

At the Grand Council meeting that night, 23 August, when the proposal to evacuate Birgu was made, La Valette, by his obstinate insistence that there could be no retreat, only confirmed the policy which he had adopted from the very beginning of the siege. His inflexible resolve and his burning belief in the righteousness of his cause, proved the moral backbone which saved Malta. When it was suggested that, before the bridge between St Angelo and Birgu was blown up, the relics and archives of the order should at least be taken for safety to the fortress, he indignantly refused. He knew that, if the Maltese and the soldiers saw that sacred relic of the Order – the hand of John the Baptist in its jewelled reliquary – being removed from the Conventual church, they would give themselves up for lost. As for the archives of their proud Order – if Malta fell to the Turks, what need would there be for archives? The Hand, the archives, the silver processional cross – all these would stay in their accustomed place to the end. And so would the defenders.

Chapter 27

Dissensions in Sicily

Mustapha Pasha now received alarming news. A large store-ship, which had been daily expected from North Africa, had been lost. It had set off from Djerba and, on passage across the 180 miles strait to Malta, had been attacked and captured by a Sicilian galley. The chief of Mustapha's commissariat told him that there was only enough flour left for a further twenty-five days. This meant that, even if the fleet and army were to withdraw at once, they would be on short rations before they reached Constantinople. In Malta itself there was no wheat or corn. The harvest, green though much of it was, had been brought in before the Turks reached the island, and nearly all the livestock had been taken to Mdina and Birgu the moment that the enemy fleet had been sighted. Mustapha and Piali at once arranged for further ships to be sent to Africa to collect supplies.

Worse than the food situation was the fact that gunpowder was running short. Despite the vast quantities of ammunition which had been transported to Malta, the Turks were now for the first time forced to husband their fire. The powder-mills and arsenals of Constantinople had provided more than enough for a siege that was expected to take only a few weeks. It was the third month, and still the island was uncaptured. Mustapha's expenditure of powder and shot had been no less prodigal than his expenditure of men. Yet neither he nor Piali dared consider depleting the ammunition supplies of the fleet, in case they were forced to fight a naval action off Malta.

Another inevitable outcome of so long a siege was that many of the guns were becoming unserviceable. The defenders observed with a quickening of hope that every day the

Turkish fire was slightly weaker. They noted how, after sunset, gangs of slaves were beginning to withdraw these guns
from the batteries that hemmed in the two peninsulas. This
action, as Balbi commented, the Turks performed in silence,
'something quite different from the shouts and cheering with
which they had first dragged them into position'.

The Sultan Soleyman was not a man to suffer failure easily.
His subordinates, aware of the ruthlessness with which he
was capable of treating even members of his own family,
feared him even more than the enemy.

Mustapha chafed not a little under the long-protracted resistance of the besieged. He looked with apprehension to the consequences of a failure in an expedition for which preparations had
been made on so magnificent a scale by his master, and with so
confident hopes of success.

He decided that, whatever happened, he would not fail to
employ every stratagem and device against the enemy to the
very end.

The Turkish sappers were forced to redouble their efforts.
Night and day they mined beneath the crumbling walls and
the breached ruins of Castile. The defenders countermined.
Maltese miners and stonemasons, tunnelling back towards
the enemy, listening in the hot darkness of the sandstone for
the tap-tapping of the Turkish working parties. As August
drew to a close, hardly a day passed without a mine or a
countermine going up with a thunderous roar. Sometimes
both besiegers and besieged were buried in the same smoking
ruin. Sometimes the miners from Birgu broke through into
the enemy galleries and, before either side could withdraw
to fire their charges, Christian and Moslem came to grips with
pick, shovel, and dagger.

Mustapha, who was still considering wintering in the
island, decided to make an attack on Mdina. If he was to
quarter his troops in Malta it would be essential for him to
hold the old capital. If he could only capture it quickly, he
would be able to use its guns, powder, and shot, against the
Knights in their strongholds. If the worst came to the worst,
and he was compelled to withdraw from Malta, it would still

be to his credit if he had stormed and captured the island's capital.

Mdina, known also as Città Notabile, had been Malta's capital since Roman times. Although the Order of St John had established themselves in Birgu, Mdina was still the only town of any size in the island. Yet, despite the fact that the Knights had improved them during the past thirty-five years, its walls were not particularly strong. If Mustapha had besieged Mdina in the beginning as he had intended, there is little doubt that he would have been successful. But to attempt it after three months' bloody fighting around Grand Harbour, and to withdraw a portion of his troops from Birgu and Senglea, was a grave error. The disheartened Moslem troops saw the action as no more than a last attempt to produce some prize for the Sultan.

It was the Arabs, during their two-hundred-year occupation of Malta, who had built most of Mdina's defences and dug the ditch which protected the city on its southern side. It was only from here that the Turks could make their attempt, for on all other quarters the walls fell steeply away down precipitous slopes. Don Mesquita, Governor of Mdina, quickly learned of Mustapha's intentions. The moment that a section of the army and a number of siege guns began to leave the main Turkish camp and take the hot dusty road to the north he made his preparations.

The Governor's garrison was very small. He had sent most of his best troops down to Birgu at the beginning of the siege. At the same time, the city was crowded with Maltese peasants and their families who had been sheltering there during the long storm of summer. Aware that Mustapha's decision to attack Mdina was a measure of his desperation, and aware also of the growing demoralization of the Turkish army, Mesquita decided that a bold appearance might be enough to discourage the invaders. Accordingly, he had many of the peasants, and even their women folk, dressed in soldiers' uniforms, and set them to patrol the ramparts in company with the real garrison troops. All his available cannon were also brought to the ready and taken round to the side from which the Turkish troops were certain to approach.

As the first of the invaders toiled up the long slopes towards the old city, they saw that their information was incorrect. This was no defenceless town with a weak garrison. The walls bristled with men and long before their first troops were within cannon-shot, the guns began to thunder – as if to show that the defenders had ample reserves of powder, and could afford to waste it. The Turks halted in consternation. The word went back 'It is another St Elmo! It is another impregnable position like those down by the water!'

The officers, who had had difficulty in urging the men to begin this new attack, were also uneasy. They reminded themselves that this was a garrison of fresh troops, not like those with whom they had been fighting for the past three months. Scouts were sent forward, some to investigate the approaches to the city, others to circumvent it and report on the state of the ramparts on the precipitous sides. One and all came back with the same story. Every section of the walls was heavily guarded.

Even on the northern walls, where in any case it would be impossible to attack, the ramparts were dense with soldiers. Such a prodigal display of manpower demoralized the Turks. Word was sent back to Mustapha that Mdina looked as strong and well-guarded as had Birgu in the first day of the siege.

The troops halted. Derisively the cannon thundered from the battlements and a few cannon balls trundled down the parched slopes towards the front ranks. A crackle of musket fire sounded from the men on the wall – ineffectual, yet depressingly suggestive of fresh and untired men whose morale was high and whose powder limitless. Mustapha listened to the reports of his officers and came to judge the strength of the city with his own eyes. Deceived by the Governor's stratagem, he saw an apparently fresh and formidable garrison. He called off the attack. There was nothing left for him now but to renew his assault on the two disintegrating bastions of the Knights and hope that, somehow or other, they would fall to him before Piali insisted on withdrawing his fleet.

The daily slackening of the Turkish fire, and the news that part of the army had been withdrawn to besiege Mdina had raised the defenders' spirits at a moment when all had been resigned to death. Now, there was even talk among Knights and soldiers alike of the possibility of defeating the Turks by themselves. Alone and unaided, it seemed that they might beat off the invaders – and what achievement could be more glorious? If they could drive off the Turk without ever a relief from that sluggard, or coward, Don Garcia, they could say to all of Europe 'Alone we did it!' The further news that all of the army was now back in line against them did not serve to quench their new confidence. The very fact that Mustapha had given up the idea of attacking Mdina seemed a further confirmation of his growing weakness. If he did not dare attempt Mdina, weakest of all the island's fortification, what hope had he against Birgu and Senglea which, desperate though their situation was, had already held out for over two months?

In Mdina itself, Don Mesquita the Portuguese Governor could afford to congratulate himself. He had no more than a handful of trained soldiers within the city, very little powder and even less shot for his old cannons. Mustapha's withdrawal seemed a miracle, and a thanksgiving service was at once held in the old cathedral. Here, where every year on 4 November a Mass was said for the repose of the soul of Count Roger the Norman (who had delivered Malta from the Arabs nearly five centuries before), they now commemorated another victory over the infidel. Built supposedly on the site of the house where Publius 'the chief man of the island' had given shelter to the shipwrecked St Paul, the cathedral was the heart of the Island's Faith. It must have seemed to many of the worshippers that the Turkish withdrawal from their walls had proved yet again that the Apostle still watched over them. It seemed an omen that not only the city, but the whole island, would be delivered from the Moslem.

During the latter part of August, the Grand Master had been unable to communicate with the Governor in Messina. He had no knowledge, therefore, that the long delayed relief force was on the point of sailing. Cut off from the outside world in his crumbling, fire-scorched peninsula, La Valette had resigned himself to expecting no help from Don Garcia, or from the other members of the Order in Europe. Had he but known, it was these late arrivals who had finally managed to activate the sluggish Governor, and to shame his advisers into taking some immediate action. Over two hundred Knights, Commanders, and Grand Crosses of the Order now waited in Messina with their troops. Anxious to be with their brethren in the fight against the infidel, scornful of the Governor's long delay, they made the small court in Messina only too anxious to be rid of them. Don Garcia daily felt the sting of their disapproval. When he protested to one of the Knights, Louis de Lastic, Grand Prior of Auvergne at not receiving from him – as was his due – the courtesy title of 'Excellency', the Grand Prior replied: 'Sire, provided that we arrive in Malta in time to save the Religion I will give you what titles you please – "Excellency", "Your Highness", or even if you wish, "Your Majesty".'

On 22 August, when the defenders of Birgu and Senglea were at their last gasp (the day before the Grand Crosses had suggested to La Valette that they should retreat to St Angelo) Don Garcia had held a review of the relief force. Eight thousand men were drawn up on the slopes above the harbour of Syracuse. Near the theatre where Aeschylus had once watched his plays performed, in front of the great land-locked harbour where, 1,900 years before, the Athenian fleet had met disaster, the troops destined for another siege were mustered under the 'lion-sun' of summer Sicily. Borne on the south wind they could hear the distant mumble of the guns, seventy miles to the south of them.

The relief force was composed of professional soldiers and adventurers from all over Europe. The Spanish contingent formed the major part but there were many Italians, Germans, French, and other European nations among the contingent. The Marshal of the Force was an Italian, Ascanio de la Corna, Vincenti Vitelli commanded a force of adventurers from Italy and other nations, and a Spaniard, Alvarez de Sandé, was in charge of the Regiment of Naples, which was composed of Spanish garrison troops. The Viceroy himself was in overall command.

The Great Siege

Don Garcia de Toledo was still not happy about the situation. As he had explained to the Grand Prior of Auvergne (when he had excused himself for his delay in sending help to Malta) it was not enough just to attempt a relief. It was all-important that it be successful. Eight thousand troops were little enough against the vast army that Mustapha Pasha had transported from Constantinople. The Viceroy did not quite realize how great a toll sickness, as well as the defenders of Malta, had taken of the Sultan's 40,000.

While the relief force waited in Syracuse for the transports to assemble, the siege of the island went on relentlessly. Mustapha and Piali, determined to crush the resistance before autumn, continued to pound the bastions of Castile and St Michael's. Already, though, there was less weight in their attacks, and even the Janissary charges had lost their fire. The long resistance of the garrisons, coupled with their losses and with shortages of food and water, had taken the heart out of the attack. Day by day, desperate though their position still was, the defenders felt new hope stir in their hearts.

Every day of the siege, the Grand Master went to the Conventual Church of St Lawrence to pray. On each occasion when there was anything approaching a victory, or a deliverance from some imminent danger, he saw that thanksgiving services were held. In his religious duties, as much as in his duties as a soldier, La Valette was meticulous. How many times had he not said 'No man can end his life more gloriously than in defence of the Faith'? Old, exhausted by three months of continuous strain and responsibility, not forgetting active fighting, La Valette in these last days of August seemed to shine among his men like a flame. His white beard powdered with sandstone dust, his once bright armour dulled and dented, he never left his headquarters in the central square of Birgu – unless it was to go to the defence of the ramparts.

Sixty-five miles west of Malta, the small barren islet of Linosa juts out of the Mediterranea Sea. It was here that, several weeks before, La Valette had sent a boat with information for the Viceroy of Sicily. Linosa, the nearest island to Malta between Sicily and North Africa, had been previously arranged as a rendezvous, or communications base, should it be impossible for boats to get through directly between Malta and Sicily.

On 25 August, unknown to La Valette, Don Garcia weighed anchor and sailed for Linosa. A final muster of his troops showed close on 10,000 men. They were embarked in twenty-eight ships and galleys. The relief force, so it seemed, would soon reach the island.

Chapter 28

The Relief

For a week there was an uneasy lull in the fighting. The bombardment of Birgu and Senglea never ceased, but the Turkish forces made no more attacks on the tottering bastions of Castile and St Michael. Then, on 1 September, Mustapha and Piali launched another mass offensive.

Rendered desperate by the lateness of the year and by their lack of stores and ammunition, it was as if they were determined, with this last throw, to make good all their losses. But the troops who now surged forward across the shell-torn waste land beyond the walls were not the same as those who had first come to Malta 'to save their souls'. It was not only the prolonged resistance of the garrisons and their bloody losses which had sapped their morale. Disease had enfeebled them and had reduced their numbers far more than had the cannon, the muskets, and the swords of the Knights.

In that hot summer the whole island around Grand Harbour stank like a charnel house. The Turks with their ignorance of the elementary principles of sanitation contrived their own ruin. Dysentery, enteric, and fever, had been active in their ranks since June and had increased throughout the following weeks. The reason why the defenders in their shattered garrisons did not suffer so much as the enemy can probably be traced to the Knights' principal avocation, that of Hospitallers. Simple though their surgery was, and ignorant though they were in many ways, they did at least understand the rudiments of hygiene. In the Hospital, where under normal conditions both rich and poor, Knight and commoner, were served their food off silver plate – to increase 'the decorum of the Hospital and the cleanliness of the sick'

– even during the siege, some attempt was made to look after the patients properly. It was no doubt for this reason that the garrisons owed their relative freedom from the diseases which decimated the enemy.

The day-long attacks of 1 September failed as had all the others. The fire had gone out of the attackers and, proportionately, the morale of the defenders had increased every day since Mustapha's failure against Mdina. Turks, Janissaries, Iayalars, Algerians, Dragut's corsairs, all were now despondent. 'It is not the will of Allah', they said, 'that we shall become masters of Malta.' Had they known what had happened to the relief force destined for the island, it is possible they would have plucked up courage and taken the initiative again.

Don Garcia's fleet, sailing westerly for its rendezvous off Linosa, had run straight into a heavy gale. The channel and the narrow seas between Malta and Sicily are notoriously treacherous. When a strong north-westerly, with all the fetch of the Mediterranean behind it, blows over these shallows a dangerous breaking surf builds up in a few hours. At the turn of the year, just as the summer was giving way to autumn, Don Garcia's fleet was unlucky enough to run into just such a typical Malta channel gale. Dispersed over the sea between Terrible Bank, Linosa, and the Aegadean Islands off the west coast of Sicily, the ships were forced to run for safety. The galleys plunged and stooped as they strained to get back under the lee of the land. Oars were shattered, sails and rigging torn away, and equipment lost.

When the bulk of the fleet reassembled off the island of Favignana, opposite to Marsala on the west coast of Sicily, the condition of the ships was such that there could be no question of an immediate return to Linosa. Not only had many of them suffered extensive damage, but their sea-sick troops were in no state to land and fight the enemy on Malta. It was not until 4 September, that the fleet was ready to sail again. This time it reached Linosa in safety, and Don Garcia de Toledo found La Valette's last message waiting for him. In it, the Grand Master explained how the whole south of the island was in the hands of the Turks and that the two ports of

Marsasirocco and Marsamuscetto were occupied by their
fleet. He suggested to the Viceroy that the two best places for
him to land were the bays of Mgarr and Mellieha in the north
of the island. Both had sandy beaches where his troops could
go ashore, and both anchorages were relatively sheltered.

The fleet left Linosa for Malta in two divisions, the advance
guard being under the command of the Spaniard Don
Cardona, with the Viceroy in charge of the main body. Bad
weather set in yet again as they neared Malta. The bulk of
the fleet, losing sight of Don Cardona over night, stood to the
north and came to anchor off the fishing village of Pozzalo at
the southern tip of Sicily. The advance guard meanwhile had
pressed on through the thickening weather and was in sight
of the island of Gozo. Now was the time when Piali's ships by
all the rules of war should have fallen upon them and destroyed them. Yet it is one of the mysteries of the siege that no
attempt seems to have been made to attack this spearhead of
Christian ships. One can only assume that Piali's captains,
not liking the look of the weather, had all retired from their
Gozo patrol and had made themselves snug in Marsamuscetto.

Don Garcia's return to Sicily, and his seeming reluctance
to proceed to Malta until he had news of the other ships,
again raised doubts among the Knights as to his intentions.
It was only when their demands for action became increasingly vituperative that he gave orders for the fleet to weigh
and stand south for Malta. Even at this last moment his
natural hesitancy seems to have come to the fore. The Abbé
Vertot in his history of the Order repeats the accusations
against Don Garcia which were current at the time of the
siege:

But the Viceroy's action again made people doubt whether he
intended to profit by his advice (La Valette's information that
Mgarr and Mellieha would be good places to land); instead of
entering by the channel between Gozo and Malta he coasted down
Malta on the western side, and let himself be seen by the Turkish
frigates which came out of Marsasirocco. It seemed that he sought
less to make a landing, than to find some fresh obstacle which would
oblige him to depart and return yet again to the ports of Sicily.

It was not until the evening of 6 September that Don Garcia's reunited fleet slipped through the Gozo channel and came round to Mellieha Bay on the north east of the island. On the morning of the 7th the long-expected, long-delayed, relief force began to stream ashore. They plunged through the shallows, with their weapons and ammunition above their heads, while boatloads of Spanish soldiers ran up on the beach at the end of the bay.

The news reached Mustapha Pasha and La Valette at almost the same moment. To the one it brought dismay, to the other the knowledge that his long ordeal was nearing its end. Yet, after so long a time of waiting, La Valette had undoubtedly expected that the relief force would be a great deal larger than it was. Accounts vary as to the exact numbers of the troops, ranging from 8,000 (the lowest estimate) to 12,000. In any event, the relief force was hardly large enough to accomplish its task if the morale of the Turks had been high. As soon as he knew the numbers of the troops, La Valette devised a cunning piece of deception. He gave orders for one of the Moslem galley slaves, who were kept in the tunnels below Fort St Angelo, to be granted his freedom. It was, the man was told, an act of clemency on the Grand Master's part. The slave was also told that 16,000 Christian troops under the Viceroy of Sicily were coming ashore in the north of the island, and that it was no use the Turkish Commander-in-Chief thinking he could prosecute the siege any longer. Whether he believed the story (or whether he was, in fact, given the illusion that he was making his escape without the garrison's knowledge) the fact remains that this slave reached the Turkish camp safely. He was interrogated by some officers, and then brought before Mustapha, to whom he repeated his information – that the Knights were jubilant, that they counted the siege as good as at an end, and that 16,000 men were landing in Mellieha Bay. Dismayed at the news, disheartened by the whole conduct of the siege, and aware that his troops were on the verge of mutiny, Mustapha ordered the immediate evacuation of the island.

The inefficiency of the Turkish high command, and particularly of the fleet, during the campaign is difficult to understand. Piali had by far the most powerful fleet in the Mediterranean, while twenty-eight galleys were all that the Viceroy had managed to raise for his invasion force. (Don Garcia had, in fact, every good reason to fear that he might lose not only his ships but also all his men.) Yet the Turkish admiral, with three times as many warships at his disposal, had never attempted to contest the landing. By all the rules, Piali should have attacked the relief force at sea and sent the Christians to the bottom – more especially when one bears in mind how irresolute had been their approach to the island. But Piali and his fellow naval commanders had assumed that the Christian fleet would try and enter either Marsasirocco, or Marsamuscetto. Accordingly, they had secured their ships in these two harbours and had barred the entrances with chains and stakes. It seems to have escaped their notice that Mgarr or Mellieha bays were perfectly adequate for landing troops – provided only that the invasion fleet did not loiter too long in these somewhat exposed anchorages. It was Piali's timidity, coupled with his evident ignorance of the geography and weather conditions of Malta, which had from the very beginning bedevilled the Turkish campaign. Don Garcia had no intention of waiting in Mellieha. The minute that his troops were ashore he intended to return to Messina, where a further reinforcement of 4,000 men was waiting.

Chapter 29

The last engagement

As Don Garcia's galleys left for Sicily, they made a short detour to the south and passed close off the mouth of Grand Harbour. They saw the Turkish flag flying over ruined Fort St Elmo and heard the thunder of the guns still bombarding from the heights of Corradino and the slopes behind Birgu. As a gesture to the Turks, and as a sign to the defenders that relief was at hand, Don Garcia ordered the ships to salute St Angelo and the flag of the Order. 'And when our armada was in a place where we could see them clearly, then each galley fired three times. . . .'

The joy of the garrison knew no bounds. These were the first Christian ships they had seen since the siege started. Their presence off Grand Harbour told its own tale. Even those who had been sceptical about the news of a relief force, now took heart. The very fact that these galleys could be at sea just off the harbour mouth proved that the Turkish fleet had lost all fighting spirit.

La Valette, eager to take the offensive as soon as possible, waited impatiently, in the hope that part at least of the relief force would try and make contact with Birgu during the night. Nothing happened. He heard the creak of wheels and groan of tackle which told him that the Turks were successfully removing their guns from the batteries behind Birgu. The Grand Master had hoped to capture them and make good some of his own losses during the siege.

Mustapha's army was now on the point of embarking. The camp on the Marsa was struck. The ships which had been lying in Marsasirocco began to make their way to the north, ready to join the bulk of Piali's fleet as it left Marsamuscetto.

Cannon that had been mounted on St Elmo and the heights of Sciberras were dismantled and taken down to the ships. The troops started to withdraw from Corradino, and from their lines behind the two peninsulas. The long entrenchments were deserted. Only the assault towers and a few cannon too heavy to remove quickly were left behind. The torn, star-shaped walls of St Elmo, whose capture had been the only Turkish triumph of the campaign, were left to silence and memory. All night long, the lights and the flares along the Marsa, and over the narrow neck of land between there and Marsamuscetto, showed where the army of the Sultan was withdrawing.

The relief force, meanwhile, had marched straight inland from Mellieha Bay and had established contact with the garrison in Mdina. Under the command of Ascanio de la Corna, the troops had taken up their station on the high ground that lies on the east side of the island, a steep ridge surmounted by the village of Naxxar. Unaware that the enemy was already in retreat, de la Corna had decided to hold this high point rather than be brought to battle in the low land. As soon as day broke, he would be able to make out the enemy's intentions. Until then he wisely decided to hold his men in check. His second-in-command, Alvarez de Sandé, was more impetuous and pressed to lead his men at once in a night attack upon the Turks. De la Corna's discretion won the day, and the relief force waited to see what the dawn would bring.

As soon as the first light flooded the island, the defenders of Birgu and Senglea looked across the scorched and cratered slopes in front of them. They were empty of the enemy. No Crescent flag waved above the long lines of trenches and emplacements. No packed masses of Janissaries poised themselves on the hillocks, ready to hurl down upon them in a charge. La Valette ordered the gates to be opened.

For the first time in months, Knights and soldiers, men, women and children from the small townships, streamed out unmolested. Weakened by their wounds and privations, scorched by wildfire, and deafened by mine and cannon, they burst out into that arid no-man's-land as if released from a long winter into spring fields. They foraged among the deserted Turkish lines, picking up here an arquebus, there a morion, here a brigantine jacket, and there a dagger from Damascus. Among the ruined sites of the batteries they found several cannon. Among the unburied dead they found jewels and purses of money, richly-worked weapons and enamelled clasps and brooches.

A body of Knights and men-at-arms at once rode round the Marsa, and up the slopes of Mount Sciberras. From that parched hill, which had cost the lives of thousands, they looked down into the harbour of Marsamuscetto. The first Turkish ships were already under way, driving out under oar through the narrow mouth past the ruins of St Elmo. The Knights spurred down to the tip of the peninsula. They rode in through the breached walls where old de Guaras and the gallant Miranda had died so bravely. Above the battered walls where sun and sea-wind had long since cleansed the air of death, they hoisted the white cross of St John. It snapped in the breeze as the first Turkish ships began to clear the harbour. Messengers were sent back to Birgu to ask for light cannons to be brought as quickly as possible to St Elmo.

On this day, 8 September, nearly four months since the Turkish fleet had first been sighted off Malta, the great invasion force began to withdraw. The moment that the first guns started to open fire on them from Sciberras and the point of St Elmo, they redoubled their efforts to get under way. Their ships, foul with weed and underwater growth from the long hot summer, stained with sun and salt water, and loaded with wounded, were very different from those which had so proudly advanced across the Ionian Sea in the early days of May.

The eighth of September was not only the day on which the siege was raised, it was also the feast of the Nativity of the Virgin. La Valette was not slow to remind his followers and the inhabitants of the island that they owed their deliverance to God, and not to man. The bells of the Conventual church of St Lawrence rang out over the shattered houses of Birgu.

I do not believe that ever did music sound so sweet to human beings. It was three months since we had ever heard a bell which did not summon us to arms against the enemy. That morning, when they rang for mass, it was at the same hour that we had grown used to expect the call to arms. All the more solemnly then, did we give thanks to the Lord God, and to His Blessed Mother, for the favours that they had poured upon us.

Through the narrow streets, still blocked by the stone barricades that had been erected as a protection against the enemy gunfire, past the ruined houses and tottering walls of their homes, the Maltese and the Knights and their soldiers made their way to offer a 'Te Deum' to the God of Victories. The island still smoked and crackled from the fierce breath of war. Every now and then, a section of the breached wall would fall away with a great tearing sigh. The streets were littered with battered cannon balls, great pieces of metal, and vast lumps of marble that had been fired by the basilisks. In the cool darkness of the small Conventual Church they saw the gleam of the silver reliquary containing the hand of St John the Baptist. Even those Knights Grand Cross who at one moment had doubted the wisdom of La Valette's decision to remain in Birgu, now recognized how right the Grand Master had been. Every position had been held to the end. The dead of St Elmo, of Birgu, and Senglea, had not died in vain.

It was at this very moment, while the survivors of the siege were giving thanks for their victory, that Mustapha Pasha realized how he had been misled as to the numbers of the relief force. From Spahis who had been scouting the enemy positions, and from ships' captains who had seen the relief arrive, he learned that only twenty-eight ships had come to the island, and that the troops landed against him numbered 8,000, possibly less. Fearful of the Sultan's anger, indignant at the way in which he felt he had been let down by the fleet and its Admiral, he ordered an immediate halt to the evacuation.

Piali, ever eager to be under way with his precious fleet across the Ionian and the Aegean before the winter storms began, opposed him. The hostility between the commanders which had for a long time been unconcealed, once more burst into flame. Mustapha was quick to point out that the Sultan was no lover of failure. Throughout the siege the army had done everything in its power to ensure success, but could the same be said of the fleet? He demanded that the troops who had already been embarked should again be landed, while Piali took his fleet seven miles up the coast to St Paul's Bay. The Commander-in-Chief intended to give battle.

The guards whom La Valette had posted on Mount Sciberras and St Elmo hastily reported to the Grand Master that the Turkish Army was disembarking. The ships were all leaving the harbour and going northwards up the coast, but the troops were reforming on the shore. A messenger was at once sent to Ascanio de la Corna to tell him that Mustapha Pasha had clearly changed his mind and was going to fight. At the same time, other horsemen were dispatched to follow the Turkish fleet along the coast.

La Valette well knew that a defeat at this moment might still lose him the island. Mustapha's forces were larger than de la Corna's, and a Turkish victory might well restore their morale. If that happened, there always remained the possibility that Mustapha might decide to winter in the island, and reduce the forts by starvation. La Valette was also aware that if the relief ended in a disaster, there would be no question of any further aid from Sicily.

Ascanio de la Corna, immediately on receiving the Grand Master's warning, brought all his troops together on the high ground of Naxxar. From there he could see the Turkish army debouching from the head of Marsamuscetto and taking the road towards him. Mustapha had landed about 9,000 men. To seaward de la Corna saw the fleet making its way slowly up the coast. Messengers came back from the north of the island and reported that the first ships were beginning to drop anchor in St Paul's Bay. It seemed that Mustapha hoped to march north, obliterate the relief force and then, with this victory to his credit, rejoin Piali's fleet. De la Corna decided to wait on his vantage point. He did not want to be lured down to give battle in the plain. He had reckoned without the temper of the newly arrived Knights of St John and of his own troops.

The impetuous Chevaliers, who had been held back so long in Sicily, were in no mood to listen to words of caution. 'There is the enemy!' they cried. 'And there in the distance are the smoking ruins where our brethren died!'

Without waiting for an order, they began to spur down from the ridge. The troops, led by de Sandé, at once followed them. Seeing that it would be better to take advantage of the spirit of his men – and profit by their impetuosity – rather than attempt a recall, Ascanio de la Corna gave the order for a general charge. The garrison from Mdina and the Maltese militia, who had been watching and waiting on their ridge to the west, followed suit. While the main body of the relief force charged down to meet the enemy head on, the forces from Mdina swung across the plain to take them on their flank.

Mustapha Pasha's decision to land his troops after they had once been embarked was a blunder. Demoralized by unsuccessful months of fighting in the island, and by their heavy losses, they were in no mood to engage a fresh and vigorous relief force. Having once embarked, and having, as they thought, put the deadly soil of Malta behind them, they obeyed this new order with the greatest reluctance. At the sight of these fresh troops pouring down upon them from Naxxar ridge, many broke and ran. Others halted irresolutely. The Knights and their Spanish troops fell upon the disorganized vanguard.

Not all of Mustapha's men were lacking in spirit. One group, who had managed to capture a small tower crowning the highest point of the ridge, opened a heavy fire on the Christians. Round this tower the main battle now developed. The Turks were determined to hold it so as to allow their army to pass in safety, and the Christians were equally determined to capture it and turn the flank of the enemy. At last, a group of Spanish infantrymen managed to storm the hillock in the face of heavy fire and took the tower at a run. '. . . And on that day, no quarter was given, and well did they redden their swords with the blood of the enemy.'

Dislodged from the tower and unable to protect the flank of their army, the Turks were now in full retreat. They poured through the valley between the ridges of Mdina and Naxxar and fled towards the sea. The long fertile plain which runs north-easterly towards St Paul's Bay was a scene of confusion and panic. Dust clouds marked the passing of cavalry and mounted Spahis. The parched earth, untended and unwatered throughout the long hot summer, shook and trembled as thousands of men struggled and fought towards the safety of the sea.

Mustapha Pasha showed himself then, as he had done throughout the siege, a man of outstanding bravery. Whatever his faults as a commander, no one could ever question his courage. Throughout the day he was constantly in the heart of the fighting. In the early stages he had been always in the van of the army. But now that what had started out as an attack, had turned into retreat, he stationed himself in the rearguard. Twice his horse was shot from beneath him. On one occasion he was nearly lost. Only a well-directed charge by the Janissaries, faithful to the last, prevented their Commander-in-Chief from being captured or killed.

As the head of his army neared St Paul's Bay, Mustapha and the rearguard took up their station in the flat land to the south, near the small bay of Salina. Mustapha saw that the pursuit was becoming disorganized, the Maltese militia and the Spanish foot-soldiers having fallen a long way behind the mounted Knights. Quickly he formed up a party of Janissary arquebusiers. At a given signal, they faced about and opened fire on the ragged line that swept down upon them. For a moment the Christian attack faltered and broke. Alvarez de Sandé, who was leading the attack, was hurled to the ground as his horse was shot from under him. A number of other Knights were also unhorsed. Several of them were wounded. Four, according to Balbi, died from strokes 'due to the excessive hotness of their armour'. Mustapha's action had its desired effect. It checked the advance guard of the Knights just at the moment his own men were beginning to embark in the boats that were waiting for them along the foreshore of St Paul's Bay.

Hassem, the Viceroy of Algiers, who had been ordered to cover the last phases of the embarkation, stationed groups of arquebusiers along the small hillocks and ridges that commanded the bay. As the Knights and men-at-arms reformed and charged, they were met with a hail of fire. Again their advance faltered and the Turkish army was given a few more minutes' grace.

The bay, no more than a mile wide at its entrance, was an extraordinary sight. Dense with shipping, its shallow blue waters were criss-crossed with the wakes of rowing boats evacuating the defeated army. Out beyond the narrow sandstone isle of Selmunett – legendary scene of the shipwreck of St Paul – the war galleys cruised anxiously to and fro. They kept an eye to the north, in case a Christian fleet from Sicily should suddenly fall upon them. Other ships and cargo vessels thronged the bay of Mellieha a mile to the north. It still seemed incredible that so large a fleet and so vast an army should be in retreat. As always in an evacuation, the sailors blamed the soldiers, the soldiers the sailors.

The main body of the Christians had now caught up with Mustapha's rear guard. Hassem's musketeers could no longer stem the weight of their attack. Relentlessly they were driven down into the sea, as all the sandstone shelves and slopes around the bay became the scene of bloody hand-to-hand fighting. The pale blue sea, only a few feet deep in many places, was a scene of horrible confusion – overturned boats, bodies rolling in the water, and men slashing at one another with axe, sword, and scimitar. From the Christians on the shore, and from the musketeers in the boats, there resounded a steady rattle of fire. Hundreds of men were killed in this last action.

By the evening of 8 September, the siege was over. Leading out from Mellieha and St Paul's Bay, the fleet of Sultan Soleyman joined up with the last store ships and transports coming up from Marsasirocco. A gentle north-westerly was blowing, as the fleet, taking the swell upon its beam, set course for Greece, the Morea, the Aegean, and Constantinople. Behind them they left a devastated island, and the slopes behind Birgu and Senglea blackened with their dead. The scene of their last action, the small enclosed bay of St Paul, was foul with bodies. 'For two or three days afterwards the water of the *cala* was so thick with enemy dead – more than three thousand – that no man went near the place because of the stench.'

Embarking among the last of his men, still protected by the fire of Hassem's gallant arquebusiers, Mustapha Pasha looked back upon the island. He saw the bare ridge of Wardia behind St Paul's Bay, and in the distance the silvery gleam along the slopes of Naxxar, and Mdina on its unconquered heights . . . He could no longer see, hidden as they were behind the other hills and ridges, the grim bastions of Senglea and Birgu – nor even the shattered walls of Fort St Elmo.

At the beginning of his diary Balbi had written:

It has pleased God this year, 1565, under the good government of the brave and devout Grand Master Jean de la Valette, that the Order should be attacked in great force by Sultan Soleyman, who felt himself affronted by the great harm done to him on land and sea by the galleys of the Knights of this Order.

Now, four months later, the fleet and army of the hitherto almost invincible Sultan had been defeated. Malta, and the Order of St John of Jerusalem, had survived. The price of victory was a high one.

Chapter 30

'We shall never take you'

'Then they came over to Birgu as much to see the Grand Master in person – that man so famed and valiant – as to see the great ruin and destruction of our battlements.' Within his lifetime, La Valette became a legend. He was the living embodiment of the Knightly virtues.

The sight which met the eyes of the relief force when they entered Birgu was horrifying. The easy victors of the last action realized now at what a cost the island had been saved. Birgu and Senglea still smoked and disintegrated from their three months of siege. Not a single house was undamaged and, in places, the breaches in the wall were so great that it seemed incredible how the soldiers of the 'Grande Turke' had failed to penetrate and overwhelm the garrisons. Hardly a man, woman, or child, was unmarked by the terrible rigours of the siege. The maimed and wounded dragged themselves about their shattered fortresses like figures risen from the dead, as if to mock these healthy living soldiers who had come so late to their relief.

On every hand they were shown places where Turks had attacked, and where men known to them by name had died. 'And here Juan de la Cerda fell . . .' 'And there a band of Maltese swimmers sallied forth . . .' 'And here the nephew of the Grand Master was cut down in front of the great tower . . .' The ground in front of Birgu still quaked and chasms opened suddenly as the roofs of the old mine-tunnellings fell in. They saw the great crumbled breach where the bastion of Castile had gone up on that fateful morning and, as Vertot tells us, 'Their hearts were filled with unspeakable anguish.'

The small kingdom of the Knights of the Order of St John lay in ruins about them. Bitterly the Maltese might have repented of their willingness to lay down their lives for this alien order of Knightly Christendom! Bitterly, as the farmer contemplated his spoiled and barren fields, he might have thought that even the raids of corsairs like Dragut had never caused such havoc. Yet the knowledge that they had been engaged in a Holy War, and that they had helped to save Europe by their efforts, sustained them. While they buried their dead, they remembered that they who were left must still bear the ordinary guilts of life, while these had gone stainless into Paradise.

The relief force brought all the provisions that they could spare into the two crippled citadels. They brought ashore cloth and bandages for use in the Hospital. Their sailors trundled barrels of wine down to refresh the garrisons. Even at that moment, when Ascanio de la Corna's men could congratulate themselves on their success over Mustapha's forces, they could see that the victory had been almost won before their arrival. The vast masses of Turkish dead – now hastily buried in common graves – the ruined cannons, and the scattered remnants of the camp at the Marsa, told their own tale. It was no army on the point of victory which had fled from Malta. It was an army that had already been defeated.

It may be it was during these first days after the siege, that some soldier, sitting round the campfire at night, began to frame the words of a song which would later become famous in the Mediterranean:

Malta of gold, Malta of silver, Malta of precious metal,
We shall never take you!
No, not even if you were as soft as a gourd,
Not even if you were only protected by an onion skin!

And from her ramparts a voice replied:

I am she who has decimated the galleys of the Turk –
And all the warriors of Constantinople and Galata!'

All was now over. The flags fluttered over the unconquered peninsulas and over the ruins of St Elmo, the fort that had died to save them. Now was the time when the Grand Master and his secretary and Grand Council could take stock of what had befallen them. They gave thanks to God for victory, but they knew how bitter a price had been paid for it. Nearly 250 Knights of the Order had lost their lives, and of those who remained, almost all were badly wounded or crippled for life. Out of the Spanish and foreign soldiers and the Maltese inhabitants, 7,000 had died in the defence of the island. Out of a garrison force originally consisting of nearly 9,000, the Grand Master had only about 600 left, still capable of bearing arms. Mustapha had been correct when he had surmised that a few more weeks must inevitably deliver the island into his hands.

'The arms of Soleyman the First,' wrote W. H. Prescott, 'during his long and glorious reign, met with no reverse so humiliating as his failure in the siege of Malta. To say nothing of the cost of the maritime preparations, the waste of life was prodigious . . .' Balbi reckons that in the course of the siege the Turks lost 30,000 men. Vertot, who had access to all the records, agrees with this figure. Boisgelin is more conservative with 25,000. Von Hammer in his *History of the Ottoman Empire* calculates that the original Turkish force (excluding seamen, galley slaves, and supernumeraries) was 31,000 – out of which 10,000 at the most reached Constantinople again.

It has always to be borne in mind that these figures are all based on Turkish or Christian records, and that no data exist regarding the losses of the Algerians, the Egyptians, or Dragut's Barbary Corsairs. If one accepts the minimum figure of Turkish losses – 20,000 – it would still seem likely that the total losses of the expedition were about 30,000. This would not take into account the ships and men lost between the island and the North African coast due to the attacks of the Sicilian galleys.

This was the last great attempt of the Ottoman Empire to break into the western Mediterranean. During the centuries that followed, occasional efforts were made to penetrate beyond the defences of Malta, but only in the most faint-hearted manner. It was the defeat of their army, and the proven inadequacy of their fleet during this Great Siege, which first checked the westward expansion of Turkish power. Their maritime pride received a final, disastrous blow at the battle of Lepanto in 1571, when the navy of the Christian league, reinforced by galleys from Malta, destroyed the greater part of the Ottoman fleet.

The news that Malta had been relieved, and the Sultan defeated, was carried all over Europe by ships, horsemen, and signal fires. From Palermo, to Rome, Paris, and even London, the bells rang in the churches and the cathedrals. Although it was natural that the Pope, that protector of the Order, should command rejoicing and festivities in Rome, it is significant that the victory was not forgotten in Protestant England. Matthew Parker, Archbishop of Canterbury (no doubt after consultation with Queen Elizabeth) appointed a Form of Thanksgiving to be used thrice weekly for six weeks after the event. Malta 'that obscure island', Malta 'that rock of soft sandstone', became known as the 'Island of heroes' and the 'Bulwark of the Faith'.

Fertile and fruitful Rhodes to which Villiers de l'Isle Adam and even La Valette had dreamed of returning, was now eclipsed. There was no more discussion about moving the Order's base and headquarters to any other part of the Mediterranean. The Sultan's attack had been successful in an unlooked for way. It had proved quite clearly to all the European and Mediterranean powers how important was Malta's strategic position, astraddle the trade route of the inland sea. There would never be any further question of Malta being considered of little consequence by the rulers of Europe.

Don Garcia de Toledo, the Viceroy of Sicily, 'when he saw from the bastion of the castle of Syracuse the Turkish fleet passing to seaward, learned without the need for any couriers, the happy success of the relief force, and the raising of the siege.' A few days later, on 14 September, he sailed south again, bringing a further 4,000 men to protect the island in the unlikely event of the Turks returning. The Viceroy was met by the Grand Master, who, with his customary politeness, made no reference to the long delays under which the Order and the island had lost the greater part of their men. La Valette entertained him and his staff to dinner in the ruins of Birgu. He had little enough provisions and wine for his distinguished guests, so Don Garcia and the other captains of the fleet produced stores for the occasion, while 'the Governor of Gozo also sent many fresh food-stuffs.'

La Valette heard from the Viceroy how, on his way south to Malta, he had passed the tail-end of the Turkish fleet, all heading in the same direction – eastwards towards Constantinople. In view of the small size of his own force, he had desisted from attack. The Grand Master may have smiled ironically, but he made no comment. Later he took the Governor on a personal tour of the island and its defences. Together they inspected the Turkish entrenchments and walked over the battered southern seawall of Senglea. They rode round to the hot slopes of Sciberras and down to the lonely fort at its far end. The Viceroy learned at first hand from La Valette of how his son had died. It was no moment for the Grand Master to upbraid him, or take him to task for his dilatory conduct throughout the long summer.

A few days later Don Garcia returned to Sicily. La Valette, contemplating his ruined defences, his barren and burnt-out island, his decimated forces, and the tragic state of the islanders, could only think of the monumental task that lay ahead. While he gave thanks to God for the deliverance, he was already preparing for the future. He was dreaming of a series of fortifications that would be impregnable, and of a city that would last as long as time.

Chapter 31

The impregnable fortress

Death by the axe, sword, or bowstring were not uncommon punishments for those who failed the Sultan. Mustapha Pasha and Piali may well have trembled for their necks when they returned in defeat to Constantinople. They took the precaution of preparing the Sultan for the disastrous outcome of the expedition, by sending a fast galley ahead of them containing their dispatches. On first hearing the news Soleyman, whose temper had grown increasingly violent during his last years – possibly due to the acute gout from which he suffered – threw the dispatches on the floor, and stamped on them.

'There can only be one Emperor on earth, and one God in Heaven!' the vizier, Ibrahim, had remarked when urging Soleyman to the expedition against Malta. But now the Sultan had to acknowledge that the Order of St John, under its Grand Master, La Valette, had defied him and survived.

'There is not one of my officers whom I can trust!' he cried. 'Next year, I myself, the Sultan Soleyman, will lead an expedition against this accursed island. I will not spare one single inhabitant!'

While the fleet rounded Cape Matapan and toiled up the Aegean, the Sultan's fury had time to abate. His first rage over, he sent a message to Mustapha and Piali, telling them to bring the fleet into harbour after nightfall. He had no wish for his subjects to see the ruin that had been inflicted upon the army. He pardoned his two commanders for their failure.

'I see that it is only in my own hand, that my sword is invincible!'

The Great Siege

Despite his words, Sultan Soleyman was never destined to lead an expedition against the Island of the Knights. In the following year, having decided that the time was not ripe for a further attack on Malta, he turned his attention to the war in Hungary. On 5 September 1566, at the age of seventy-two, while conducting the siege of Szigetvár, Sultan Soleyman died. In the course of a long and brilliant reign, perhaps the most glorious period in the history of Islam, he had only met with two reverses worthy of the name. The one was his failure before the walls of Vienna in 1529, and the second – and by far the most damaging – was at Malta.

The only Moslem commander present at the Great Siege who later distinguished himself in battle was El Louck Aly, Governor of Alexandria, who was present at the battle of Lepanto in October 1571. When the Christians under Don John of Austria attacked the Turkish fleet, only El Louck Aly's squadron achieved any success. Completely out-manoeuvring Andrea Doria, El Louck Aly drove in the right wing of the Christians. When the Turkish centre, under its commander-in-chief Aly Pasha, collapsed and the Turkish fleet was routed, El Louck Aly alone managed to escape, together with the greater part of his squadron. Another who survived to fight at Lepanto – that last great naval battle in which the oared galley predominated – was the Chevalier Romegas. Romegas was perhaps the finest seaman that the Order of St John ever produced, and his name deserves to rank in history with that of his redoubtable adversary, the corsair Dragut.

The noble Greek, Lascaris, whose desertion to the cause of the Knights served them so well – particularly in the first great attack on Senglea – also survived the siege. He returned to the Faith of his fathers, and his bravery had so impressed the Grand Master that La Valette arranged for a pension to be paid to him for the rest of his days. Of the Maltese heroes of the siege there is no record, only legend. Like the ordinary soldiers of the time, their names were not considered important enough for official documents or histories. Only a few of them, like Luqa Briffa and Toni Bajada have survived in Maltese stories. The latter has a street named after him in the fishing village that now stands on the site of the last Turkish defeat, St Paul's Bay.

Don Garcia de Toledo passes into obscurity soon after the siege was raised. On the evidence of one authority, it is said that La Valette complained to Philip II of Spain about his Viceroy's behaviour. Certainly the Grand Master had good reason to complain of a policy which had left him without aid or assistance (except for the 'Little Relief Force') for nearly four months. This was especially the case since he had had two definite assurances from Don Garcia that he would come to the assistance of the island – the first, before the end of June, and the second, before the end of August. Historians of the Order have been quick to make Don Garcia the villain of the piece, and to try and find some deep-seated scheme behind his conduct. It seems much more likely that the Viceroy of Sicily was concerned first and foremost for his own domain, and that he could not raise enough troops and transports to meet his early, and optimistic, promises. Whatever way the fault lay, it seems that he incurred his sovereign's displeasure. Soon afterwards he was relieved of the Governorship of Sicily and retired to Naples, 'where he passed the remainder of his days, without public employment of any kind, and died in obscurity'.

Francisco Balbi da Correggio, whose day-by-day account of the Great Siege is by far the most accurate document we possess, survived a further twenty-four years. He was sixty years old when he fought as an arquebusier in the Spanish corps defending Senglea. An entry in the chronicle of the Italian town Correggio for 12 December 1589, has been recorded by Sir Harry Luke:

It is believed that the death of Francisco Balbi da Correggio, a wandering poet who wrote in Italian and Spanish and who was ever persecuted by men and by fortune, occurred on this date away from his native land. He is mentioned favourably by the celebrated Tiraboschi and the historian Colleoni – [The first edition of Balbi's account of the siege was published in Alcala de Henares in 1567, and a second edition in Barcelona in 1568.]

Honours were showered upon Grand Master La Valette by all the kingdoms of Europe. Philip II sent him a jewelled sword and poniard, the hilts of enamelled gold set with pearls and faceted diamonds. '*Plus quam valor valet Valette*' ran the punning device. The king's envoy who brought him this token of honour, pronounced a eulogy which would have embarrassed even the Sultan Soleyman. The defence of the island, the coastline of Malta, the figure and features of the Grand Master, all were celebrated in verse and histories. Incidents and details of the siege were reproduced in many contemporary drawings, maps, and broadsheets. The earliest of these, now in the Royal Malta Library, was printed in Germany in 1565 – only a month or so after the siege had been raised. It shows the dispositions of the Turkish army and fleet, their camp on the Marsa, and the embattled walls of St Elmo, St Angelo, and St Michael.

The two villages of Birgu and Senglea were not forgotten in the distribution of honours that followed the Great Siege. The first was renamed 'Vittoriosa', 'The Victorious City', and the latter, 'Invitta', 'The Unconquered'.

The Pope, Pius V, mindful that the Order came under his personal protection, sent the Grand Master a cardinal's hat. La Valette, with careful modesty, and disclaimers as to his fitness for such an honour, declined it. He would not be able, he said, to fulfil his duties as a cardinal adequately since, as Head of the Order, most of his time must be given to its affairs. As Grand Master, he must also have reminded himself, he enjoyed a cardinal's distinction – but without being obligated to the Pope, or involved in Vatican politics. La Valette's refusal of a cardinal's hat has sometimes been attributed to modesty. It is more likely that it was common sense.

Throughout the autumn and the winter of 1565, the Grand Master, his Council, and all the inhabitants of the island laboured to repair the defences in case another siege should follow. La Valette was also busy soliciting financial help from the sovereigns of Europe. Such was now the prestige of his name, and the fame of the island, that contributions were neither slow in coming or small in amount. The members of the Order, almost all of whom were men of wealth, also helped to refill the depleted treasury. The galleys of the

Order, refitted and re-equipped, were ready by the following year for the lucrative task of raiding the Sultan's supply lines.

On 28 December 1565 the Italian Engineer Francesco Laparelli (who had been specially chosen by the Pope for this task) reached Malta. He brought with him plans for new defences, and for a new city. Laparelli and La Valette have sometimes been given all the credit for deciding that Mount Sciberras was the ideal site for the new home of the Order. Such a proposal, in fact, had been made by several engineers who had visited the island before the Great Siege. Among them was Count Strozzi (who had first suggested the erection of Fort St Elmo) and Antonio Ferramolino (who had re-designed St Angelo and the defences of Birgu). The fact remains that it was La Valette's practical genius, his ability to restore the Order's finances, and his quick grasp of Laparelli's plans, which gave birth to the city that bears his name.

Mount Sciberras, dominating Grand Harbour from the north and Marsamuscetto from the south, was clearly a perfect situation for the new home of the Knights. On 28 March 1566, its foundation stone was laid. The Grand Master and all the Knights met formally on those slopes, where the flower of the Turkish army had died, to inaugurate the city. It was called after its Grand Master – *Humillima Civitas Valettae* – the Most Humble City of Valette. This was no more than a euphemism, one may think, for what was to become the most aristocratic and exclusive fortress in Europe – a city often referred to in later days as '*Superbissima*', the 'Most Proud'.

Throughout 1566, while more than 8,000 workmen toiled on the slopes of Sciberras, levelling sections of the ground and raising the first walls, the island was protected by a garrison of 15,000 soldiers. They had been sent to Malta by Philip II, in expectation of a further Turkish attack. But the Sultan was engaged in Hungary, and the walls began to rise in peace above the craggy sides of Grand Harbour and Marsamuscetto. While the galleys cruised southwards to the Barbary coast, and eastwards to the Aegean, and the young Knights

went on their Caravan to learn the hard trade of the sea,
La Valette stayed day and night in his new city. There he
interviewed envoys, there he held meetings with his council,
supervised the affairs of the Order, and conferred with the
engineers and masters of fortifications.

Three years after the siege, in July 1568, La Valette succumbed to a stroke after a day's hawking under the hot sun.
He was carried to the Magistral Palace in Birgu through the
restored, but still narrow, streets that had witnessed his
greatest triumph. He lingered on for several weeks, still
conscious enough to make his final depositions, to arrange
for his household slaves to be set at liberty, and to appeal to
his brethren to live together in peace and unity, and to up-
hold the ideals of the Order. On 21 August 1568, the silent
crowds in the streets heard that the Grand Master, Jean
Parisot de la Valette, was dead.

Obedient to his last commands, the Knights of the Order
had his body placed aboard the admiral's galley, and rowed
across Grand Harbour to the city that bore his name. Four
other galleys, shrouded in black, accompanied this greatest
of Grand Masters on his last voyage. The coffin was borne
through the new streets of Valetta. It was laid to rest in the
chapel dedicated to the Blessed Virgin, Our Lady of Victory.

La Valette now lies in the great crypt of the cathedral of St
John's. Beside him rests an Englishman, his secretary and
faithful friend, Sir Oliver Starkey – the only man other than
a Grand Master to be buried in the crypt.

The inscription on La Valette's tomb was composed in
Latin by Sir Oliver Starkey. Translated, it reads:

Here lies La Valette, worthy of eternal honour. He who was
once the scourge of Africa and Asia, and the shield of Europe,
whence he expelled the barbarians by his holy arms, is the first
to be buried in this beloved city, whose founder he was.

Around him lie the Grand Masters who were to follow him
in later centuries. Above, on the tessellated floor of the great
cathedral, shine the arms and the insignia of Knights, who,
for more than two hundred years, were to maintain the
impregnable fortress of Valetta.

Bibliography

Abela, Commendatore Fra F. G., *Della Descrittione di Malta* (Malta, 1647).

d'Aleccio, Matteo Perez, *I veri Ritratti della guerra & Dell' Assedio dati alla Isola di Malta dall'Armata Turchesa l'anno 1565* (Rome, 1582).

Balbi, Francisco da Correggio, *La Verdadera relaçion de todo lo que el año de MDLXV ha succedido en la Isla de Malta* (Barcelona, 1568).

Baudouin, J., *Histoire des Chevaliers de l'Ordre de S. Jean de Hierusalem* (Paris, 1624).

Boisgelin, L. de, *Ancient and Modern Malta & the History of the Knights of Jerusalem* (London, 1895).

Bosio, G., *Dell'istoria della Sacra Religione et Illma. Militia di San Giovanni Gierosolimitano* (Rome, 1594).

Bowerman, H. G., *The History of Fort St Angelo* (Valetta, 1947).

Brantôme, L'Abbé de, *Œuvres du Seigneur de Brantôme* (Paris, 1740).

Brydone, P., *A Tour through Sicily and Malta* (London, 1773).

Cavaliero, R., *The Last of the Crusaders* (London, 1960).

Cambridge Modern History, vol. III, *The Wars of Religion* (1907).

Corso, C., *Commentarii d'Antonfrancesco Cirni Corso . . . e l'Historia dell'Assedio di Malta diligentissimamente raccolta, insieme con altre cose notabili* (Rome, 1567).

Cousin, R. J. D., *The Siege of St Elmo* (Malta, 1955).

Crema, Cavaliere F. T. da, *La Fortificazione, Guardia, Difesa e espugnatione delle fortezze* (Venice, 1630).

Curione, Celio Secondo, *Nuova Storia della Guerra di Malta*. Translated into Italian from the original Latin by Dr E. F. Mizzi (Rome, 1927).

Currey, E. Hamilton, *Seawolves of the Mediterranean* (London, 1910).

Downey, Fairfax, *The Grande Turke* (London, 1928).

Floriana Pompeii, *Discorso intorno all'isola di Malta e di cio che porra succedere tentando il Turco dal impresa* (Macerta, 1576).

Bibliography

Gauci, Gaetano, *Il Grande Assedio di Malta* (Malta, 1891).

Gravière, Jurien de la, *Les Chevaliers de Malte et la Marine de Philippe II* (Paris, 1887).

Hammer, J. Von, *Histoire de l'Empire Ottoman depuis son origine jusqu'à nos jours*. Translated from the German by J.-J. Hellert (Paris, 1841).

Hughes, J. Quentin, *The Building of Malta 1530–1795* (London, 1956).

Laking, Sir G. F., *A Catalogue of the Armour and Arms in the Armoury of the Knights of St John of Jerusalem in the Palace, Valetta* (London, 1905).

Lucini, Anton F., *Disegni della Guerra, Assedio et Assalti dati dall' Armada Turchesa all'Isola di Malta l'anno MDLXV* (Bologna, 1631).

Luke, Sir Harry, *Malta – An Account and an Appreciation* (London, 1949).

Macerata, Paolo F. da, *Difesa et Offesa delle Piazze* (Venice, 1630).

Molle, Stefano, *L'Ordine de Malta e la Cavalleria* (Rome, 1929).

Pantaleone, H., *Militaris Ordinis Johannitorum Rhodiorum aut Melitensium Equitum . . . Historia Nova* (Basle, 1581).

Porter, Whitworth, *The History of the Knights of Malta* (London, 1883).

Pozzo, B., *Historia della sacra religione militare di S. Giovanni Gerosolimitano, detta di Malta* (Verona, 1703).

Prescott, W. H., *History of the Reign of Philip II* (London, 1855).

Ryan, F. W., *Malta* (London, 1910).

Schermerhorn, E. W., *Malta of the Knights* (London, 1929).

Taafe, J., *History of the Order of St John of Jerusalem* (London, 1852).

Vassallo, G. A., *Storia di Malta* (Malta, 1848).

Vendôme, P. Gentil de, *Della Historia di Malta et Successo della guerra seguita tra quei Religiosissimi Cavalieri et il potentissimo Grand Turco Sultan Solimano l'anno 1565* (Rome, 1565). (More than twenty other editions in four or five languages, including an unusual edition by Hubert Pernot (Paris, 1910) with a Greek epic poem by A. Achélis based on the Great Siege.)

Vertot, L'Abbé de, *Histoire des Chevaliers Hospitaliers de S. Jean de Jerusalem* (Paris, 1726).

Viperanus, J. A., *De Bello Melitensi Historia* (Perugia, 1567).

Zabarella, Conte Carlo S., *Lo Assedio di Malta* (Turin, 1902).

Zammit, Sir T., *Malta – The islands and their history* (Malta, 1926).

Zammit, Sir T., *Valeta – An Historical Sketch* (Malta, 1929).

Notes

None of the dialogue in this book has been invented. The speeches of the Grand Master and others have been taken wherever possible from the earliest available sources. At the head of the notes to each chapter I have indicated in order the principal authorities from whom quotations have been made.

CHAPTER I

Fairfax Downey, *The Grande Turke* (London, 1928).
R. J. D. Cousin, *The Siege of St Elmo* (Malta, 1955).
Conte Carlo S. Zabarella, *Lo Assedio di Malta* (Turin, 1902).
E. Hamilton Currey, *Seawolves of the Mediterranean* (London, 1910.)
J. Taafe, *History of the Order of St John of Jerusalem* (London, 1852).
The Cambridge Modern History, vol. III (1907).

For the description of the Divan of October 1564, and of its conclusions, I am principally indebted to J. Von Hammer's *History of the Turkish Empire*, in the French translation of J.-J. Hellert (Paris, 1841).

CHAPTER 2

Louis de Boisgelin, *Ancient and Modern Malta* (London, 1895).
Sir Themistocles Zammit, *Malta – The islands and their history* (Malta, 1926).

The document of the Emperor's gift of the Maltese archipelago to the Order is in the Royal Malta Library. It was issued in 1530 in the name of the Emperor Charles V and of his mother, Queen Joanna.

CHAPTER 3

Conte C. S. Zabarella, ibid.
J. Baudouin, *Histoire des Chevaliers de l'Ordre de S. Jean de Hierusalem* (Paris, 1624).

For much of the information on the Mediterranean galley I am indebted to Jurien de la Gravière's *Les Chevaliers de Malte et la Marine de Philippe II* (Paris, 1887). Gravière quotes Forfait, a French marine engineer who had made a specialized study of the galley. Forfait calculated that in a flat calm a galley could maintain about 4½ knots for the first hour, 2¼ to 1½ for subsequent hours.

One of the largest vessels of the period was the Great Carrack of Rhodes, which the Knights brought with them when they left that island and which subsequently ended its days in Malta. It has been described by J. Taafe in his *History of the Order*:

It rivalled with our lifeboats in this, that however pierced with multitudinous holes, no water could sink it. When the plague was at Nice, and the mortality so frightfully huge that the stench of the corrupted air made the birds of the sky drop down dead, not a man was ever sick aboard it, which is chiefly attributed to the great quantity of fires kept by the workmen to supply the requisite screws, nails, and other irons. . . . [It] had eight decks or floors, and such space for warehouses and stores, that it could keep at sea for six months without once having occasion to touch land for any sort of provisions, not even water; for it had a monstrous supply for all that time of water, the freshest and most limpid; nor did the crew eat biscuit, but excellent white bread, baked every day, the corn being ground by a multitude of handmills, and an oven so capacious, that it baked two thousand large loaves at a time. That ship was sheathed with six several sheathings of metal, two of which underwater, were lead with bronze screws (which do not consume the lead like iron screws), and with such consummate art was it built, that it could never sink, no human power could submerge it. Magnificent rooms, an armoury for five hundred men; but of the quantity of cannon of every kind, no need to say anything, save that fifty of them were of extraordinary dimensions; but what crowned all is that the enormous vessel was of incomparable swiftness and agility, and that its sails were astonishingly manageable; that it required little toil to reef or veer, and perform all nautical evolutions; not to speak of fighting people, but the mere mariners amounted to three hundred; as likewise two galleys of fifteen benches each, one galley lying in tow off the stern, and the other galley drawn aboard; not to mention various boats of divers sizes, also drawn aboard; and truly of such strength her sides, that though she had often been in action, and perforated by many cannon balls, not one of them ever went directly through her, or even passed her deadworks.

CHAPTER 4

Celio Secondo Curione, *Nuova Storia della Guerra di Malta*. The original in Latin, dated 1565, and translated into Italian by Dr E. F. Mizzi (Rome, 1927).

Antonio Ferramolino was the Italian engineer and architect responsible, under Grand Master D'Omedes, for most of the fortifications between 1541 and 1550. He was succeeded by Pedro Pardo. La Valette's engineer for most of the works constructed during the year preceding the siege was Evangelista. R. J. D. Cousin gives the number of Gozitans captured in Dragut's great raid of 1551 as 'seven hundred men and between five and six thousand women and children'. This seems a large estimate, being almost the total population of the island.

For much of the information about the state of Malta's defences prior to the Great Siege I am indebted to J. Quentin Hughes, *The Building of Malta 1530–1795* (London, 1956). The Royal Malta Library and the Archives of the Order also contain much invaluable information about the fortifications, including the original plan of Fort St Elmo, dated 1552. (See page 75.)

CHAPTER 5

We are extremely fortunate in having an excellent eyewitness account of the day-to-day fighting and events of the Great Siege. This was written by Francisco Balbi da Correggio, a sixty-year-old poet, writer, and soldier of fortune, who served in the garrison of Senglea through the whole siege. The Royal Malta Library has two copies of the 1568 Barcelona edition of his work.

Antonfrancesco Cirni 'Corso', a Corsican cleric, who came to Malta with the main relief force was the only other eyewitness to record the siege. Unlike Balbi, who was present from beginning to end, Cirni only saw the very last phase of the campaign. His material, however, was diligently gathered by him from the actual survivors of the siege. Pierre Gentil de Vendôme published his *History of Malta and the Siege*, in Rome, only a few months after the island had been relieved. His material was also gathered from survivors and from members of the relief force.

541 Knights and servants-at-arms who were present in Malta in the spring of 1565 were divided among the various Langues as follows:

	Knights	Servants-at-arms
Provence	61	15
Auvergne	25	14
France	57	24
Italy	164	5
England	1	–
Germany	13	1
Castile	68	6
Aragon	85	1

Notes

CHAPTER 6

Von Hammer in his *History of the Ottoman Empire* gives the following breakdown of the Turkish forces embarked at Constantinople: 7,000 Spahis from Asia Minor. 500 Spahis from Karamania. 500 Spahis from Mitylene. 4,500 Janissaries. 3,000 irregular troops. 12,000 irregular Spahis. 3,500 irregulars from Roumelia.

Balbi's figures are: 6,300 Janissaries. 6,000 Spahis from Anatolia. 500 Karamanian Spahis. 2,500 Roumanian Spahis. 400 Iayalars from the Islands. 3,500 Iayalars from the Balkans. 4,000 volunteers. 6,000 levied troops.

Although it is natural to exaggerate the size of one's enemy, Balbi is quite conservative in most of his estimates, and his whole account is sober and painstaking. There seems no real reason to doubt his figures, which give a grand total of 29,200. This, of course, does not include Dragut's corsairs, Hassem's Algerians, or the Egyptian troops. At the height of the siege, before sickness and wounds had taken their toll, I see no reason to doubt that there were about 40,000 troops investing the island.

CHAPTER 7

John Taafe, ibid.

Jurien de la Gravière, ibid.

The ill-feeling that undoubtedly existed between the Maltese aristocracy and the Knights of the Order of St John is not difficult to explain. The Knights did not consider the local nobility (mostly of Siculo-Aragonese descent) suitable for inclusion within the Order. E. W. Schermerhorn in *Malta of the Knights* (London, 1929) makes the following comment:

> To the educated and aristocratic Maltese, well-informed on local history, the memory of the imperious Order that took away their parliament and free institutions, interfered with the sacred privileges of their bishopric, snobbishly refused membership to the sons of families whose titles of nobility ante-dated the occupation of Rhodes . . . is simply not to be discussed or defended in any well-bred circles.

CHAPTER 8

John Taafe, ibid.

Antonio Ferramolino, who was sent by the Emperor Charles V to advise Grand Master D'Omedes in 1541, had pointed out all the weaknesses in the defensive system of the island. He had even suggested that Birgu should be evacuated and the Convent moved to Mount Sciberras. There can be little doubt that La Valette had his advice in mind when he began the construction of Valetta.

The descriptions of St Elmo are taken from the works of Bois-gelin and Bosio. The latter's *History of the Order* (Rome, 1594) is comparatively well-documented.

Piali's concern over the necessity for occupying the harbour of Marsamuscetto proved the stumbling block on which the Turkish campaign came to grief. There was, in fact, very little danger to his fleet if it had remained in Marsasirocco throughout the summer. *The Mediterranean Pilot*, vol. 1 (Admiralty, London, 1951) devotes a section to the Gregale and its prevalence. In some five years of sailing around Malta and the central Mediterranean I have rarely encountered N.E. winds of any strength in the summer months.

In this chapter and several others, I have quoted from General Whitworth Porter's *History of the Knights of Malta* (London, 1883). The scarce 1883 edition is almost double the size of the six or seven other editions of this work. About three-quarters of the entire publication was destroyed by fire, and the edition as a whole was never reprinted.

CHAPTER 10

I have quoted in this and other chapters from W. H. Prescott's *History of the Reign of Philip II* (London, 1857). The first two volumes of this history were published in London in 1855, and the great American historian was working on the third volume at the time of his death in 1859. The second volume contains a clear and accurate account of the Great Siege, based mainly on Balbi's memoirs. The chapters devoted to the siege have been translated into Maltese and issued as a separate volume in Malta.

CHAPTER 11

Brantôme, L'Abbé de, *Œuvres du Seigneur de Brantôme* (Paris, 1740).

The great French historian and biographer (1540–1614) came to Malta shortly after the siege. He met La Valette and the other Knights. I have made use of the Paris, 1740 edition from the Royal Malta Library in the course of this work, although there is little doubt that Lalanne's twelve-volume edition (1864–96) is the best. The Abbé de Brantôme was a great admirer of the Order, and even took part in several Caravans in the galleys.

For the information about the life of Dragut I am indebted to many authorities – among them, Von Hammer, Jurien de la Gravière, and E. Hamilton Currey. The following is a brief sum-mary of his raids on the Maltese island:

1540. Attacks Gozo.

Notes

1544. Attacks Gozo. During this raid it is said that Dragut's brother was killed and that the Governor of the Citadel had the corpse burned. Dragut swore revenge. At the same time he is reputed to have had a prophetic intimation that one day he, too, would meet his death 'in the territory of the Knights'.

1546. Raids Gozo again.

1547. Raids Malta, landing in Marsasirocco.

1551. Two raids on Malta, one in spring and one in summer. This time he uses Marsamuscetto as his headquarters. Beaten off by the Knights from Birgu, he switches his attack to Gozo and carries off almost the entire population into slavery.

1563. Another raid on Gozo.

1565. Joins Mustapha Pasha and Piali as their adviser for the siege. Wounded by splinters from a cannon-ball, he dies in his tent on the Marsa, 23 June, the day that St Elmo fell.

CHAPTER 12

Von Hammer, ibid.
Balbi, ibid.

CHAPTER 13

W. H. Prescott, ibid.
J. Taafe, ibid.

Bosio, Vertot, Taafe, and other historians of the Order all indict Don Garcia de Toledo for pusillanimous conduct, if not worse. Prescott has the following comment: '. . . The Viceroy, far from quickening his movements, seemed willing to play the part of the *matador* in one of his national bullfights – allowing the contending parties in the arena to exhaust themselves in the struggle, and reserving his own appearance till a single thrust from his sword should decide the combat.'

CHAPTER 14

Bosio and Vertot mention Vitelleschi as the Knight chosen to deliver the mutineers' message to La Valette. Zabarella, without stating his authority, awards this dubious honour to the French Knight, Bonnet de Breuilhac. This may well be no more than national partisanship. It is noticeable that Zabarella, throughout his account of the siege, gives the lion's share of honour to the Italian Langue. Both Vitelleschi and de Breuilhac died in the fall of St Elmo.

The original of the mutineers' letter has not so far come to light. My translation is based on that quoted by earlier authorities. It seems quite likely that the original may have been destroyed, either immediately after the siege or at a later date, to avoid any imputation of cowardice resting upon men who had died so bravely.

CHAPTER 15

Balbi, ibid.
Jurien de la Gravière, ibid.
E. Hamilton Currey, ibid.
The lines

> *One of the saintly murderous brood*
> *To carnage and the Koran given . . .*

are from Thomas Moore's poem 'The Fireworshippers'.

CHAPTER 16

W. H. Prescott, ibid.
A portrait of that redoubtable sea-captain and warrior, Dragut, Governor of Tripoli, is to be seen in the Palazzo Reale, Milan. Jurien de la Gravière wrote the following about his death – it might well serve as his epitaph: '*Il est mort sans déclin, dernière faveur de la fortune pour un homme qu'elle avait toujours gâté.*'

CHAPTER 17

R. J. D. Cousin, ibid.
P. Gentil de Vendôme, ibid.
E. Hamilton Currey, ibid.
J. Taafe, ibid.
L'Abbé de Vertot, ibid.
The lines 'From the lands where the elephants are . . .' are taken from James Elroy Flecker's *Hassan* (London, 1922).

CHAPTER 18

All La Valette's actions, from the very beginning of the siege, show that he had made up his mind there could be no withdrawal from Malta, as there had been from Rhodes. As for the cruelty displayed by both sides during the siege, Moritz Brosch's comment in vol. III of the *Cambridge Modern History* seems apt:

In the matter of tolerance towards those of differing faith the Sultan was the superior of those with whom he fought. The exaction of a tithe of their boys from the defeated Christians was an act of cruelty, but apart from this no one was persecuted in Soleyman's time, when the Inquisition was carrying on its deadly work in Spain and in the Netherlands. In view of all this, it cannot be said that in the wars of Soleyman barbarity was

Notes

to be found only on the side of the Turks. *In several points it is undeniable that the Ottomans were better, the Spaniards and Imperialists worse than their reputation.* [My italics.]

CHAPTER 19

For the information about La Valette's actions and words during this critical stage of the siege I have relied principally upon Balbi, Cirni Corso, Vertot, and Brantôme. Bosio also has a number of anecdotes relating to the Grand Master.

CHAPTER 20

Lascaris was the name of a Bithynian family who had given three Emperors to Nicaea during the thirteenth century. After the fall of Constantinople many of them were exiled by the Turks, others killed. Lascaris survived the siege and was awarded a pension from the funds of the Order by La Valette.

The stake palisade, which played so important a part in the defence of Senglea during this first attack, was another of La Valette's brilliant improvisations. An error made by a number of authorities, including Boisgelin and Prescott, is to suggest that this palisade ran from the tip of Senglea across the mouth of the creek to the end of Corradino. This would have been impossible, because of the depth of water, as well as the nature of the bottom. (The creek is now 7 fathoms at its entrance, but was probably never less than 5 fathoms.) Perez d'Aleccio's engravings (made prior to 1600 and based on the evidence of survivors of the siege) show quite clearly that the palisade ran parallel to the western shore of Senglea.

CHAPTER 21

For much of the information contained in this chapter I am indebted to C. J. Ffoulkes's *The Armourer and his Craft* (London, 1912), also to Sir G. F. Laking's *A record of European Armour and Arms* (London, 1920) and his *Catalogue of the Armour and Arms in the Armoury of the Knights of St John in the Palace, Valetta* (London, 1905).

CHAPTER 22

Balbi, ibid.
Porter, ibid.

There is no doubt that the Chevalier de Lugny's cavalry action deserves to rank with that of de Guiral's battery (which destroyed the ten boatloads of Janissaries in the first attack on Senglea).

Without a certain element of luck, and without the opportune exploitation of that luck, Senglea would have been lost on both these occasions.

CHAPTER 23

Balbi gives the figures of the enemy killed in the first attack on Senglea as 4,000. This may well be an exaggeration. Vertot is even more lavish in his assessment of the casualties.

During the great debate in Messina on the question of sending relief to Malta, Giannino Doria – nephew of the famous Admiral – was one of the principal advocates of the Knights. The opposing party were in favour of La Valette accepting terms, as Villiers de l'Isle Adam had done at Rhodes. Alvarez de Sandé, later the second-in-command of the relief force, is also reported to have been in favour of La Valette surrendering.

CHAPTER 24

The quotation regarding the number of cannon shots fired during the great siege is from Jurien de la Gravière. If anything, his figure of 70,000 cannon shots may be taken as an underestimate. It has to be remembered that a great many of the cannon balls fired at St Elmo were easily reclaimable and could be used again. A number of cannon balls have been dredged out of Grand Harbour, and off the point of St Elmo, in recent years.

Sir Harry Luke describes the plant which grows on Fungus Rock in his book on Malta. Its botanical name is *Fucus coccineus melitensis* and, like the unique lizards which live on the islet of Filfla, it appears to be unknown in other parts of the Mediterranean.

CHAPTER 25

Vertot, ibid.

The description of Mustapha's infernal machine is taken from Balbi. The latter had a good opportunity to view it, for he was in the garrison of St Michael at the time of the attack.

CHAPTER 26

For the description of the Grand Council meeting on the night of 23 August, I have drawn upon Balbi, Antonfrancesco Cirni Corso, and Celio Secondo Curione; as well as later commentators such as Vertot, Boisgelin, Zabarella, and Taafe. There seems to me no doubt that La Valette's action in refusing to evacuate Birgu and withdraw into St Angelo was the decision that saved the island.

Notes

During the latter part of the siege, the chronology of the various commentators and historians varies considerably. Wherever possible I have followed Balbi, but in certain places I have preferred the dates given by Cirni and Curione. W. H. Prescott followed Balbi almost entirely. It is true that Balbi was present throughout the whole siege, but he did not publish his account until two years later. Cirni and Curione published their accounts within the same period and, although they were not present, probably had more access to the records than Balbi. The Abbé de Vertot, writing more than a century later, also had access to all the records and archives. Balbi's account, nevertheless, is far the best – the simple, unvarnished tale of a fighting soldier.

CHAPTER 27

W. H. Prescott, ibid.
Vertot, ibid.

Don Mesquita, the Governor of Mdina, plays only a small part in the histories of the siege. The fact remains, that, on at least two occasions, his actions were decisive. His concealment of the weakness of Mdina was one. The other was his enterprising cavalry attack on the Turkish base in the Marsa, at the moment when Mustapha Pasha had almost succeeded in taking Senglea.

CHAPTER 28

The importance of the Hospital during the siege must not be forgotten. Roderick Cavaleiro in *The Last of the Crusaders* (London, 1960) has this to say about its functions:

> The Hospital was obliged to provide for the sick and wounded of all races, creeds and colours, free of charge. No sick man was to be denied treatment, though if he were a Protestant, a Greek schismatic or a Moslem, he was to be confined to a separate ward. Slaves, too, were admitted. . . .

The gale which wrecked the fleet carrying the relief force had its parallel during the second siege of Malta. On 9 July 1943, a somewhat similar, and unexpected, gale nearly caused havoc among the Allied Fleet which was then crossing the Malta Channel for the invasion of Sicily.

CHAPTER 29

All the quotations in this chapter are from Balbi. His estimates of casualties are usually reasonable, but on this occasion it would seem that victory inspired him to exaggeration. In the withdrawal from

St Paul's Bay he gives the Turkish losses as 3,000, and the Christians as no more than eight.

CHAPTER 30

Balbi, ibid.

The song 'Malta of gold, Malta of silver . . .' is translated from Hubert Pernot's French translation of a Cypriot sixteenth-century song. It is quoted by him in his (Paris, 1910) edition of Vendôme's *Le Siège de Malte*. In this same edition there is a curious and rare poem by A. Achélis. Based on Vendôme's account of the siege, this is an epic treatment of the event written in Modern Greek and divided into twenty chapters.

Balbi lists all the Knights killed in the siege, and later historians such as Zabarella have followed his list, with only a few alterations and additions. Vertot rates the Christian losses even lower than Balbi, but as a historian of the Order he was very much concerned with its aggrandizement.

CHAPTER 31

Vertot records that the Sultan's projected second expedition against Malta was postponed because the great arsenal at Constantinople was destroyed by a spy sent there for this purpose by La Valette. It is a curious tale, but I have been unable to find any evidence for it. Unfortunately, Vertot rarely gives any indication of his sources. It is only on his authority that we have the statement that La Valette complained to Philip II about the behaviour of Don Garcia de Toledo.

The dagger and poniard given to the Grand Master by Philip II are now in the Bibliothèque Nationale, Paris. They were among the numerous treasures looted from Malta by Napoleon when he captured the island in 1798.

In his *History of the Knights of Malta* (1883), General Whitworth Porter wrote with a prophetic insight:

English hearts and English swords now protect those ramparts which formerly glistened with the ensigns of the Order of St John; and should occasion ever demand the sacrifice, the world will find that British blood can be poured forth like water in defence of that rock which the common consent of Europe has entrusted to her hands. On such a day the memory of this Great Siege will have its due effect, and those ramparts already bedewed with so much noble blood, will again witness deeds of heroism, such as shall rival, if they cannot excel, the great struggle of 1565.

In Malta's longest siege, from 1940 to 1943, British blood was, indeed, 'Poured forth like water in defence of that rock.'

Glossary

ARMET: A helmet with a movable visor.

BASILISK: A large cannon firing a 48- to 200-pound ball. Called after the legendary monster whose glance and breath were fatal.

BASTION: A defence work consisting of two faces and two flanks, all the angles being salient.

BRIGANTINE JACKET: Jacket of leather with small overlapping iron plates attached to it.

CARAVAN: A term used by the Order of St John to denote a year's duty on active service in the galleys.

CASQUE: Any piece of head armour, but generally an open helmet.

CAVALIER: A defensive work within a fortification, or one rising higher than the main rampart.

COUNTERSCARP: The slope of a ditch opposite the parapet, or the parapet itself.

COUNTERWALL: A wall erected opposite that of the enemy. In siege terms, often a wall erected within the main defences as a secondary defensive system.

CULVERIN: Originally a very long cannon, but by the sixteenth century any large cannon.

CURTAIN: Part of a rampart bordered by a parapet that connects the flanks of two bastions or towers.

DEMI-BASTIONS: A half bastion, with a single face and flank.

DOUBLET: Close-fitting body garment, belted at the waist. In military terms usually of leather, with sometimes the addition of chain mail.

ENCEINTE: The principal line of fortifications enclosing a place, or the area thus enclosed.

FASCINES: Bundles of rods or sticks bound together and used in the construction of earthworks.

GALLEAS: A large galley with three masts and fifteen or more oars each side.

Glossary

GALLEY: Vessel principally propelled by oars. In the sixteenth century almost invariably a warship.

GALLIOT: A galley propelled by both sails and oars, but smaller than a galleas.

MORION: An open helmet without visor, usually worn by men-at-arms.

OUTWORK: A defensive work constructed outside the enceinte, either in or beyond the ditch of a fort.

PASHA: Ottoman title signifying a General, Admiral, or Governor. The title was divided into three grades, denoted by one, two, or three horsetails – the latter being the senior rank.

PORTCULLIS: A grating or framework made of bars of wood or iron, sharp-pointed at the lower end, and sliding vertically in grooves on either side of the portal of a fortified place.

RAMP: Gradual slope from the interior of a fortification to the level immediately inside the parapet.

RATAL: A Maltese measure of weight equivalent to about $1\frac{3}{4}$ imperial pounds.

RAVELIN: A detached work with two faces meeting in a salient at the front and open at the rear. Usually placed in front of a curtain to protect it and the shoulders of adjoining bastions.

SALADE: An open helmet, affording no protection to the face.

Index

Index

Index

Index

Index

Index

Mustapha, *continued*
138; transports ships overland, 148–9; attacks Birgu and Senglea, 148–204; animosity towards Piali of, 188–9, 212–13; his supplies running low, 196; abortive attack on Mdina of, 197–200, 205; hears of Relief, 207; orders evacuation of Malta, 209–11; halts evacuation, 212–14; final defeat, 214–17; courage of, 215; return to Constantinople of, 223

Nakshivan, 14
Naples, 43, 87
Naxxar, 20, 210, 213–17
North Africa, 15, 19, 47, 86, 143, 196, 202, 220

Omedes, Juan d', Grand Master of the Order of the Knights of St John of Jerusalem, 36, 39, 234
Oran, 158, 160
Order of the Knights of St John of Jerusalem, *see* Knights of St John

Palermo, 221
Palestine, 24
Pantaleone, H., *Militaris Ordinis Johannitorum Rhodiorum aut Melitensium Equitum*, 230
Pardo, Pedro, 37, 75, 233
Paris, 221
Parker, Archbishop Matthew, 221
Paschal II, Pope, 24
Passaro, Cape, 104
Penne, Barras de la, 33
Peñon de la Gomera, 15
Peñon de Velez, 45
Pereira, Guevarez de, 194
Pernot, Hubert, 11, 241
Persian Gulf, the, 14
Pessoa, Chevalier, 193
Phillip II, Emperor of Spain, 15, 43, 44, 46, 58, 87, 103, 175, 225, 227, 241
Piali, Admiral, 15, 18, 50, 57, 90, 164; captures Djerba, 48; co-commander of the Armada, 48–9; biography of, 48; raids Italy, 48; his galley, 51–2;

Councils of War of, 63, 67–8, 88–9, 114, 124; wishes to occupy Marsamuscetto, 68, 90, 235; wounded, 79; orders attack on St Aubin, 80; rivalry with Army of, 80; meets Dragut, 85; to respect Dragut, 88; hinders attack on St Elmo, 90; inefficient fleet of, 102, 188, 206, 208; stops reinforcements, 114, 132–3; worried by course of campaign, 118; and death of Dragut, 125; to attack Birgu and St Angelo, 147; in charge of operations against Birgu, 165, 168–9; animosity towards Mustapha of, 188–9, 212–13; refuses to winter in Malta, 188; sends supply ships to Africa, 196; his timidity and ignorance ruined campaign, 208; refuses to land again, 212–13; fleet of, carry out evacuation, 216; returns to Constantinople, 223

Piccolo Soccorso, 143–5
Piron, 149
Pius IV, Pope, 43, 71, 175, 221
Pius V, Pope, 226
Polastron, Chevalier, 183–4
Pont, Martin Juan del, 152
Popes *see* Paschal II; Pius IV; Pius V
Porter, General Whitworth, *The History of the Knights of Malta*, 140, 230, 235, 238, 241
Pozzalo, 206
Pozzo, B., *Historia della sacra religione militare di S. Giovanni Gerosolimitano detta di Malta*, 230
Prescott, W. H., *History of the Reign of Philip II*, 82, 140, 166, 220, 230, 235, 236, 237, 238, 240
Provençal Langue of the Order of the Knights of St John of Jerusalem, 28, 60, 65, 109–11, 137, 146, 233

Quinay, de, 157

Ravelin, 37, 38, 69, 74, 91, 95, 96, 98, 101, 105, 108, 116, 118, 122, 129
'Red Apple', the, 52
Reggio, 87

Index

Index